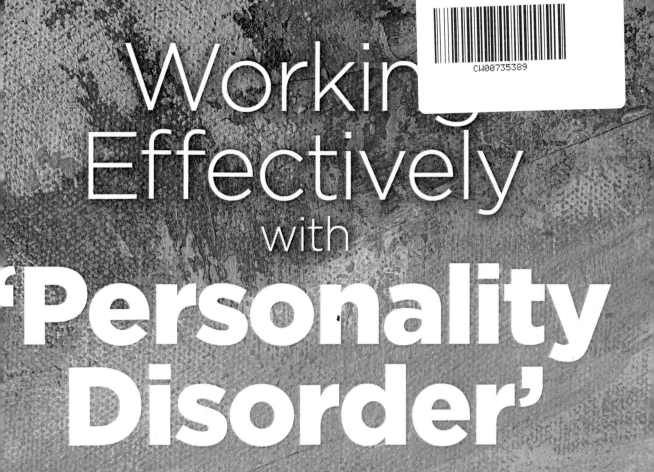

Working Effectively with

'Personality Disorder'

Contemporary and Critical
Approaches to Clinical and
Organizational Practice

Edited by Jo Ramsden,
Sharon Prince and Julia Blazdell

Working Effectively with 'Personality Disorder'

© Pavilion Publishing & Media

Published by:
Pavilion Publishing and Media Ltd
Blue Sky Offices
Cecil Pashley Way
Shoreham by Sea
West Sussex
BN43 5FF
Tel: 01273 434 943
Fax: 01273 227 308
Email: info@pavpub.com

Published 2020

A catalogue record for this book is available from the British Library.

ISBN: 978-1-912755-97-4

Pavilion Publishing and Media is a leading publisher of books, training materials and digital content in mental health, social care and allied fields. Pavilion and its imprints offer must-have knowledge and innovative learning solutions underpinned by sound research and professional values.

Editors: Jo Ramsden, Sharon Prince and Julia Blazdell
Production editor: Ruth Chalmers, Pavilion Publishing and Media Ltd
Cover design: Phil Morash, Pavilion Publishing and Media Ltd
Page layout and typesetting: Phil Morash, Pavilion Publishing and Media Ltd
Printing: Ashford Press

To all the service users, activists, colleagues, survivors and friends who have inspired us: thank you.

Contents

About the authors

Melanie Anne Ball started her career employed as a Peer Worker in a residential therapeutic community. Since then, she has been privileged to work across the sector, undertaking a variety of different roles in a diverse range of settings, including CAMHS, adult inpatient and community services, high secure services, and in a prison. Mel has also worked nationally and internationally for a number of years as a public speaker, trainer, researcher and consultant for organisations and communities. Currently employed as the Trustwide Lived Experience Practice and Peer Support Lead for Central and North West London NHS Foundation Trust, she teaches at Canterbury Christ Church University, Abertay University and is a Teaching Fellow at London Southbank University.

Dr Kimberley Barlow MBChB BSc MRCPsych is the Clinical Lead of the Cassel Hospital, an NHS Tier 4 Specialist Inpatient and Community Based Personality Disorder Service which is located within West London NHS Trust. She is a Consultant Psychiatrist in Medical Psychotherapy having qualified in medicine in 1999 from the University of Edinburgh and training in psychiatry and psychotherapy at South West London and St George's NHS Trust and the Tavistock and Portman NHS Foundation Trust. Early in her career she worked at the Henderson Hospital, a therapeutic community in Sutton, and this set her on the path of working relationally. As well as working in specialist mental health settings she has also worked in male and female prisons. Between 2016 and 2019 she was a member of NHSE clinical reference group for specialised services. These experiences have exposed her to the inherent disconnects and anti-relational practices and policies of the commissioning system and the detrimental impact these have on peoples lives. She is keen to work with others on the development of reflective and comprehensive services which better the needs of people with complex relational difficulties and increase the availability of treatment.

Jina Barrett is an organisation consultant, executive coach and consultancy supervisor in the public sector and in private enterprise. She contributed a psychoanalytic and systemic organisational perspective to both (i) the National Personality Disorder Development Programme, through the Camden & Islington NHS-sponsored multi-agency project, LiveWork, from 2005-2011, and (ii) to the development and delivery of the national training framework, the PD KUF (Personality Disorder Knowledge and Understanding Framework) from 2007-2018. Her professional background is in social work, and in psychoanalytic psychotherapy in the NHS. She currently works as an internal consultant with Camden and Islington NHS Community Division. On behalf of the Portman Clinic, she contributes to developing organisation support initiatives in forensic and custodial settings. In independent practice, with a range of associates, she co-designs and delivers consultation training as part of leadership development for organisational change.

Nick Benefield has retired as Department of Health Lead for Personality Disorder and Joint Head of the NHS/NOMS Offender Personality Disorder Team. He trained in social work and as a Jungian psychotherapist. He has a background in the therapeutic treatment of young offenders, inner city community social group work and community mental health services. He has worked as a clinician, trainer, manager, commissioner and policy maker and has an ongoing interest in the development of psycho- social relational environments in criminal justice and wider health, social and educational settings.

Dr Julia Blazdell (editor) works as a Network Co-ordinator for the Managed Clinical Network for Personality Disorders in West London Health Trust and is a freelance lived experience consultant, researcher and trainer.

Sue D Ellis is a contented and fulfilled Wife to David, Mother of two and grandmother of five. A Librarian and Person-centred Counsellor, Sue has enjoyed a varied career in statutory, academic and third sectors. The last ten years has been applying academic learning; BA 1st Class Honours in Counselling and an MSc Working with Personality Disorder – Extending Expertise and Enhancing Practice, and personal experiential learning in the field of personality disorder and mental well-being. Resolute and passionate, Sue believes that with kindness, care, empathy and validation everyone can become self-fulfilled and reach their personal potential by overcoming adversity.

Dr Neil Scott Gordon has recently retired to his native Scotland after 40 years working in the NHS as a Senior lecturer, Organisational Consultant and Forensic Psychotherapist. He was most recently a Senior Fellow and Academic Consultant in the Institute of Mental Health, Nottingham University, where he was Head of Doctoral Programmes and Masters Programme Lead for the national Personality Disorder, Knowledge and Understanding Framework (KUF). Neil has co-authored a textbook *Working Positively with The Challenges Of Personality Disorder In Secure Settings: A practitioner perspective*, and published articles and chapters on a range of topics including: personality disorder and trauma, organisational change, mental health education and qualitative research.

Rex Haigh is a Medical Psychotherapist who studied social sciences at Cambridge, before his medical qualification in Oxford then training and working as a GP in Cornwall. He went on to specialise in psychiatry, psychotherapy and group analysis. He has been an NHS consultant in Berkshire since 1994, was

Clinical Advisor to the English Personality Disorder Development Programme (2002-11) and part of the NICE guideline development group (2007-9) for Borderline Personality Disorder. At the Royal College of Psychiatrists, he was the founder of 'Community of Communities' quality network (2002) and the 'Enabling Environments' award (2009). He was appointed Honorary Professor of Therapeutic Environments at Nottingham University's School of Sociology and Social Policy (2016) and is involved with several third sector mental health organisations. His clinical interests are modified therapeutic communities, relational practice, ecotherapy, and service user co-production.

Dr David Harvey is a Consultant Clinical Psychologist and Cognitive Analytic Therapy Practitioner working in Leeds and York Partnership NHS Foundation Trust Forensic Services. He has worked for fifteen years in services supporting people with complex mental health needs and trauma histories who may pose a risk of harm to others or themselves. This work has included psychological risk assessment and management in the NHS, Probation, Courts, Children's Services, Prisons and the Third Sector. He has a particular interest in how effective working and proportionate risk management by professionals, services and organisations can be disrupted by their own powerful emotional reactions to the work.

Alan Hirons is an Occupational Therapy Clinical Specialist at Leeds Personality Disorder Services. Alan qualified as an Occupational Therapist at the College of York St John in 1999 and completed an MSc Working with Personality Disorder – Extending Expertise and Enhancing Practice at the Open University in 2014. After working in a variety of mental health settings, he has worked in the Leeds Personality Disorder Services since 2004 across both the community and offender services as a manager, clinician and trainer. Over the years, Alan has been involved in the development of a number of dedicated occupation focussed and generic interventions for people with 'personality disorder'.

Mary McMurran PhD is a registered Forensic and Clinical Psychologist, a Fellow of the British Psychological Society, and recipient of the Division of Forensic Psychology's Lifetime Achievement Award in 2005. Formerly a Professor at the University of Nottingham, she now practises independently. She has published widely on personality disorders, alcohol-related aggression and violence, case formulation, and treatment engagement. She has worked as a clinical and forensic psychologist in the Prison Service and the NHS and is currently a member of the Parole Board for England & Wales.

David Pilgrim is Honorary Professor of Health and Social Policy, University of Liverpool and Visiting Professor of Clinical Psychology, University of Southampton. With a mixed clinical and research background in clinical psychology in the British NHS and mental health policy, his relevant interest here is in the ethics of healthcare and the social context of patient presentations. He approaches all topics from a philosophical position of critical realism and has published widely in this regard. His book *Critical Realism for Psychologists* has been published recently by Routledge.

Sharon Prince (editor) is a Consultant Clinical & Forensic Psychologist and is the Clinical Lead for the Personality Disorder Services within Leeds and also the Strategic Lead for Psychological Professions within Leeds & York Partnerships NHS Foundation Trust. The award winning Personality Disorder Service has a national reputation for being psychologically informed and for continuous innovation. For over twenty years, her career has been spent working with service users who have been marginalised and excluded from services, and with whom services have often struggled to provide accessible and acceptable services. She is passionate about psychologically informed mental health care and how both psychological and social models can be employed to improve service user, carer and staff experiences.

Dr Jo Ramsden (editor) is a Consultant Clinical Psychologist and Clinical Lead for the Yorkshire/Humberside Personality Disorder Partnership (YHPDP). YHPDP is part of Leeds Personality Disorder services and works in partnership with the national probation service as part of the national Offender Personality Disorder (OPD) strategy. Jo is interested in and committed to finding a way of working with people who are, typically, excluded from services and/or whose contact with services has been damaging. The importance of organisational anxiety is, she believes, paramount to helping us find a way of working restoratively with some of the more intractable difficulties and damaging practices. Services and providers can work better where they are able to examine themselves.

Sue Sibbald is a Peer Specialist at Sheffield Health and Social Care Foundation Trust and has worked there for eight years running groups for people who are labelled with 'personality disorder' and their family and friends. Sue was also Co-Chair of the Consensus Statement for people with complex mental health difficulties who are diagnosed with a personality disorder 'Shining lights in dark corners of people's lives' alongside Norman Lamb MP.

She also has done work with NHS England NHS Digital and NCISH (The National Inquiry into Suicide and Safety) and has done work privately with LACNetwork and Sheffield University health service. Recently Sue was awarded a British Empire Medal for her services to mental health in the New Year's Honours List 2020.

Sarah Skett is a Registered Forensic Psychologist, and an Associate Fellow of the British Psychological Society. She has worked with offenders for nearly 30 years, including men, women and young offenders. She has experience of undertaking assessment and treatment interventions with serious violent and sexual offenders, mainly serving indeterminate sentences, and was the Regional Psychologist for the Midlands, overseeing the strategic and professional development of Her Majesty's Prison and Probation psychology teams. She has worked as a commissioner for HMPPS (formerly the National Offender Management Service), and since 2012 is the Head of the Joint Offender Personality Disorder pathway for both the NHS and HMPPS, establishing with colleagues a network of services underpinned by 12 core principles and a set of evidenced based quality standards for people likely to meet the diagnostic criteria for 'personality disorder' and who are also high risk of harm to others.

Dr Ruth Sutherland is Principal Clinical Psychologist at Leeds Personality Disorder Managed Clinical Network/Pathway Development Service. Ruth qualified as a Clinical Psychologist from the University of Leeds in 2004 and is also an accredited Cognitive Behavioural Psychotherapist. She has worked in a range of adult mental health settings with people with complex needs and joined Leeds Personality Disorder services in 2014. Ruth has a range of roles in the service, including psychological therapy, service development, training, supervision and consultation. She is particularly passionate about her role as service lead for Service User and Carer Involvement, holding the firm belief that coproduction is the best way to develop and deliver effective services for people with 'personality disorder'.

Bernie Tuohy has worked for an award winning Third Sector partner 'Community Links' as a Regional Housing and Resettlement Caseworker; working within the 'Regional Pathway Development Service' for the past 10 years. The Regional Pathway Development Service was formed in 2008, as a Partnership between Leeds Partnership NHS Foundation Trust (LYPFT) and Community Links.

Bernie is a qualified further education teacher and provides regional workforce development training 'KUF awareness of Personality Disorder', alongside bespoke training to housing providers.

Bernie has previously developed mental health partnerships within the deaf community and has previously coproduced a paper for *Mental Health Today* 'Listening to Deaf people' (Tuohy & Cooper, 2007) and authored 'The Challenges and Pitfalls of Working with Sign Language Interpreters' in the *Healthcare Counselling & Psychotherapy Journal* (2004).

Foreword

This thought-provoking volume addresses an important and timely issue: how to work differently with people with personality disorder – something that is badly needed. People with the complex emotional, interpersonal, and social difficulties that characterise this condition all too often derive little benefit from the help provided by traditional health care and social services. Indeed, many find that these services add to their burden and the chronicity of their problems. The editors are to be congratulated for tackling such an important multifaceted problem and for assembling an intriguing array of viewpoints that not only challenge current thinking but also offer practical alternatives that reflect a sensitive understanding of the problems and experiences of clients. It is especially useful to have a volume exploring these issues based on experiences in the UK because the last few decades have seen a variety of innovations that deserve wider dissemination. Although the volume's authors, including service-users, consider these changes just the beginning, these initiatives have created services that are different and often better than those available in other places, especially North America, where services are largely confined to one-to-one treatment when it is actually available.

As the eclectic array of chapters argue, major changes are needed in all aspects of our understanding and treatment of this disorder. Even the term "personality disorder" is problematic carrying as it does connotations and stigmas that add to the burden of those who suffer with it. Although I use the term here for convenience, we badly need less pejorative and more constructive terminology. As the volume documents, we also need new ways to conceptualise and treat this condition. This is challenging because personality disorder is enormously complex in nature and origin and the problems faced by those suffering from it vary widely from person to person. Such complexity and variability present significant challenges for diagnostic assessment, the characterisation of these problems, treatment, and service delivery.

When exploring these issues, authors are essentially grappling with the consequences of a quirk of human nature that when faced with complex problems such as personality disorder, we tend to opt for simple solutions that invariably turn out to be wrong. The problem plagues approaches to personality disorder and accounts for many of the frustrations those with the disorder experience when seeking help.

Problems begin with contemporary diagnostic classification. Faced with the multi-faceted, multi-levelled nature of personality disorder, contemporary psychiatry uses a count of relatively superficial features to assign people to categories that show limited resemblance to the problems of actual individuals and have few specific treatment implications. An important theme of the volume is the need for a more systemic approach that seeks to understand the disorder in the context of the person's life and development in a way that captures the nuances and individuality of clinical presentations.

But, it is not only psychiatric nosology that has opted for a simple solution. Treatment has followed a similar path adopting relatively fixed treatment protocols based on traditional models of individual therapy. Although the last few decades have seen progress in developing effective interventions, there is a long way to go. Our therapies are not as effective as we originally thought and some commonly used therapies have limited relevance to treating the levels of severity typically encountered by community mental health services. And, even after completing current therapies, many participants have substantial residual difficulties especially with relationships and with building a satisfying life. The volume explores these problems from diverse perspectives emphasizing the fundamental importance of the treatment relationship and the need for an eclectic approach that combines useful interventions of all effective treatments.

The volume also emphasises that besides developing more effective treatment, we also badly need to find more effective ways to deliver care so as to make it more accessible and more relevant to patients' needs and problems. A valuable feature of the volume is the preparedness to think outside the box in this regard. One approach that is especially interesting is the establishment of treatment networks – something pioneered in the United Kingdom. The idea makes sense. We are a sociable species designed to live in networks and most of our time is spent in one kind of network or another, with our families, at work, in community activities, and often in our leisure time. Since the difficulties that our patients experience find expression in their personal networks, it makes sense to treat their problems within a network of care. There are also practical reasons to organise care in this way. Besides the problems addressed by traditional therapies, people with severe personality difficulties also have a panoply of social problems, medical conditions in addition to mental health problems, occupational challenges, and housing difficulties. The idea of providing the services needed under a single umbrella is appealing. Apart from the benefits of coordination, the network model recognises that treatment not only occurs in practitioners' offices but also in the way the diverse components of care are delivered throughout a system of care. Since all interactions with network staff can contribute to positive outcomes, this offers a powerful treatment model.

Finally, I want to draw attention to the fact that in pursuing new ways to work with personality disorder, the editors have not only identified critical issues and brought together authors with interesting viewpoints that often differ from traditional positions, they have also done something else that is equally important: they have created a volume that reflects not just an academic interest in personality disorder but also a deep concern for all aspects of the wellbeing of those forced to cope with the disorder and the challenges it presents. The tone of the volume reminds us that effective treatment is not simply a matter of finding the right interventions, it also requires that we get the tone right and that outcome ultimately depends on the quality of relationship clinicians establish with their clients. Having read the book, the reader cannot help but ponder on how this is best achieved in their own practice.

John Livesley
Professor Emeritus, University of British Columbia, Vancouver

Introduction

Jo Ramsden, Sharon Prince and Julia Blazdell

Over the past 20 years, those involved in the field of 'personality disorder' have seen a number of policies, reports and initiatives designed to ensure access to effective services (e.g. National Institute for Mental Health in England, 2003; Department of Health, 2009). Despite these initiatives, the history of these services is scarred with testimonies from people with 'personality disorder' diagnoses who have been isolated, stigmatised and re-traumatised.

It is common for those of us involved in this field of work to see young people repeatedly set on pathways which will inevitably compound their difficulties; to see people sent away from home and placed in hospital settings that create dependency and isolation. Many of us recognise the fact that individuals frequently experience obstructed, problematic, hopeless pathways and live day-to-day managing overwhelming distress with little help or support. It is common for us to work with people whose experience of services is to have been lied to, punished, disliked, discriminated against and excluded.

Many of us feel that public money is often wasted on ineffective and highly expensive services. We see exhausted and overwhelmed service providers working – with few resources – with people who present profound relational and risk management challenges. We know and understand the complex dynamics which are inevitable when working with this service user group but, overwhelmingly, we see problematic responses to these complexities. We see services failing to learn, failing to innovate and failing to be bold in providing something different and something meaningful.

In amongst all this we know that there are creative networks of learning – people who are providing progressive services for and with the client group, working bravely and compassionately. Our frustration is that these networks and this learning repeatedly fail to inform dominant discourses about what 'personality disorder' is and how to work with it.

Our ambition for this book is to articulate a different way of working which is built on our learning and all the things that experienced practitioners and other service providers know to be important. We want to acknowledge the critical debate that currently rages among professionals and service user groups (often on social media) about the diagnosis of 'personality disorder'. We know, for example, that using the term 'personality disorder' in the title of this book may alienate and/or anger many people who – for very good reasons – refuse to identify with it. Of fundamental importance for this book is, therefore, the need to speak 'truths' about the experience of 'personality disorder'. We attempt (throughout the book but particularly in Part 1) to represent some of the perspectives held by practitioners (including those with lived experience) which underpin a widespread understanding that the way we do things could be so much better.

Part 1 illustrates how many practitioners and others believe that our current service provision is based upon a set of flawed assumptions which act, insidiously, to problematically position those with lived experience of the 'disorder' as powerless and ill. We share these views and see, within our own working lives, how many people who struggle every day with the problems associated with 'personality disorder' are offered meaningless services and remain excluded, stigmatised and without help. We also share the view, held by many within our 'personality disorder' community of practice, that biomedically based, pathology-focused assumptions (which underpin much of our traditional response to people with 'personality disorder') remove powerful personal stories of oppression and abuse. These assumptions have the potential to position specialist services as the truly helpful ones and to de-emphasise the importance of services which work more holistically, less 'expertly' and often with a wider, more socially focused agenda.

As a consequence, we are concerned with 're-thinking' services that work to help those with 'personality disorder'. Fundamentally, this book argues for a paradigm shift in how organisations understand and respond to people who, through social injustice and the misuse of power, live every day with emotional challenges associated primarily with the interpersonal realm. The perspectives articulated in **Part 1** underscore the importance not necessarily of treatment but of compassion and validation (**Chapter 1**), relationships (**Chapter 2**), co-produced stories and personal meaning (**Chapter 5**). **Chapter 4** invites us to interrogate the very basis of our service delivery and, in doing so, to engage in 'an honest appraisal of the social and existential challenges' faced by those we work with (Pilgrim, this edition).

Part 2 of the book seeks to articulate how we act to ensure that those perspectives inform our delivery of services. While we are aspirational, we are also pragmatic, and this book is not intended to outline a way of working which is impractical and/or overly prescriptive. We recognise the limits of our current knowledge, and the importance of learning from communities of practice and of continually adding to what we know to help us do things better. The second part of the book strives, therefore, to assist existing services to shift their thinking, to innovate and to learn through a set of guiding principles for governance. Our ambition for these principles is that they work to hold a frame which frees workers to be less expert (less fearful), more creative and perhaps more humane than they tend to be within traditional service models.

Key assertions underpinning the need for a paradigm shift

The need for a paradigm shift in how we respond to 'personality disorder' is based on three key assertions which are picked up throughout the book.

The first assertion is that working with people who face serious emotional and relational challenges leads services themselves to become 'disordered'. To put this another way, it is a central claim that the impact of being in relationships with people (particularly people who behave in often disturbing ways) inevitably (and universally) leaves workers feeling fearful, incompetent, overwhelmed, etc. The emotional impact of the work leads to the development of practices which work to serve the organisation in the management of its anxiety at the expense of those who use the service (see **Chapter 6**).

Throughout the book there are examples of how we have become lost: commissioning services which prevent relational approaches (see **Chapter 3**); illogically confusing conduct with illness (see **Chapter 4**); compounding exclusion and stigmatisation through upholding the importance of specialism (see **Chapter 7**); overlooking the importance of personal stories and meaning and becoming stuck in intractable debates (see **Chapter 5**). By focusing on the emotional impact of the work we suggest that practising in ways which ill serve our clients is the unintentional, unconscious consequence of workers and organisations feeling frightened, overwhelmed, angry, etc. Losing our minds is, we would suggest, inevitable.

In her seminal paper, Isabelle Menzies Lyth (1960) illustrates how the emotional impact of the work of caring for other human beings leads those in caring roles to become lost through 'social defences'. These defences operate to distort an innately humane response to those in serious distress. They are hard to notice, given that they are often organisationally sanctioned and professionally reasoned. It is only, perhaps, with the benefit of decades of learning – and trying to learn – about what works, that we can see how lost we have become. As part of this, we want to acknowledge the truth of what we hope may, in time, be reconciled: abuses have been perpetrated against people with the diagnosis by those working (and occupying powerful roles) in services that are supposed to help them. At the same time, a lack of organisational wisdom has meant that those workers have had little support in managing the stress and anxiety which is an intrinsic part of the task of caring for people who have experienced extremes of trauma and behave in distressing ways as a consequence. Many of us working with people with 'personality disorder' have failed to notice what is happening to us and how the conditions are frequently put in place for power to be misused and 'unconscious abuses' to be enacted (Hinshelwood, 2014).

In the second part of the book, it is argued that a meaningful response to this group of service users can only be delivered if the emotional impact is acknowledged and ways of managing it – of ensuring that services can keep their minds – are made explicit in operational and service delivery models. Essentially, we will work effectively where it is acknowledged that managing the emotional impact of the work is a significant aspect of it (see **Chapters 6** and **12**).

The second key assertion is that our current conceptualisation of what constitutes 'intervention' is too narrow. For many professionals working in services for people with 'personality disorder', their work is focused on alleviating individual intra-psychic problems (usually defined through expert assessment). We have, however, collectively failed to define authoritatively what interventions 'cure' people and, instead, have become reliant on proving effectiveness using outcomes which are incapable of measuring the complexity of the issues (see **Chapter 11**). It is also interesting to note that, in line with the argument outlined in **Chapter 4** (which states that our service delivery is really concerned with risk and the management of incorrigible conduct rather than treatment), the evidence base for interventions is concentrated on those who cause the most harm to self or others. As the authors of **Chapter 8** acknowledge, the evidence base is sparse for personality disorders which are not classified as either 'borderline' or 'anti-social'.

Arguably, in mindlessly trying to 'treat' people, many services – in managing their own anxiety about lack of treatment progress – contribute to stigmatisation by blaming those who do not 'recover' (e.g. for lacking insight or being hard to engage) (see **Chapter 5**). We are often preoccupied with contributing towards evidence bases for particular theoretical modalities and evaluating our own services, at the expense of considering the needs of those for whom these 'treatment' services are meaningless. When we 'look up' and remember that our work is often based upon a set of flawed assumptions we are reminded also that, for many people, expert, professional psychological or medical treatment is irrelevant. It is at these moments we might discover other ways of helping people.

Chapter 8, in particular, articulates the issues around intervention and defines what may helpfully constitute a way forward. These authors define 'up-to-date' interventions as any deliberate and conscious activity which has:

> '... the potential to "create" evidence and experience for service users of the efficacy and utility of engaging safely with other people in the service of immediate survival, emotional regulation and the development and maintenance of quality of life.'
>
> (Hirons & Sutherland, this edition)

A contemporary approach to intervention, therefore, requires radically re-designed services and an appreciation that 'interventions' can be provided in much broader social contexts than have been traditionally considered. If we embrace the potential of employing someone's everyday environment to provide learning opportunities then we are more able to utilise a wider range of available resources and to shift the emphasis from the question 'are you able to engage with what we offer' to 'how can we provide what you need' (**Chapter 7**). In **Chapter 10**, the authors uphold intervention as partnerships – working flexibly across service boundaries to ensure a more holistic, socially focused approach. These authors acknowledge the complexity and emotional challenges inherent in sharing authority with other providers and argue for a focus on the emotional processes which undermine effective partnership work. In **Chapter 7** the authors argue for a widening of the role that specialist services occupy to ensure that practice across specialist and generic, statutory and third sector services is increasingly trauma-informed and responsive not to 'illness' but to intelligible behavioural responses to adversity.

The third and final assertion is that we are failing to notice that we are lost and, as a consequence, we are perpetuating exclusion, isolation, trauma and dependency through services which are unwilling or unable to develop and adapt. Many of the chapters highlight the failure of services to 'look up' from a very narrow, professionally defined understanding of what constitutes a meaningful service. In **Chapter 13**, Neil Gordon writes: 'I begin writing with a sense of regret that, although well intentioned, we may as a community of practitioner/educators have been narrow in our approach'.

In **Chapter 5** the role that psychiatric classification has played in restricting our knowledge about what 'personality disorder' is, and how to help people, is acknowledged. This chapter goes further by identifying how the traditional medical approach has prevented us from being able to learn from those who have been diagnosed. Personal, idiosyncratic, internal experiences of the diagnosis, of what it feels like to suffer in this way and of what helps, are all lost through the diagnostic process and the service delivery models which stem from it.

This chapter goes further by arguing that investment in personal meaning helps us to transcend paralysing debates about diagnostic labels. In **Chapter 9**, the importance of co-production in helping to shift our thinking and to start developing progressive, inclusive services is most clearly articulated. Barriers to co-production are discussed in this chapter and the avoidance of co-production is upheld as a consequence of organisational anxiety associated with the sharing of power. In **Chapters 9 and 13**, the authors argue that services will only adapt to provide a meaningful response when they genuinely – and fearlessly – commit to co-producing knowledge and 'practising near' to those who use their services.

Building on these assertions, a paradigm shift is proposed which privileges individual personal meaning alongside structures and processes that support staff to intervene as collaboratively as possible and with a mind on the social injustices that have led individuals to seek their help. We invite the reader to consider that services are better delivered when providers are outraged by the failures which have led to the difficulties faced by their clients, and when they work humanely and relationally to support traumatised and fearful people in whatever way has meaning for them.

The importance of hope

Frequently, people accessing 'personality disorder' services encounter despairing professionals and rejecting services. These responses are often based on service expectations about recovery and pathways which hold little realistic meaning for the person using the service.

This book does not ignore the disturbing aspects of the work of caring for people who present in a way that is consistent with a 'personality disorder' diagnosis and, as such, is a manifesto for hope, regardless of what we acknowledge is often highly challenging work. In contrast, we would argue that hopelessness is largely a product of collusive expectations about recovery which, in reality, constitute organisational attempts to manage anxiety. In other words, workers are frequently hopeful about recovery journeys which fail to take into account what individuals need, want and value. Instead, we tend to invest hope in pathways that are professionally defined and built on illogical assumptions about how individuals approach the world. We ignore the impact of trauma and of insecure attachment experiences, and create instead an image of 'recovery' which assumes entirely different developmental experiences. Once again, we can see how services become lost, deviating from the service user's experiences and needs. Throughout the book there are clinical examples of people who do not fit traditional therapeutic narratives of 'recovery' or 'gaining insight'. These examples illustrate the importance of meeting people where they are, of investing in co-production and 'practising near' the personal meaning that those using services have about their problems and their needs. They illustrate how we might learn from and authentically hold hope for people when we approach our task more mindfully and more collaboratively.

Finally...

The ideas and approaches in this book are not new; they are, instead, gathered from many who have been working in this field and thinking about how to progress things for years. There are many others who could have contributed. This book is, therefore, an acknowledgment of all the brave, innovative, compassionate work that has been happening for many years and which has brought us to this point. On behalf of all of those who have contributed and/or who have inspired us and taught us, we hope that this book presents a viable, realistic alternative which is challenging to established structures and traditional approaches. We hope it presents a distillation of much that is most important for the future of services with people who are suffering in the way that we understand 'personality disorder' to mean. We hope that it articulates a way of thinking that enables providers to work differently and more effectively. Our ultimate ambition is that providers might be inspired to adopt approaches which enable those who use services to feel more empowered, valued and safe.

References

Department of Health (2009) *Recognising Complexity: Commissioning Guidance for Personality Disorder Services*. London: Department of Health.

Hinshelwood RD (2014) Abusive help – helping abuse: The psychodynamic impact of severe personality disorder on caring institutions. *Criminal Behaviour and Mental Health* **12** (S2) S20–S30 doi.org/10.1002/cbm.2200120604

Menzies Lyth IEP (1960) A case study in the functioning of social systems as a defence against anxiety: a report on a study of the nursing service of a general hospital. *Human Relations* **13** (2) 95–121. doi.org/10.1177%2F001872676001300201

National Institute for Mental Health in England (2003) *Personality Disorder: No Longer a Diagnosis of Exclusion*. London: Department of Health.

Part 1

Contemporary and Critical Perspectives on 'Personality Disorder'

Chapter 1:

Life and Labels: Some Personal Thoughts about Personality Disorder

Sue Sibbald

I was born in Leeds in 1963, a time when the asylums existed, where they housed people for years on end and often for very nefarious reasons.

My mum was labelled with schizophrenia the year I was born. She was, at first, on wards in the general hospital, and then was consigned to an asylum after a few years. There were good times: she took us to the library, played musical songs on the piano, and we went to the café and pinched sugar cubes from the bowl. However, my mum could be very unpredictable in her illness and she would spend long spells in bed, and go out on spending sprees. She lost herself; she lost her mind. For a child that was really hard: her absences, the not knowing who would be there and sometimes her anger and the police cars turning up. So scary for a small child. I had my dad and brother and sisters. We coped. My dad had little help back then and social services actually asked to take us into care, but my dad refused. He was a strong man who loved his children, so he managed.

For me, as a sensitive soul, this lack of connection with my mum caused me lots of distress and later in life, as an adult, it led to me breaking down. I know that I had no memory of some events; my sister told me about them later. The start of dissociation.

As a child I played out all day and sat in my tree at night pretending to be an owl. As I grew older I began to slowly unwind and I began to turn up late for school and didn't put much work in. I guess things began to slide.

A funny moment in retrospect was when my dad told me I couldn't go to see Soft Cell play at a local gig in Leeds, before they were famous. So I ran away from home and went on a mini tour with them in their white van … I went back home as I ran out of money. My only means of earning were a Saturday job at a sports shop and babysitting.

I scraped into polytechnic to study public administration, a course which was just awful for me. I hardly attended lectures and during that time my girlfriend dumped me, which led to a week in bed depressed. I felt like my mum. I dropped out of poly and worked in a nightclub in Leeds six nights a week, where I took drugs and drank. It was around this time that I first self-harmed and took an overdose. I lived in a shared house. One of my friends was a nurse, so that was useful. I thought all of this was normal. I didn't see anything wrong with me, even though I started to suffer panic attacks, particularly in restaurants, and I avoided eating out for three years. I thought having a mental health condition was my mum – that person zapped by electroconvulsive therapy who had lost her mind – and that was not me. I was scared of psychiatrists and mental health hospitals. Visiting my mum had felt traumatic. As a small child I thought the psychiatrists would section me and take me away to the scary asylum. I kept away. I carried on. I lost weight. I couldn't eat. Much of it was due to severe anxiety. I carried on…

But great things can happen, and I met my wife when I was 24. We were both DJs and our love of music was the thing that brought us together. I moved from my hometown of Leeds to Sheffield to be with my wife and ended up working in The Leadmill live music venue and nightclub. I lasted 20 years there. From DJ and working in the cloakroom, I finally ended up managing and part-owning the venue. I did well for myself and I worked hard. Due to being an insomniac I could work very long hours and do difficult shift work.

Around the age of 46 I left The Leadmill to work for a local college training door supervisors. I began to dissociate while training. I lost time and it often led to panic attacks. I began to see images in the house of a dead person. (I now name it 'death'. It is black, witch-like, with flowing raggedy cloaks.) I began to unravel. I ended up seeing a counsellor. Then I was referred to my CMHT, where I was labelled with 'borderline personality disorder'. I was apparently well-kempt, although my psychiatrist could have done with a haircut. I told him I would be dead before he cured me.

I had never heard of the label and I had no idea at that moment what a stigmatising label it was. People I knew had never heard of it. The stigma wasn't coming from them. What I discovered later on was that the stigma was coming from lots of professionals who didn't know how to help.

My thoughts on the 'personality disorder' label

The label of 'borderline personality disorder (BPD)/emotionally unstable personality disorder (EUPD)' is controversial. Just to explain: the name 'BPD' comes from the Diagnostic Statistical Manual (DSM), from America (American Psychiatric Association, 2013), and the name 'EUPD' comes from the International Classification of Diseases (ICD) diagnostic manual, from the World Health Organisation (2018). In order to get the diagnosis you have to meet several criteria. I was told I had BPD so I must have had five or more of the nine criteria listed in the DSM. The whole diagnosis for 'personality disorder' is very fuzzy and leads to much confusion, in my opinion.

Some people hate the label. It has led to them being refused treatment: gate-kept out of services, being told they are manipulative, attention seeking, mad and bad, their trauma not acknowledged. They have been forgotten, locked up in prison or in forensic units, restrained – piling trauma upon trauma. Many have had their children taken away from them. With no support offered, they are left out in the wilderness. Some of my friends have died by suicide. One was turned away from A&E twice in one night. She was told she was attention seeking. She died by suicide later that night, crashing her car into a tree.

It is mainly women who are given the diagnosis of BPD. Many men are given the diagnosis of antisocial personality disorder or autism. It is seen by some as the dustbin diagnosis: the one you are given if you don't recover, or if psychiatric medication doesn't work or if you complain. Oh, those hysterical women!

Other people embrace the label. They feel that it validates their experiences of being invalidated as children. They've received help at the right time and have experience of working with amazing professionals. I have friends who no longer meet the criteria for the diagnosis and I would probably count myself in this camp. But if something catastrophic were to happen in my life I think I would need support. You never recover, you just learn to live with the difficulties your past life has thrown at you. Some days are better than others.

There are some very vocal user-led groups out there who campaign for the label to be dropped, such as Survivors Not PD (@SurvivorsNotPD). They do not believe in the construct of personality disorder. They are against the pathologising of their survival from trauma and being blamed for their own distress. On social media they use the hashtag #traumanotpd.

Other people find the label useful as an explanation as to why they have felt that way for the whole of their lives. They find it validating. There is a huge Facebook group called Personality Disorder Awareness Network and a few big Twitter accounts where people talk about the diagnosis and how it is for them.

My belief is that a label should only be given by mutual consent and that people who don't agree with the label should still be helped. I do think the name needs to change to something that mentions trauma, but we need to recognise that trauma is not always the big T of sexual abuse or childhood neglect. It can be the trauma of invalidation from parents for someone who is exquisitely emotional; others may just find life difficult and overwhelming.

We should have awareness that something traumatic has happened to people who are given this label (although some people aren't ready to be asked that question, so be careful when asking). However, frequently people are blamed for their behaviour: 'your personality is disordered'; 'you should be recovered'; 'it's your choice if you attempt suicide'; 'think about what your kids would think about your self-harm'. It becomes all about what is wrong with you. But when you have experienced trauma in all of its forms, life is hard. I have needs that were not met in my childhood and I will play them out as an adult. It wasn't until I had therapy, which I will discuss later, that I became aware of the patterns I was repeating as an adult.

What people need

I don't choose to self-harm. The shame I feel when I have done so is huge. I am overwhelmed. My emotions engulf me and the only way I have learnt to escape is through self-harming. I must mention that I have been treated abominably by some staff in A&E: having my feet slapped; told my bed is for an ill person, not for those who overdose. Being told that I have 'personality disorder' so it must be all my fault, not the fault of the trauma from my childhood. I have also been treated with respect and compassion in the past. I have not had to go to A&E for five years now, so I am not sure if it has improved in my area. However, I still see people on social media tell their stories of awful victim-blaming treatment.

The label itself causes the blame. It is located in me, my personality is disordered. For me, the blaming from staff comes from their feelings of powerlessness, of not knowing how to help. So, they project those feelings back onto the person and start the name calling because it can't be their fault. Many people feel they are blamed for not recovering, when it is often the case that the person is not given the right support at the right time. So, for me, a name change in itself won't be enough. What is also needed is trained staff who know how to help in a trauma-informed way. It takes time to help people. There are no quick fixes so patience and good relationships are required. Relationships are so important for people who have had little or no experience of them in their lives. The myth that people with the label should have strict boundaries, that they must not get attached, so must be kept out of services is just rubbish. How do people learn about positive relationships if they aren't allowed one? There should be limits which are flexible but safe and human and which can be negotiated. I love the Boundary Seesaw Model (Hamilton, 2010), which talks about how the best boundaries are where you are involved enough to nurture and empower someone, where you are the negotiator. You are not tipped too far into being controlling and end up with a boundary like a brick wall which is punishing. Nor do you have a hole in your wall where you are over-involved and too placatory with the person, where you are the pacifier. Being in the middle of the seesaw, being balanced, is key.

Services – how they can change and what they should offer

When I was diagnosed I discovered there was hardly anything for me in my area and I wrote a letter. Not one wrapped round a brick, although maybe it should have been, but one asking why there were no National Institute for Health and Care Excellence (NICE) recommended therapies in my area. I specifically wanted dialectical behavioural therapy (DBT), as it had received the greatest number of randomised controlled trials (e.g. McMain *et al*, 2016). There are other therapies as well, since DBT doesn't help everyone.

Eventually I was invited to join the Sheffield Health and Social Care Foundation Trust 'Personality Disorder' strategy team. Here I was tasked, alongside a psychologist colleague (and now good friend), to create some training for staff and a group for people labelled with 'BPD' or who may have had a trauma background and who find managing emotions difficult. We co-produced these sessions and then I went on to train to bring a family group back to the Trust. The group has been running for about six years now and is for family and friends of those with the label of 'personality disorder', although you do not need to have a family member with the label. I do other work now around suicide awareness training for staff, which is co-produced with other work colleagues.

Due to campaigning and some forward-thinking staff, my Trust now have full DBT, cognitive analytical therapy (CAT) and cognitive behavioural therapy (CBT) programmes in a specialist service, with a hope to bring mentalisation-based therapy (MBT) on board in the near future. I like to think I have played my part in my local area to get things up and running and I have recently been working with others both inside and outside the NHS to get the right help for people. My hope is that this is all trauma-informed. I think that people can get involved and change things from within a service. But I think it is equally powerful to work outside: to campaign for better things such as the label change, the construct, and the right type of help for people.

One thing that I have noticed over the years is the fact that 'personality disorder' is at the bottom of the mental health pile. People talk about 'serious mental illnesses' (e.g. schizophrenia) and how the physical health of people with those illnesses should be looked after. However, the Consensus Statement for People with Complex Mental Health Difficulties who are Diagnosed with a Personality Disorder (Personality Disorders Commission, 2018) states that people with the diagnosis die early. For women, lives can be curtailed by 19 years; for men, by 18 years. Some people will die by suicide. But it would seem that the NHS ignores the plight of people who attract a personality disorder diagnosis. I often wonder if it is due to the constant blaming of someone with this label: 'If only you would quit the drugs, the drinking and get a grip on your eating disorder then you might live a bit longer.' All of these issues are often co-morbid alongside a 'personality disorder' and I guess people learn to cope with abuse, neglect and overwhelming emotions in all sorts of ways. I know for me I used to take drugs and drink when I was younger to try and mange my overwhelming emotions. I couldn't cope with life. People labelled with 'personality disorder' should have their physical health taken care of as well as their mental health. These two things are not separate and a great book I read around trauma is Bessel Van Der Kolk's (2014) *The Body Keeps the Score*. In the book he shows how trauma is so intrinsically linked with not only the mind but also the body. His book makes much sense to me and makes a great case for people being looked after in a more holistic way – I guess total care of the body and mind.

Another thing that worries me is the growth of the private sector and the warehousing of people who are kept in on a section for far too long. It's worrying that these private services are making money from their patients. I have known people who have been in prison and in the forensic system or locked rehabilitation who have become institutionalised – have received little or no therapy and come out being so reliant on people to look after them. It then becomes work to help people live a life again and to regain their independence. Often people are left with little hope. I think the lack of a meaningful therapeutic relational environment doesn't help. Also, being away from family and friends for such a long time does not help people live the life they need. We need better help in people's local community. So: what does a good service look like?

For me, the word 'relationships' comes to mind. It is those relationships that matter to people and those connections we forge that help us to discover what might help us. They help show us how to be with people and try to live the best life we can with the resources that we have. The people who helped me most who work as mental health professionals are those who have been able to sit with me, sit by me, metaphorically 'hold me', while I have gone through some really tough times in my life. I was lucky to have twice-weekly therapy for three years and it was that relationship that helped me move on in my life. Without it, I would never have been able to write this chapter or be the co-chair of the Consensus Statement for 'Personality Disorder'. The relationship with my therapist was one of respect, of understanding, of me being able to tell everything in a safe space and for her to be able to hold me, move me forward and to help me understand my past and how it still operates in the present. It was a relationship like no other as, of course, I knew little about her, which at times felt strange and often frustrating. But I have not overdosed for five years now and I understand myself so much better, and with her help I have discovered what makes my life worth living. I still have down times and feelings of dread and anxiety, but the way I respond has changed and I feel better able to explore the world without the constant dread that something bad will happen. I still get those days, but I either sit with the feelings or accept that this is how it is for now. Or I do the things that help me get through the difficult times. That includes medication, but also things such as yoga, mindfulness and being outside in my garden, walking or being with my family and my cat Mowgli.

Other good relationships I had in the mental health system were with my psychiatrists, both of whom were kind and were led by me and what I thought I needed, and with my two care coordinators, who supported me when times were bad. All of these people made mistakes from time-to-time. But, on the whole, it was important to have people I could rely on, even when they messed up. And I guess learning from them what it was to be human – warts and all – made it possible for me to learn to trust again. What truly mattered was that all of them were kind, and for me kindness matters so much. If you burn out, or lose the ability to empathise and be kind, I think it is time to think about finding a new job, as it is core to what helps people. I know I may be lucky. I hear stories of people who have been harmed by professionals, which is really sad, and something that people should keep talking about. A problem that often exists is that workers are not given the support they need, or the time and space to think or reflect, due to the government cuts to mental health services over the past few years. There are fewer workers due to the cuts and also a shortage of trained staff in some areas. I guess well supported and trained workers are key to helping people, and also having a trauma-informed organisation, where people are thinking about what effect their behaviour and the organisation's systems are iving on people who have suffered trauma in their lives. This is often forgotten the system and in the target-driven organisations that exist these days. How we are with people is so important and an organisation can cause iatrogenic harm in the way that it operates. An example for me was not being called back when I was under the Home Treatment Team, which may seem small, but when you are in a mental health crisis and are in need of support it really matters.

Another thing I think is important for people is that they have a choice of therapies and other interventions to help, as one approach does not fit all. People who responded to a survey for the Consensus Statement stated that they wanted this choice and many were interested in creative-type interventions. Often the case is that there is only one therapy offered and that therapy might not be the right one for that person. We need to invest more in doing the things that help an individual rather than pushing people through a factory machine, as one size does not fit all. My idea of the help that I need may be outside the mental health system, in third sector or voluntary organisations, and may not include therapy but rather an art group or just being involved in things in my own community.

Community matters in mental health. Being part of something. Feeling like you belong. But many local day services have been closed due to the government's austerity programme. Where I am in Sheffield there is a social enterprise called Sheffield Flourish that is both online and offline. It has a gardening project, a football project and other groups which help to bring some of our mental health community together. There is also a service user network run by the Trust and a group called Challenge Sheffield. They all help to bring people together. There is the great service user led crisis house in Leeds which does a lot of other work too, which helps create a sense of community. We need more of this, as the Consensus Statement also said that peer support was also important to people. I think this should be made available in and outside of the mental health system.

The Consensus Statement

I was asked to join the Commission for 'Personality Disorder' by my psychologist colleague. I went to my first meeting not knowing what to expect. I was quite nervous as there were some really well-known people there and I felt like a small fish in a big sea. Also what I discovered was that there was a lot of disagreement, particularly around the label.

I managed to speak a bit but I was exhausted after the meeting. They felt tense. I felt tense. After attending a couple of meetings, I was asked if I would apply to be the co-chair, which I did, and I was voted in. Who would have thought it: me becoming a co-chair with Norman Lamb MP! I still feel strange about it – I was someone who came from nightclubs to co-chairing the Commission.

The British Psychological Society (BPS) for whatever reason failed to release monies to fund the project and subsequently Emergence, the service user-led organisation which was managing the Commission alongside McPinn Foundation, went into liquidation. This was the end of the Commission and I personally felt embarrassed and frustrated and angry at the BPS.

From the embers of the Commission came the Consensus Statement (Personality Disorders Commission, 2018), as people did not want to give up on advocating for those labelled with 'personality disorder'. The person who brought it all together and worked so hard to keep things on track was clinical psychologist Alex Stirzaker. Her hard work and determination meant the Consensus Statement was possible.

The main areas of discussion were about the label, which we seemed to get bogged down with for quite a while. However, after time people came to the consensus that the label needed to change. Also, people from various areas of expertise came up with the best practice for helping people, from young people to those in the criminal justice system. People with lived experience were also asked their opinion on what helped. All of this was done without any funding and for me it was a bit of a miracle that it came together.

The Consensus Statement was launched at the Palace of Westminster with everyone who had been involved, and I was asked to speak alongside Alex Stirzaker and Sir Norman Lamb. The BBC also did a piece on News at Ten, which was exciting. I had the Home Affairs correspondent Mark Easton round at my house interviewing me, which once again felt strange, it felt a bit like imposter syndrome. For me, the Consensus Statement was a positive move forward and I have personally spoken about it at a few conferences and to another mental health trust.

The consensus statement advocates for a change to the 'personality disorder' label but also recognises some of the complexity of doing this. In the meantime, and until an alternative emerges, we highlight the importance of recognising the role of trauma in people's lives, and also of intervening as early as possible. We argue for a wide range of interventions and for the importance of recognising the multiple ways in which people are failed. Working to develop safe, compassionate care across a whole system is an ambition for the consensus committee, who argue that it is no longer an option to ignore the needs of people in this group.

A final word on the importance of validation

The last thing I would like to mention in this chapter is validation, and I would like to do it by way of a blog I wrote some years back. Wherever I go, when I am doing public speaking or training staff, I talk about validation, as it is my belief that it is emotional first aid for those in a mental health crisis. For me, validation means acknowledging and accepting another person's feelings, thoughts, behaviours and internal experiences as valid. It requires empathy and communication that the other person's reactions make sense. It is how we can connect with others through showing that you understand what the other person is feeling, thinking or believing, and communicating that back to them. Here is the blog:

'Some of the things validation helps with are communication, building trust and it can help lessen distress for someone by showing you just "get it". Invalidation causes the person to get more upset and this happens to many people who self harm and attend A&E. They often feel that they're not taken seriously. When I am educating people about validation this is the story I tell...

One day my daughter had gone off on a bike ride with my wife and I was outside gardening. Suddenly I heard the car pull in and I thought "hmm ... what's happened here?" My daughter appeared on the path, her chin wobbling, looking really upset.

I asked her "what's wrong? What's happened?" She replied that her chain had broken on her bike and she wasn't able to go on her bike ride.

I said, "oh no! You really wanted to go on that bike ride. You must be so sad" (validation).

She started crying and I asked her what she wanted to do. She replied, her voice faltering, that she just didn't know. I saw there was rhubarb growing in the garden. My daughter loves baking. I said, "how about you make a rhubarb crumble? I can cut you some". She said "OK" and after a few more tears off she went into the house and baked a delicious rhubarb crumble.

Now take two... rewind... If she had come down the path and I'd said, "oh you can go on a bike ride another day. Listen, big girls don't cry!" (invalidation) I know she would have become really upset, more than likely run down the path into the house slamming doors and more importantly I wouldn't have got that rhubarb crumble!!'

(BPDFFS, 2016)

But this is what happens in life, particularly with those who seek help for self-harm. They are often ignored or treated with disdain, and those overwhelming emotions that often bring people to self-harm are completely invalidated. A few validating statements such as 'It looks like you're having a really tough time right now' or 'You must be really hurting right now' would help. It's not necessarily agreeing with the self-harm, it's about letting the person know the real emotional pain they are in.

I also think people could learn a thing or two from the people on Twitter with mental health difficulties. Watch how they validate each other on a daily basis, show empathy and really help each other. We know how it feels and we know how to help. It can be peer support at its best.

I'm wondering how people use validation in their work or day-to-day life? I use it at work with my colleagues and my family. It truly helps with relationships.

References

American Psychiatric Association (2013) *Diagnostic and Statistical Manual of Mental Disorders* (5th edition). Washington, DC: American Psychiatric Association.

BPDFFS (2016, 29 May) The Rhubarb Crumble – a lesson in validation [blog post]. Retrieved from bpdffs.wordpress.com

Hamilton L (2010) The Boundary Seesaw Model: good fences make for good neighbours. In: A Tennant and K Howells (eds) *Using Time, Not Doing Time: Practitioner Perspectives on Personality Disorder and Risk*. Chichester: Wiley Blackwell.

McMain ST, Guimond T, Barnhart R, Habinski L & Streiner DL (2016) A randomized trial of brief dialectical behaviour therapy skills training in suicidal patients suffering from borderline disorder. *Acta Psychiatrica Scandinavica* **135** (2) 138–148. Doi: 10.1111/acps.12664

Personality Disorders Commission (2018) *'Shining Lights in Dark Corners of People's Lives': The Consensus Statement for People with Complex Mental Health Difficulties who are Diagnosed with a Personality Disorder*. Retrieved from mind.org.uk

Van der Kolk B (2014) *The Body Keeps the Score: Brain, Mind, and Body in the Healing of Trauma*. New York: Viking.

World Health Organization (2018) *International Classification of Diseases for Mortality and Morbidity Statistics* (11th Revision). Geneva: WTO.

Chapter 2:

Personality Disorder: Breakdown in the Relational Field

Nick Benefield and Rex Haigh

When human development is disrupted, the psychological, social and economic consequences can reach into every area of an individual's personal and social world, resulting in alienated and chaotic lives and repercussions throughout their communities. The causes of this disruption may cover the whole range of physical, environmental, psychological, social and economic factors: from an unlucky genetic inheritance to a difficult birth, child abuse, inadequate parenting, failed attachment, trauma or emotional deprivation. The causes can also be poverty: material poverty, or the poverty of expectation that leaves individuals feeling powerless to have any impact on the world in which they live.

Over-riding differences in class and educational advantage confer upon some strong constitutions – or a range of poorly understood protective factors – which may be sufficient to enable the individual to withstand the impact of these environmental failures and emerge from their early experience to live what appears to be a thriving and healthy life. However, very many people end up in a situation where they are excluded from mainstream society, rejected by those who might be able to help them and destined to live lives of unremitting frustration, without the happiness and fulfilment that most of us would consider just and expect for ourselves and our families.

The people who have ended up in this excluded and marginalised state, and often their families, have little psychological sense of their place among others or where they fit into society. School, working lives and almost any pro-social relationships are difficult or impossible to establish and sustain. They often experience the world as a hostile, unhelpful, threatening or undermining environment; live in a marginalised underclass with high levels of substance misuse, self-harm and criminality; and suffer severe, enduring and disabling mental distress. People in this situation will often use a considerable range of statutory services to little benefit.

A minority will receive a formal diagnosis of 'personality disorder' ('PD') and so gain access to PD intervention services. However, the majority will receive an ambiguous and often prejudicial formulation of their difficulties and will be more likely to meet a range of unsatisfactory public service responses. Dependent on the immediate presenting difficulty, this response will often be inconsistent and have little relevance to the core psychosocial problem faced by individuals who are trapped in the experience of a failing relationship with the world around them (Moran *et al*, 2016).

The policy context

In mental health services, resistance to change is not a viable option if we are to improve services and outcomes. In the 2000s, government policy sought changes to practice in order to achieve three objectives: to improve health and social outcomes, to reduce social exclusion and to improve public protection (Department of Health, Home Office, 1999; National Institute for Mental Health in England, 2003; Joseph & Benefield, 2012). It required a culture of altruism and cooperation in the face of intensifying market competition between health providers, which operated at at least two levels: clinical competition between different treatment 'brands', and economic competition between commercial, public and third sector resourcing mechanisms. The specifics of collaboration included regular events such as an active learning network, quality networks to share and disseminate best practice and generating an unthreatening spirit of friendly rivalry (Haigh & Brookes, 2010).

However, despite high-quality innovations and widespread acclaim from service users, the community-based programme (the 'National Personality Disorder Development Programme') was closed in 2011. Since then, any coordination of these efforts (for non-residential services, at least) has been undertaken by voluntary organisations, such as service user groups and the British and Irish Group for the Study of Personality Disorder (BIGSPD). NHS foundation trust providers and local commissioning groups have generally overseen a competitive ethos to provide 'evidence-based' services with few new resources.

For residential 'severe personality disorder' services, NHS England has been involved in drawing up service specification and commissioning 'Tier 4' provision – but this covers only a fraction of the need. So far it has made little progress towards a more suitable and sustainable commissioning solution, and no progress in gaining recognition of the scale of need in the wider population.

Evidence from the eleven English pilot projects started in 2003–4 demonstrates that good answers do exist (Crawford *et al*, 2007), but that they do not lie in a traditional mental health treatment model or straightforward social policy. They include sophisticated cross-agency work that takes in the experience and expertise from various sectors: including health, social services, offender management, housing, social security, employment and the voluntary sector (Wilson & Haigh, 2011). Most importantly, they also involve new forms of partnership with service users themselves – where they can feel themselves as active agents in their own recovery, rather than passive recipients of technical expertise. In parallel with the National Community PD Programme, the Home Office and Department of Health were working to develop services for high risk offenders with personality disorders and initiated as a joint Dangerous and Severe Personality Disorder (DSPD) policy programme (1999). The approach was to pilot new assessment and treatment services within prison and probation services. Following evaluation, this initiative was superseded by the Offender Personality Disorder (OPD) Programme (2011) a new joint programme between the Ministry of Justice and NHS England. Whilst still focussed on high risk offenders this current programme is jointly commissioned and seeks to develop and research a range of new initiatives for those offenders with complex needs in both prison community probation settings.

This is a field that is more complex than can be addressed by a disease model or unitary interventions, and there is a need to continue to encourage evaluated and researched service innovation, and establish a workforce equipped to meet the demand for skilled and specialist intervention. To be effective, this will require closer collaboration across public services to ensure the relevance of personality disorders is understood and informs policy, strategy and service provision across the fields of health, social care, education and criminal justice. Above all else, the quality of relationship between all professionals and service users is vital to support the work, as a new form of partnership. This needs to be based on the recognition and acceptance of complexity and the commitment to important biopsychosocial principles (Engel, 1980; Bolton & Gillett, 2019), with different roles and responsibilities being actively aligned and coordinated.

However, the commissioning of services has increasingly become based on singular service specifications and dependent on contract monitoring and performance (Appleby *et al*, 2010). The current climate for commissioning and delivering of public services creates a pressure to simplify interventions based on economic efficiency and contractual precision. The need to identify effective interventions and implement them at scale can tend towards a more mechanised, industrialised and uniform model of delivery. The specifications often tend to favour services with sharply defined inclusion and exclusion criteria. This can leave people with more complex problems, who are the most in need, without access to satisfactory interventions. In this way, the whole system is in danger of being led toward the false efficiency promised by the quantification and costing of all services as discrete elements, without considering the relationships, overlaps and coordination between them. Treatment becomes 'one size fits all', while many of the people who need it most do not fit at all.

A model of human development

The starting point for relational-based services has to be what we already know: that human development for everybody has a common basis. In **Figure 2.1** we provide a diagrammatic representation to bring together a wide range of existing theories, as a 'Unified Model of Human Development' underpinned by a 'relational field', which assumes inter-relatedness as a primary condition. This is represented in the diagram as the coloured background. It is in keeping with the group analytic idea that the relationships between people are as important as individuals themselves (Cohn, 1993), and with social ecology approaches that give priority to interconnected, ecological views of life sciences, and modern mathematical ones, rather than mechanistic ones based on Newtonian physical sciences (Capra, 2005). Another fundamental cornerstone of this model is the way in which nurture and environment impacts on biopsychosocial development (Bolton & Gillett, 2019).

The details of the model are based on a range of theories which explain emotional experience, identify life events and predict life outcomes, and it incorporates the main areas of current thinking behind the concept of 'human development'. The life course narrative is a maturational process from birth to death; it must be understood as a complex system, with similar chaotic dynamics to the weather, rather than as a single causal chain of events and consequences. A simplistic, single problem approach is insufficient: solutions require a more whole-person and whole-life framework. For example, an early adverse event which appears objectively trivial may have disproportionate and severe consequences throughout somebody's life. This could be something unpleasant said at school, a moment of perceived rejection by a parent, a pervasive atmosphere of disquiet – or any number of potential experiences. Such an event will not have a single definitive effect, but will also modulate further development by changing the way in which experience is perceived and responded to. And so on, ad infinitum.

With this in mind, we have tried to prevent the model becoming deterministic, and to steer a course between clarity and complexity in an area where finding a common understanding of language often makes it difficult to find the right terms. We have accommodated the ideas of systems theory, including complexity and chaos theories: complexity to accommodate the multiple and interlocking feedback processes that lead to continually changing emergent outcomes that cannot be predetermined (Butz, 2018), and chaos theory in which sensitivity to initial conditions and fundamental uncertainties lead to very limited and short-term areas of predictability such as the 'butterfly effect' (Gleick, 2011).

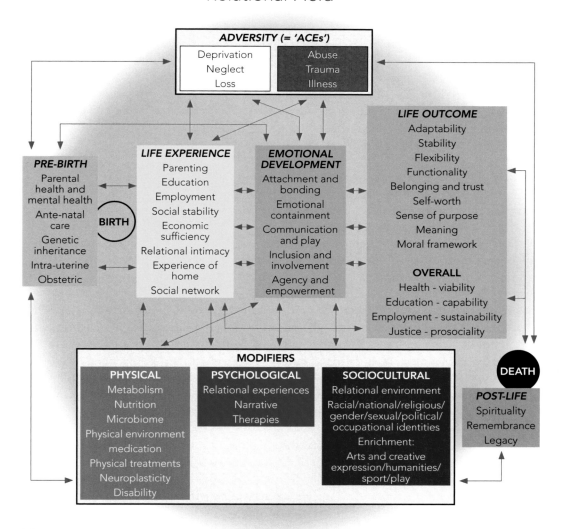

Figure 2.1: A Unified Model of Human Development

An understanding of individual development involves both conscious and unconscious processing, and the whole range of risk and resilience factors, represented by the graduation of colours in the background. It establishes the centrality of the interface between each individual and their world, both internal and external. Although the arrangement of elements is linear, the feedback loops and multiple interactions are indicated by the use of the numerous multidirectional arrows.

The three main areas before 'outcome' are presented, somewhat artificially, as boxes. The centre of the developmental process is 'emotional development' (Haigh, 2013). The others are 'pre-birth' and 'life experience', and all contain numerous elements. 'Pre-birth' covers genetic heritability, parental health and antenatal and birth factors. 'Life experiences' covers the range of individual and social relational experiences that provide the external support for emotional development and stability. 'Emotional developmental' stages assert the importance of a maturing and stable sense of identity, and contribute directly to the development of cognitive and executive capability (Shonkoff *et al*, 2011).

Negative factors that are sometimes called 'adverse childhood experiences' ('ACEs') (Felitti *et al*, 1998; Rutter *et al*, 2007) affect emotional development by omission (such as deprivation or poverty) or commission (such as trauma or abuse): they are shown as a box containing these influencing factors. The other main 'biopsychosocial' factors, which can be positive or negative, are grouped in another box of 'modifiers'. The relationship between these three elements of modifying influences involves a complex inter-relationship with a constant process of feedback, progression and regression; this can also include epigenetic factors. Sociocultural inheritance and expectations will have a variable impact on emotional development. Aspects of emotional development will continue to be strengthened or undermined by the quality and timing of life experiences and the opportunity for experiential provision and learning. In the area of emotional development, issues of adversity, as a result of either commission or omission, can have a significant influence on levels of risk and resilience at an individual level, undermine one's sense of wholeness, and directly affect stability and confidence in a 'lived' life.

'Life outcome' is a moving target (therefore itself also subject to and providing dynamic feedback in the system) and is depicted as another box containing a list of qualities, all of which are dimensional in nature, spanning negative to positive outcomes, with most people existing somewhere between the extreme points. More positive outcomes here indicate the optimal expected results of a satisfactory combination of pre-birth factors, life experience and emotional development. These can be considered as levels of individual capacity and capability and, in the societal sense, show how the individual responds across the four domains of health, education, employment and justice.

'Post life' recognises the significance of individuals' spiritual or religious life, with its expectations of remembrance and legacy, how they may influence the way their life is led, and their acceptance or rejection of life experience. Some religions, for example, have a focus on the afterlife as the defining factor of how one lives one's life in the here and now. The model also acknowledges the interconnected ways in which bereavement and legacy can have significant effects on the life courses of others in the wider relational field (Casement & Tacey, 2006).

Relational practice

Working with this model in mind, close attention must be paid to the quality of relationships, which need not to be undermined by bureaucratic processes. Without this approach, development of services and practices can result in commodification of care and loss of person-centredness. It requires acceptance of a psychosocial way of working which is at odds with the current policies and procedures in most mainstream services.

It also requires attention to non-specific factors in the setting, such as the therapeutic environment, ethos and therapeutic philosophy – rather than concentrating on specific or manualised therapy techniques. An example is the current provision of 'Improving Access to Psychological Therapies' (IAPT) services which seek to provide a management model for distress, rather than understanding the need for a long-term relational intervention (Dalal, 2018). These evidence-based techniques are only one part of a successful service: if a service cannot engage those most in need of help, often in chaotic personal circumstances, any number of randomised controlled trials showing positive results are not relevant.

Good relational practice is driven by a partnership and demands engagement between experience of the service user and expertise of the professional. It also requires the professional to have a good understanding of their own emotional responses. This capacity, to maintain a separate position and yet identify with the service user's position, is at the heart of relational practice. This can unsettle professional roles and require working in more open (and perhaps exposing) ways, across professional boundaries, that some clinicians may find unfamiliar and unwelcome. However, the benefits of improved relationships, care and ultimately outcomes, almost certainly outweigh professional and territorial considerations.

This relational approach cannot be 'claimed' by any specific psychotherapeutic school: the development and maintenance of the therapeutic relationship and therapeutic environment is seen as the main priority. Whatever the therapeutic model, the quality of the relational process is of key importance.

Formal diagnosis and standardised treatment protocols are insufficient. A fundamental requirement is to rely on personal narratives and meaning, which require both the expertise of the professionals and close collaboration with the service user: a formulation is constructed which makes sense of a person's lifelong experiences, and also explains why that person fits the formal diagnostic categories. Making narrative-based meaning of someone's life might also need to include spiritual, cultural, political factors. This becomes a multi-dimensional account, with features of complexity and uncertainty that cannot be accommodated within a diagnostic category (World Psychiatric Association, 2003). Going further, another relational initiative has come from the British Psychological Society, which has recently made a comprehensive case for a new way of thinking about how mental distress is understood and dealt with: the 'Power-Threat-Meaning Framework' (Johnstone et al, 2018). It emphasises that the key question is not 'What is wrong with you?' but rather 'What has happened to you?' Posing this question is central to the intervention, and encourages a deepening of the narrative at the heart of the individual's difficulties.

One needs also to be aware of the context in which the formulation is constructed and delivered: if it is delivered from 'on high' by an 'expert' professional by whom the service user feels quite intimidated, that power relationship would result in a very different outcome from co-production of the formulation in the context of a trusting and established therapeutic alliance. The power imbalance can also be addressed by having an expert by experience present – representing a 'third position' in the conversation (Shonkoff, 2007). Power needs to be located, held and exercised in the context of the relationships between people, and their understanding of each other's roles – not simply in the individuals themselves.

Furthermore, standardised intervention protocols are inadequate without the necessary enrichment of experience (Ryan et al, 2018; Winnicott, 1962). This requires a significant depth of the therapeutic relationship and provision of a facilitating environment – which is considerably more sophisticated than a simple operational protocol can prescribe.

Negative experiences of current mainstream practice often cite discontinuity, lack of reliability and short-termism as problems. We believe that successful relational practice requires a continuity of care and long-term pathway planning so that those needing services actually feel that there is a 'caring matrix' that supports them, through the various vicissitudes that are often part of a successful relationship with both individual therapists and the whole relational field. Although certain elements of this may be discrete time-limited interventions (for example, support for housing), the whole-system ethos of relationality can ensure that it is all experienced as coherent – and that one is not being treated as a number, or as a problem. This requires a management approach that values relationships above procedures, and support for positive risk management at senior levels within an organisation.

Part of these 'ups and downs' is how services manage the breakdown of therapeutic engagement. In the whole-life perspective of treating those with these complex conditions, breakdowns are almost inevitable and certainly should be expected. The response to them must not be perceived as exclusion or rejection, but as an important part of the whole process that can, and should, be managed in a way that is ultimately helpful. It should not only serve the needs of organisations seeking to limit their workload in the face of limited resources, nor should it allow burnt-out practitioners to escape the needs of vulnerable people with claims of 'manipulativeness', 'attention seeking' or 'lack of motivation'. Those practitioners need better selection, induction, training, supervision and support.

Relational practice provides an operational process to allow authentic interpersonal experience and opportunities to find one's place among others, to feel emotional connectedness and internalise positive emotional experience.

User-friendly, relationally based services cannot be designed without service users' active collaboration. This is co-production, or 'co-creation', and is an aspect of 'asset-based community development' (Mathie & Cunningham, 2003). It can be achieved by recruiting 'experts by experience', 'peer mentors', 'people with lived experience' or service users who are currently receiving treatment themselves. Many factors need to be considered to ensure good 'co-production' or 'co-creation', but the underlying success depends on diminishing the sense of 'us and them'. It is important to include the 'staff on the ground', as they can feel disconnected and uninvolved if only senior clinical and management staff meet with the experts by experience to plan services.

Although the broader philosophical objectives are clear – to develop ways of working that prioritise responsive and relational practice – this cannot be achieved without a clarity of purpose that ensures professional boundaries are kept in mind. This needs to be through reflective and relational work which relies on maturational processes and evolving relationships; it cannot be achieved by standard operational procedures alone.

Figure 2.2 illustrates some of these principles, which are required to produce an environment in which relational practice can thrive. The outer field is 'real life' – and although its relational nature is always present, this effect is as often negative as it is positive, particularly for more vulnerable individuals. The next 'level of containment' is a deliberately constructed therapeutic environment – such as in a criminal justice 'psychologically informed planned environment' (PIPE), a 'psychologically informed environment' for homelessness services or a therapeutic community (Johnson, 2010; Haigh, 2007a, 2007b; Haigh et al, 2012). This is not only relevant for those trained as therapists – everybody in a therapeutic environment is an essential participant in the relational field, and will need to be included in processes of training, support and oversight.

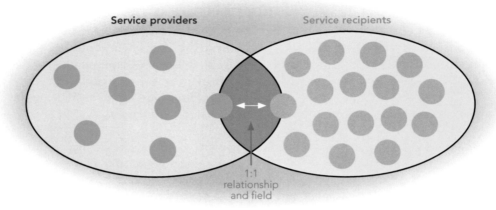

Relational Field

Figure 2.2: Relational Field at System, Environment, Group and Dyadic Levels

The figure shows that a therapeutic environment comprises groups of those who provide a service, and of those who receive it – usually described as staff and service users. The dyadic relationship between individual staff and service users is portrayed at the intersection of the two groups. It is worth noting that, when working outside a specific therapeutic environment, however difficult and non-therapeutic the surrounding setting may be, this can still be a creative and transformational space – although it may lack the power of the whole system to engage and sustain the therapeutic effort.

The diagram also demonstrates the need for an enabling or facilitative space, which the 'relational field' needs in order to be effectively buffered from the disturbances in the wider system. These disturbances might mean budgetary restrictions, changes of higher-level policy, wider social changes or many other perturbations. The essential task, to maintain the integrity of the setting, is to have a structure of management and quality of leadership that allows the relational field to be maintained, and used to positive therapeutic effect, whatever the 'external world' throws at it.

A set of value-based standards to define the diagram's 'therapeutic environment relational field' has been developed as 'Enabling Environments' which identify the necessary conditions to create and maintain a relational milieu (Haigh *et al*, 2012). The values and the standards are shown in **Table 2.1**. **Figure 2.3** shows the required inputs and anticipated outputs in existing forms of relational environments (Wilson & Haigh, 2011).

Values and Standards for Enabling Environments
BELONGING The nature and quality of relationships are of primary importance
BOUNDARIES There are expectations of behaviour and processes to maintain and review them
COMMUNICATION It is recognised that people communicate in different ways
DEVELOPMENT There are opportunities to be spontaneous and try new things
INVOLVEMENT Everyone shares responsibility for the environment
SAFETY Support is available for everyone
STRUCTURE Engagement and purposeful activity is actively encouraged
EMPOWERMENT Power and authority are open to discussion
LEADERSHIP Leadership takes responsibility for the environment being enabling
OPENNESS External relationships are sought and valued

Table 2.1: The Enabling Environments Values and Standards

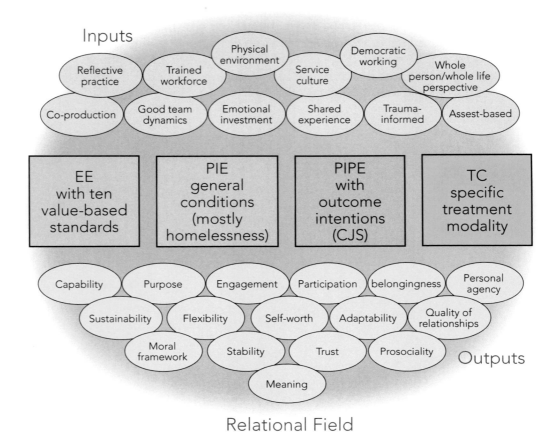

Figure 2.3: Inputs and Outputs

A way forward

In the matter of public policy making, we often provide policy interventions that are out of synchrony with our generally accepted views of how human behaviour is understood and can be influenced or changed. In general, society sees a move to simplification as more likely to provide a solution than managing the 'messiness' of a whole-person/whole-life framework. Public policy may be undermined because it is not based on a sufficiently robust model of understanding how humans develop and how their behaviour may be driven, or changed (Shonkoff, 2007), by factors not addressed by the policy initiatives themselves.

Closer collaboration across public services could be achieved by a commonly understood, simple, unified model of human development as outlined above. This would ensure that the relevance of presenting disorders, conditions and problems is more broadly understood, and interventions are designed and delivered on a whole-person/whole-life basis across the fields of health, social care, education and criminal justice. This could provide the starting point for agreement on a framework for human development that will underpin decision-making and the foundations on which public service provision and professional practice can be improved. With any new policy initiative, its intended impact needs to be considered in terms of this wider framework in order that its effectiveness can be realised, whole-system contradictions anticipated and the risks of fragmentation reduced. Policies could be considered within the context of other related policy initiatives. This would prevent parts of the overall structure being left out, or working against each other, and causing inefficiencies, ineffectiveness and wastage at best or morbidity and mortality at worst.

This absence of coordinated policy is reflected at central government level by the separation of the departments and organisations responsible for health, social care, housing, justice, education and public health: they are often dealing with the same problems – of disrupted human development – in inefficiently different or competing ways. This also results in gaps or conflicts between competing service provisions.

Figure 2.4 proposes a higher-order system which could bring about rich, complex, evidence-based and appropriate growth of the field, by active collaboration between four key areas of responsibility. Those involved are policy makers and commissioners, clinicians and other professional staff, academics, patients and the public.

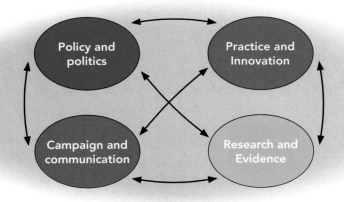

Figure 2.4: A Collaborative System

The four areas of responsibility on which it is based are:

1. Experience of the delivery of front-line services (with effective leadership and innovative practice).

2. Coordination and focusing of research and evidence gathering.

3. Policy setting in a context of politics.

4. Campaigning through informed patient and public awareness.

A more effective interaction between these four elements is required. Policy and the wider political infrastructure – including commissioning, informed by and linked to practice, its leadership and innovations in line with the changing research and evidence background – are in themselves often not coordinated. The power of the wider patient and public voice, the pressures for progressive and modernising change, are often radical, but generally service changes trail some way behind both evidence and practice. Policy, dominated by the short-termism of politics, struggles to lead and generally fails to act with coherence and coordination.

The relationship between the functions needs to be more conscious and planned. The inter-relationship between these four distinct elements is hypothesised as being necessary in order that the effectiveness of each results in a more coordinated outcome from the development of services to those with complex psychosocial needs. As we have laid out above, too often those with complex needs experience services as partial and fragmented in their usefulness.

A more actively coordinated system could avoid the 'top-down' model of service development that is frequently used for health innovations. This generally involves identifying a problem, developing and defining treatments, several stages of research to compare them and analyse what works for whom, and implementing the conclusions on a wide scale. But for personality disorder, there is no single accepted approach and the evidence base is immature: there is never likely to be a single or simple solution. However, there are several principles which are valued to both professionals and to service users – which were the subject of earlier sections of this chapter.

To be effective in the wider system, services must not exist in isolation. To work effectively between professions, organisations and sectors, shared ownership and equality of partnership is needed. This is clearly 'relational practice' applied at a different level of operations – the relationship between organisations, and their representatives. When done successfully, joint operations across integrated pathways become possible, and networks of cooperation and collaboration can develop. This is the ideal of properly 'joined-up' services, which will be able to give service users the experience of being treated as a whole person by a system that 'cares', rather than receiving fragments of 'care' which are often disconnected.

Training – particularly for appropriate attitudes – is essential for all levels of staff. For many of those in senior administrative, management and leadership roles it is essential to understand the difference between 'procedural' and 'relational' practice. In management theory this is sometimes described as the difference between 'transactional' and 'transformational' leadership. It is only through challenging attitudes such as 'that is the way we do it here' and 'if it isn't broken, don't fix it' that progressive innovation and system adaptation can happen.

From 2004, the National Programme developed an awareness and skills training escalator (NIMHE, 2003). This workforce initiative was commissioned as a collaborative enterprise between academic institutions, a service user organisation and an NHS mental health service. In the last fifteen years, the courses have been delivered in a wide range of service settings and are a requirement in specialist personality disorder services in health and criminal justice settings. The development of these programmes and modules has drawn upon a wide range of professional expertise, thereby creating an effective cross-disciplinary collaboration. Academic fields that have a claim to parts of the developmental narrative currently include the following:

- psychiatry
- psychologies (social, developmental and experimental)
- psychotherapy (psychoanalysis, group analysis, systemic, integrative)
- medical sciences (genetics, pharmacology, biochemistry, physiology, clinical studies)
- neurosciences (neurobiology/-anatomy/-physiology, and neuroimaging)
- social sciences (sociology, anthropology, critical theory and feminism, phenomenology and hermeneutics, criminology, disability studies, human geography, education, economics)
- humanities (philosophy, spirituality, arts, linguistics).

Relevant contemporary research is undertaken in all these fields, and there is a large literature base. However, the depth of understanding is much greater within the boundaries of each area of study than in the relationships between them. Overall, the current state of our knowledge is variable and there are overarching themes that remain conceptually and scientifically incomplete.

Although there is a substantial 'what works' literature, professional and ideological rivalries hamper a more integrated understanding of the 'whole picture'. In psychotherapy, psychoanalysis is often dismissed as old-fashioned and no longer relevant (Salkovskis & Wolpert, 2012), while the growth of cognitive behavioural therapy has caused similar antagonism in the opposite direction (Shedler, 2010). Psychiatry has been criticised for its diagnostic approaches (Johnstone, 2014) and the influence of the pharmacological industry (Moncrieff, 2008). Nature versus nurture arguments are sometimes unhelpfully polarised, with specialist fields competing to grow and survive by bidding for the resources to undertake their work.

This all leads to little impetus to work across fields to 'join up' the rich but disparate knowledge base about human development, particularly when so much of the relationship between the different parts is of an abstract or ill-defined nature. To change this would require specialist areas of theory and practice to locate themselves in the wider developmental context: whole-person and whole-life. This would allow determination of the key collaborations necessary to make specific policy or service interventions more connected, relevant and effective. We suggest that it is possible to provide a broad consensus on human development, and its course over time, as a basis for a greater common understanding of how we are, how we progress or change, and how a complex rather than simplistic approach is vital.

Summary

In this chapter we argue that as individuals we cannot avoid the centrality of relationship between ourselves and our world. At different moments this involves a focus on another individual, a group of 'others', society, and now, importantly, the 'global group'. In our rapidly changing digital world with new forms of contact, we are at risk of losing the importance and nuance of relationships.

We believe that we need to focus on the common experience we all have of a birth-to-death process of relationships, with all the complex, messy and unsettling processes involved. This is the fundamentally common shared ground with others in our relational world. For those individuals with the most adverse experiences in development, the boundary between themselves and their environment is the area in which distress and disorder is most experienced. Understanding the dynamics and potentiality of the relational field is essential if we are to guard against the conscious and unconscious defences of denial, splitting and avoidance. Reducing human life to a linear explanation is not the answer.

In order to ensure the appropriate provision of services and support, a fundamental change in attitude and approach is required. Understanding ourselves and others requires active efforts to resist the simplistic, and make the extra effort to embrace the complicated.

Professional leadership and baseline training and education across public services is required. Relational practice, with sufficient knowledge of the dynamics of development, needs to become the 'standard operating system' for work in all public services.

References

Appleby J, Ham C, Imison C & Jennings M (2010) *Improving NHS Productivity: More With the Same Not More of the Same*. Retrieved from kingsfund.org.uk

Bolton D & Gillett G (2019) *The Biopsychosocial Model of Health and Disease*. Cham: Palgrave Macmillan.

Butz MR (2018) *Chaos and Complexity: Implications for Psychological Theory and Practice*. Boca Raton: CRC Press.

Capra F (2005) Complexity and life. *Theory, Culture & Society* **22** (5) 33–44.

Casement A & Tacey DJ (2006) *The Idea of the Numinous: Contemporary Jungian and Psychoanalytic Perspectives*. London: Routledge.

Cohn HW (1993) Matrix and intersubjectivity: Phenomenological aspects of group analysis. *Group Analysis* **26** (4) 481–486 Doi: 10.1177/0533316493264008

Crawford M, Rutter D, Price K, Weaver T, *et al* (2007) Learning the lessons: A multi-method evaluation of dedicated community-based services for people with personality disorder. Retrieved from http://www.netscc.ac.uk/hsdr/files/project/SDO_FR_08-1404-083_V01.pdf

Dalal F (2018) CBT: *The Cognitive Behavioural Tsunami: Managerialism, Politics, and the Corruptions of Science*. Abingdon/New York: Routledge.

Department of Health, Home Office (1999) Managing dangerous people with severe personality disorder. Available from: http://www.homeoffice.gov.uk/cpd/persdis.ht

Engel GL (1980) The clinical application of the biopsychosocial model. *Am J Psychiatry* **137** (5) 535–544.

Felitti VJ, Anda RF, Nordenberg D, Williamson DF, *et al* (1998) Relationship of childhood abuse and household dysfunction to many of the leading causes of death in adults: The Adverse Childhood Experiences (ACE) Study. *American Journal of Preventive Medicine* **14** (4) 245–258.

Gleick J (2011) *Chaos: Making a New Science (Enhanced edition)*. New York: Open Road Media.

Haigh R (2007a) New kids on the block! The government-funded English personality disorder services. *Therapeutic Communities* **28** (3) 300.

Haigh R (2007b) The New Day TCs: Five radical features. *Therapeutic Communities* **28** (2) 111–126.

Haigh R (2013) The quintessence of a therapeutic environment. *Therapeutic Communities* **34** (1) 6–15.

Haigh R & Brookes M (2010) Special Edition: Personality Disorder. *Mental Health Review Journal* **15** (4).

Haigh R, Harrison T, Johnson R, Paget S, *et al* (2012) Psychologically informed environments and the 'Enabling Environments' initiative. *Housing, Care and Support* **15** (1) 34–42.

Johnson R (2010) PIELink – A practice exchange for psychologically informed environments. Retrieved from www.pielink.net

Johnstone L (2014) *A Straight-Talking Introduction to Psychiatric Diagnosis*. Ross-on-Wye: PCCS Books.

Johnstone L, Boyle M, Cromby J, Dillon J, *et al* (2018) *The Power Threat Meaning Framework*. Retrieved from https://www1.bps.org.uk/system/files/user-files/Division%20of%20Clinical%20Psychology/public/INF299%20PTM%20overview%20web.pdf

Joseph N & Benefield N (2012) A joint offender personality disorder strategy: An outline summary. *Criminal Behaviour and Mental Health* **22** (3) 210–217.

Mathie A & Cunningham G (2003) From clients to citizens: asset-based community development as a strategy for community-driven development. *Development in Practice* **13** (5) 474–486.

Moncrieff J (2008) *A Myth of the Chemical Cure*. London: Palgrave Macmillan.

Moran P, Romaniuk H, Coffey C, Chanen A, *et al* (2016) The influence of personality disorder on the future mental health and social adjustment of young adults: A population-based, longitudinal cohort study. *The Lancet Psychiatry* **3** (7) 636–645.

National Institute for Mental Health in England (2003) *Personality Disorder: No Longer a Diagnosis of Exclusion. Policy Implementation Guidance for the Development of Services for People with Personality Disorder*. London: Department of Health.

NIMHE (2003) *Breaking the Cycle of Rejection: The personality disorders capabilities framework*. London: DH.

Rutter M, Beckett C, Castle J, Colvert E, *et al* (2007) Effects of profound early institutional deprivation: An overview of findings from a UK longitudinal study of Romanian adoptees. *European Journal of Developmental Psychology* **4** (3) 332–350.

Ryan S, Benefield N & Baker B (2018) Socially created activities in psychologically informed planned environments: Engaging and relating in the offender personality disorder pathway. *Journal of Forensic Practice* **20** (3) 202–210.

Salkovskis P & Wolpert L (2012) Does psychoanalysis have a valuable place in modern mental health services? No. *BMJ: British Medical Journal* (Online) 344 e1211.

Shedler J (2010) The efficacy of psychodynamic psychotherapy. *American Psychologist* **65** (2) 98–109.

Shonkoff JP (2007) A science based framework for early childhood policy. Retrieved from http://www.ncsl.org/Portals/1/documents/cyf/HarvardChildPolicy.pdf

Shonkoff JP, Duncan GJ, Fisher PA, Magnuson K, *et al* (2011) *Building the Brain's 'Air Traffic Control' System: How Early Experiences Shape the Development of Executive Function*. Harvard University: Center on the Developing Child.

Wilson L & Haigh R (2011) *Innovation in Action* [online]. Retrieved from http://personalitydisorder.org.uk/wp-content/uploads/2015/06/Innovation-in-Action.pdf

Winnicott DW (1962) Ego integration in child development. In: DW Winnicott, *The Maturational Processes and the Facilitating Environment*. London: Taylor & Francis.

World Psychiatric Association (2003) Idiographic (personalised) diagnostic formulation. *The British Journal of Psychiatry* **182** (S45) s55–s57.

Chapter 3:
The Scale of the Problem

Sarah Skett and Kimberley Barlow

Introduction: What is the problem?

Relationships are at the heart of all things 'personality disorder'. They are at the heart of the problems and distress affecting people likely to meet the diagnostic category, and they should be at the heart of how services are both organised and provided to support those people. Unfortunately, this is very often not the case.

It is striking that different public services, such as teaching, housing and homelessness and the criminal justice system, as well as mental health, all speak of relationships as being necessary to achieve their outcomes. At the same time, these services are organised in such a way as to make it very difficult to actually maintain consistent, effective and therapeutic relationships, from policy and strategic initiatives, to service design both within and between services.

In addition, from a mental health perspective we are getting better at understanding prevalence, which highlights the disparity between service capacity and the scale of need that is out there. There are other groups in the population with unknown levels of need, as they are hidden in other systems such as criminal justice, are misdiagnosed or are 'invisible' to the system. This chapter is an attempt to argue that the scale of the problem needs to be understood and described across a range of different levels/modalities: need, cost, policy, systemic, service and individual. It is not an exhaustive list or review of the literature or prevalence studies; nor is it an exposition on the issues to do with the diagnosis or definition of 'personality disorder' itself; but it does aim to highlight the scale of the task ahead.

Problems relating to the scale of need

Problems related to an individual's interpersonal relationships are very common. For example, Yang *et al* (2010) completed an epidemiological study which showed that only 23% of a standard population they sampled had no personality 'pathology' at all, as measured by the screening version of the Structured Clinical Interview for DSM–IV Personality Disorders (SCID–II). Further, they found associations between more severe personality 'pathology' and childhood institutional care, expulsion from school, contacts with the criminal justice system, economic inactivity and greater service contact with primary and secondary care. One of their conclusions was the observation that as severity increased, so did the complexity of need and the likelihood that individual 'personality disorder' diagnostic categories would overlap, and become less useful and distinctive.

The implication of this study is that three quarters of the adult population demonstrate interpersonal problems of some kind. By this measure, 'personality pathology' is normal and everywhere. Not only that; the study also resonates with the increasing findings that these kinds of issues are rooted in our developmental histories, and probably therefore describe a 'normal' and to some extent protective response to such experiences. At what point these problems constitute a 'disorder', an 'illness' or a 'mental health problem' rather than simply being symptomatic of humanity is another question, informed by an increasing de-medicalisation agenda, and a groundswell led by experts by experience and professionals to view these problems in a more holistic and non-labelling way.

Although the use of different methodologies and diagnostic tools makes it difficult to draw a clear picture, literature regarding prevalence consistently indicates that the problems associated with a 'personality disorder' diagnosis are very common. For example, NIMHE's publication *'Personality Disorder: No Longer a Diagnosis of Exclusion'* (2003) states that between 10–13% of the adult population could be considered to satisfy the diagnosis for 'personality disorder', and that there is equal distribution between men and women in number. However, there are qualitative differences, in that 'anti-social personality disorder' is more common among men, and 'borderline personality disorder' more common among women. The Yang *et al* (2010) study takes a more global view, as the authors have incorporated and attempted to understand the dimensional (rather than categorical) aspects of a complex inter-relationship of symptoms which also will vary somewhat over time and context.

The Care Quality Commission (CQC) (2017) describes an estimated 1.8 million people accessing some kind of adult mental health or learning disability service at some point in 2015/16. It goes on to describe around 3,500 beds located in 'locked rehabilitation' wards (services which ought to be caring for patients with greater need) and around 3,700 beds in low, medium or high secure hospitals. The total bed capacity for inpatient mental health services is therefore around 7–8,000 beds. This number will include all levels of mental health need, including serious mental illness, anxiety, depression and learning disability. Bed numbers in the NHS have fallen across the board, including those providing services for mental health, from

299,000 in 1987/8 to 142,000 in 2017 (Ewbank *et al*, 2017). The largest reductions have taken place in mental health beds (including learning disability services), as a result of a policy to provide care in the community. In addition, despite a call from NHS England for clinical commissioning groups to increase spending generally on mental health by £1 billion (NHS England Five Year Forward View 2014), a King's Fund analysis (Gilburt, 2016) has shown that in real terms 40% of trusts have seen a decrease in income.

The Care Quality Commission (CQC) (2017) describes an estimated 1.8 million people accessing some kind of adult mental health or learning disability service at some point in 2015/16. They go on to describe around 3500 beds located in 'locked rehabilitation' wards, and around 3700 beds in low, medium or high secure hospitals. The total bed capacity for inpatient mental health (excluding acute inpatient beds) is therefore around 7-8000 beds. Anecdotally it has been estimated by clinicians in the field that around a third of people who are currently in 'locked rehabilitation' wards would satisfy the primary diagnosis of 'personality disorder'. There is no consensus on the definition of 'locked rehabilitation' wards other than they are units which people cannot freely leave. They are not specifically commissioned to offer evidence-based treatment for personality disorder. There are concerns that they are being used as long stay wards in which people become institutionalised. They are also expensive and are most often provided to the NHS by private healthcare companies.

Bed numbers in the NHS have fallen across the board including those providing services for mental health from 299,000 in 1987/8 to 142,000 in 2017(Ewbank *et al*, The King's Fund, 2017) .The largest reductions have taken place in mental health beds as a result of a policy to provide care in the community. This had led to a polarisation in treatment options for personality disorder, either 'locked rehabilitation' wards or community-based treatment. There are only 55 beds commissioned by NHSE to treat patients who need the containment of an inpatient setting. Despite a call from NHS England on Clinical Commissioning Groups to increase spending generally on mental health by £1 billion, (NHS England, *Five Year Forward View*, 2014), a King's Fund analysis (Gilburt, 2016) has shown that in real terms 40% of trusts have seen a decrease in income leading to a depletion of funding available for community-based treatment. Although 84% of trusts offer dedicated personality disorder treatments there is wide variability in terms of accessibility and quality (https://www.ncbi.nlm.nih.gov/pmc/articles/PMC5623882/) leaving large numbers of people without access to appropriate treatment.

Anecdotally it has been estimated by clinicians in the field that around a third of people who are currently in 'locked rehabilitation' wards would satisfy the diagnosis of a 'personality disorder'.

Let's compare this provision to the need described in the prevalence studies for 'personality disorder'; for ease we will assume this is a 10% prevalence figure (as described in NIHME 'No Longer a Diagnosis of Exclusion, 2003). The population of England and Wales is approximately 59 million (ONS, 2018a); discounting those under 18, this leaves approximately 46.5 million adults. Ten per cent of this number is nearly 4.6 million people. Not all of these people will suffer to the degree where they require specialist mental health treatment, however Wilson and Haigh (2011) provide a good summary of studies up to 2011 and describe 'the burden of morbidity and mortality' that is found in a cohort of people with a diagnosis of 'personality disorder'. This cohort of people:

> '... are more likely to experience adverse life events including relationship difficulties, housing problems, homelessness and unemployment. They are also found to have frequent and escalating contact across a range of services including mental health, social services, A&E, GPs and the criminal justice system. The presenting problems tend to be characterised by recurrent episodes of deliberate self-harm, substance abuse, interpersonal problems, anxiety, depression, brief episodes of psychosis, eating disturbances and sometimes violence, more commonly as victims than as perpetrators.'

The degree of suffering experienced is well illustrated by considering the estimated rates of 'personality disorder' among those who are at risk of or complete suicide. Doyle *et al* (2016) found a 20-fold increase in suicide risk for patients diagnosed with 'personality disorder' versus no recorded psychiatric disorder. This was further increased in those diagnosed with 'borderline personality disorder' and where there was co-morbid alcohol misuse: 37 and 45-fold increased risk respectively.

Black *et al* (2004) have estimated that at least three-quarters of people with 'borderline personality disorder' have had at least one suicide attempt, and the risk of completed suicide among these patients may be as high as 10%.

The prevalence of 'personality disorder' in community probation and prison cohorts, although not critically examined for many years, is high. Between 60 and 70% of the prison population met the criteria for at least one form of 'personality disorder' (Singleton *et al*, 1997; Fazel & Danesh 2002). A small-scale study in Lincolnshire (Brooker *et al*, 2012) suggested that this was 50% of the probation caseload, prior to the split between the National Probation Service (NPS) and Community Rehabilitation Companies (CRCs). The prison population is approximately 83,000 (as of 28 September 2018: HMPPS, Population and Capacity Briefing, 2018), which equates to approximately 49,800–58,100 people who might satisfy a diagnosis of 'personality disorder' who are currently in prison.

The developing dataset from the Offender Personality Disorder pathway programme has identified more than 30,000 offenders (approximately 2,000 are women) who show characteristics that could be diagnosed as 'personality disorder'. These cases are drawn from the higher risk National Probation Service caseload only, not those managed by CRCs; in the case of men, they also have to be deemed to be a 'high risk of harm to others' at some point in their current sentence (Skett *et al*, 2017). Thus one third of the NPS caseload currently consists of people who both present a risk to others and have a potentially significant mental health problem.

It can be postulated that certain symptom clusters are more likely to present to mental health services than others (those who are more emotionally distressed, or self-harming), and that those who satisfy a diagnosis of 'anti-social personality disorder' will be more likely to be present in the criminal justice population and not seek traditional mental health services. However, the scale of this need set against the capacity of the NHS or the criminal justice system to offer a service is alarming: the traditional provision of mental health services would appear to be woefully inadequate. Indeed, the question is whether it should fall to the NHS alone to provide services for such a number of people who exhibit this degree of distress and/or risk to others.

Economic cost

In 2009, the National Institute for Health and Clinical Excellence (NICE) stated that the economic costs of people with the most complex problems were high, given that they place the greatest demand on a range of services such as accident and emergency (A&E) and frequent admissions to mental health services. This did not include, when considering criminal justice, frequent and repeated offences and repeat prison sentences, and costs associated with the consequences for victims and their families.

The CQC (2017) examined hospital episode statistics (a database containing all hospital admissions, A&E attendance and outpatient appointments) and estimated a cost of £10 million in one year attributable to likely 'personality disorder'. This will be a huge underestimation as it would have relied on being able to identify likely personality disorder at admission/presentation. Further, a study by Rendu *et al* (2002) showed that complex emotional need significantly predicted increased total costs of service.

The key questions are whether evidence-based services are being delivered (therefore maximising expected outcomes), whether earlier access to services may prevent future increased cost to the system overall, and whether the current service configuration is the most efficient and cost-effective way of doing things.

In the United Kingdom the cost of a single suicide is estimated to be £1.6m (Knapp & Iemmi, 2014), the cost of a single homicide is just under £3.3m, and the cost of a violent offence with injury is £14k and one without injury £6k (Heeks *et al* 2018). A report by Zala and McCrone (2017) cited in the Consensus Statement (British Psychological Society, 2018) claimed that while evidence-based psychological treatment was more costly in the short term (£751), participants demonstrated an immediate reduction in self-harming and suicidal behaviour, as well as a reduction in violence (when compared to standard care). A reduction of one violent incident without harm would pay for nine such episodes of care, a prevented suicide would pay for 2,130 episodes of care, and a prevented homicide 4,394 episodes of care. It is accepted that this is a very simplistic comparison, but providing preventative services in the short term could lead to greater long term benefits.

The Leeds Personality Disorder Managed Clinical Network connects professionals across Leeds and offers up to two years' clinical case management focusing on the development of collaborative relationships and supporting people to develop self-management and social integration skills. Kane *et al* (2016) showed that this service achieved substantial reductions in healthcare usage and expenditure in the short to medium term following intervention.

Clearly, the economic case for providing evidenced based and effective services is easily made. Yet, a report by the Healthcare Quality Improvement Partnership (Safer Care for People with Personality Disorder, 2018) concluded that 'patients with personality disorder who died by suicide or committed homicide were not receiving care consistent with NICE guidance'.

Problems from a policy perspective

Through the early 2000s there was increasing awareness of issues to do with 'personality disorder', in particular where serious offending was related to severe interpersonal difficulties. The 1996 murder of Lynn and Megan Russell by Michael Stone suddenly and violently exposed a serious failing of mental health services in England and Wales. Michael Stone was convicted in 1999; it emerged that he had been discharged from mental health services just prior to the murders, which led to an inquiry into his mental health care. The Right Honourable Alan Milburn, then the Secretary of State for Health, proposed to change the Mental Health Act (1983) to allow the detention of 'dangerous people with personality disorder' even if they had not committed any crimes. Thankfully, this unethical proposal was dropped, but what remained was a change in the Mental Health Act (1983, revised 2007) which allowed people diagnosed with personality disorders to be treated and detained in mental health facilities – prior to this, people with such a diagnosis tended to be actively excluded from services and deemed 'untreatable'.

The policy document *Managing Dangerous People with Severe Personality Disorder (DSPD)* (Department of Health and Home Office, 1999), a direct consequence of the Russell murders, then led to policy guidance in the form of the National Institute for Mental Health in England's (NIMHE) *Personality Disorder: No Longer a Diagnosis of Exclusion and Breaking the Cycle of Rejection: The Personality Disorder Capabilities Framework* (2003a). This political and public awareness kick started a groundswell of policy change which led to improved funding and services and a change in the law. The funding for the DSPD programme was an average of £150,000 per patient per year, ranging from around £300,000 in a high security hospital to around £80,000 in a high security prison. The community personality disorder programme, however, did not attract anything like the same level of funding – £6.8 million per year for the whole of England and Wales.

Further policy change came in 2011 when the Department of Health and Ministry of Justice's joint publication of the *Response to the Offender Personality Disorder Consultation* directly led to the instigation of the Offender Personality Disorder pathway programme. This followed evaluation and criticism of the DSPD programme's limited ability to deliver a pathway of services to the number of people who had committed offences that needed it.

It could be argued therefore that we are in a very different place now than we were in the 1990s, when patients with a diagnosis of personality disorder were actively vilified, stigmatised and excluded from services. To a certain extent this is true: the 2007 revisions to the Mental Health Act (1983) no longer allow exclusion on the basis of diagnosis; there is more funding in the criminal justice system as part of the OPD pathway; and there is still a programme of workforce development – the Personality Disorder Knowledge and Understanding Framework (KUF) – which was commissioned by the Department of Health in 2007, and is now largely managed through the OPD pathway.

However, other subsequent policy changes have had a significant negative impact. The creation of NHS England and clinical commissioning groups following the 2012 Health and Social Care Act was the biggest re-organisation to the structure of the NHS since its inception in 1947. It abolished primary care trusts and strategic health authorities and transferred healthcare funding to hundreds of CCGs. It also allowed private (for profit) organisations access to the healthcare market. The Secretary of State for Health was disinvested of the responsibility for the health of citizens, and CCGs could independently decide how to spend their budget. This 'decentralisation' should have allowed CCGs to plan locally for their populations, leaving more specialised services and those needed by a fewer number of patients (such as specialised mental health provision – Tier 4 level and secure services) to be commissioned by the national NHS England.

In reality, it has led to wholescale disinvestment of community mental health services, and in particular a worsening of provision for those people diagnosed with 'personality disorder'. Some CCGs may have prioritised the development of specialist services for 'personality disorder' but many did not, and further, after the first personality disorder programme officially ended around 2011, existing community services at Tier 2 and 3 which had thrived as part of the programme were not continued. Patients were more likely to access services in independent (private) beds and out of area, leading to difficulties with family and local ties. This disrupted pathways of care and stranded patients in specialised services at Tier 4 and above. In addition, the reduction in long-term therapy and closure of day hospitals, and the drive to short cycles of care, all compromised the ability to form therapeutic and trusting relationships which should be at the heart of services.

The criminal justice system has also seen major reform via the Transforming Rehabilitation (TR) initiatives that cleaved probation services in two, a national probation service (NPS, dealing with higher risk cases) and community rehabilitation companies (CRCs, managing lower risk cases and also providing much of the standard resettlement work formerly undertaken by probation and prison staff, such as accommodation support). Again, CRCs opened the door to both private and voluntary sector providers to form consortia and bid to run these justice services under commercial contracts. Whereas before there were two public services providing offender management and reducing reoffending interventions (HM Prison Service and probation trusts – including probation staff being co-located in prisons), now there are separate CRCs, an NPS, HMPS and privately managed prisons which are each responsible for disparate strands of a criminal justice pathway. Previously high-performing prisons had to stop their resettlement work and hand it over to CRCs who then failed to provide. Recently, Working Links, a CRC providing services in Wales and the South West, has gone into administration, and there is widespread public criticism of both the way these contracts were managed and the organisation of the system itself. *The Guardian* (Grierson, 2018) reported that CRCs would be 'bailed out' by the public purse to the tune of £500 million to prevent widespread failure and in May 2019 the government announced that CRCs would no longer manage people convicted of offences and that this task would revert to the NPS (HM Government website, 16 May 2019), thereby implicitly accepting that the previous reform was a failure, and meaning more restructuring and upheaval in a critical public service.

This change all happened roughly at the same time as the severe cuts to public funding following the financial crash and the subsequent 'austerity' rhetoric, leading to 'benchmarking' of prison staffing numbers and large numbers of, often experienced, staff leaving the service. The drastic cut in prison officer numbers between approximately 2012 to 2016, driven by the need to save money, has been publicly acknowledged as a mistake by a subsequent Conservative minister (the Right Honourable Rory Stewart, speaking on the Today programme, August 2018). Recognition of these difficulties at the system level is not to belittle the superb work undertaken by individuals in all of these organisations who were, and are, trying to provide a good service.

Policies that were meant to improve services (and in particular improve efficiency and cost effectiveness) have done the opposite, leading to broken or no pathways of care, and a failure of policy to both understand and describe the need for services to be integrated and connected.

Problems from a system perspective

> 'This is not a case of a man with a dangerous personality disorder being ignored by agencies with responsibilities for supervising and caring for him. He received a considerable degree of attention over the years in question. The challenge presented by cases such as Michael Stone's is that his problems are not easily attributable to a single feature of his condition or to combinations of them. Further, he did not easily fall into the province of one agency or a combination of them.'
> Report of the independent inquiry into the care and treatment of Michael Stone.
> (NHS South East Coast, 2006, pp4–8)

The current methods of providing or commissioning public services tend to 'split off' an individual's problems and have different services, not usually co-ordinated, tackle them. This leads to a range of systemic problems when viewed from the individual's perspective.

The 'cliff edge' problem is illustrated by considering someone coming to the end of their prison sentence who is homeless. It is very unlikely that this person would be prioritised for housing by a local authority (for example, some local authorities in London will only house people who have lived in the borough for ten years or more). Without an address it is unlikely the person will be able to get stable employment, and we know that this is a major protective factor for future abstinence from offending. This is despite the possibility that the prison has worked hard (and spent public money) to help the person address their potential re-offending. Thus the pathway of recovery, or desistance from offending, meets an abrupt cliff edge.

The 'see-saw' problem is related, but occurs when someone requires contemporaneous services from different agencies; so, for example, the person's mental health and offending are linked and therefore both of these issues need to be addressed together. However, services, particularly those in the community, are rarely able to address forensic issues alongside mental health, and people with significant forensic issues are often excluded as being unmanageable.

The 'catch 22 problem' traps people in circular stagnation, exemplified by someone with significant substance misuse problems who also has problems with emotional instability and requires mental health support. The mental health service will likely insist the substance misuse is tackled first, as this would not allow the person to be responsive to the psychological therapy offered; but the substance misuse is itself a symptom of the mental health problem, and is not likely to abate until this underlying issue is tackled.

Services themselves can become trapped by attempting to offer things that are actually the purview of other statutory agencies; for example, a primary mental health service decides to offer supported housing to meet a need. Ultimately there is overlap with other statutory services, inefficiency and potential confusion about who is doing what.

Services are commissioned and operate in silos; responsibilities rarely encompass a whole-person approach. In the NHS, personality disorder services are commissioned differently depending on the tier the person potentially falls into: tier 1–3 services are commissioned by local clinical commissioning groups and relate to more local geographies, whereas tiers 4–6 are commissioned by NHS England on a regional or national basis; there is thus an artificial break between locally and nationally commissioned services, which rely on each other to provide a complete care pathway.

Some people who struggle with very complex, severe and enduring interpersonal problems commit offences, and some will be serious sexual and violent offences, as described in the Yang *et al* work on severity. It is important to note that most people likely to meet the diagnosis 'personality disorder' do not commit offences. However, there are a significant minority of people who do, and very often their needs are complex and cut across traditional diagnostic criteria. A high proportion of this population will at some point in their lives access both mental health services and criminal justice system services. When examining the developmental trajectories leading to the development of serious offending and severe interpersonal problems, they are often very similar, if not identical, consisting of multiple and serial adverse childhood experiences (ACEs) (Skett & Lewis, 2019).

Problems from a service perspective

'Many clinicians and mental health practitioners are reluctant to work with people with personality disorder because they believe that they have neither the skills, training or resources to provide an adequate service, and because many believe there is nothing that mental health services can offer.'

(NIMHE, 2003)

Tackling the pervasive and longstanding multifaceted problems presented by people likely to be diagnosed with personality disorder is complex, hard and exhausting. It often requires working with people with fluctuating motivation, but clear distress and very limited quality of life. It requires a dedicated, well-trained and well-supported staffing group. However Haigh in 2007 pointed out that often there is a lack of understanding of needs, and a poorly trained workforce offering ineffective treatment interventions. A vicious cycle ensues whereby inadequate service design compounds the complex interpersonal issues, often increasing distress, making further problems more likely and reducing the likelihood of positive future engagement. The care system (both prison and health,) as it is organised, perpetuates and re-enacts the fractures that underpin the interpersonal difficulties and undermine the potential development of a therapeutic environment/relationship.

There are some clear service models emerging associated with better success in outcomes. Wilson and Haigh (2011) describe general conditions that appear essential to the success of a service, including a focus on human relationships, the psychosocial environment, investment in the programme, importance of leadership, effective team work and establishing good networks and partnerships.

W. John Livesley's work (2017) describes how treatment should be integrated, trans-theoretical and modular, paying attention to the person as a whole. It should integrate different (evidence-based) treatment approaches with proven general characteristics of treatment, including structured approaches, using relationships as a mode of intervention in their own right to increase trust, consistency of approach and staffing, validation of the person as a whole, motivating the person and helping the person to reflect.

However, in reality, what is found is far from this basic ideal, with services organised in such a way as to either be totally ineffective or lead to unintended worsening of symptomology and iatrogenic effects. Unfortunately, findings in 2007 (Crawford, 2007) that 'many individuals with complex emotional needs have treatment histories punctuated by revolving door care, including multiple admissions, inadequate care planning, infrequent follow-up, incomplete treatment, and unmet needs' were echoed in a survey by the CQC in 2017.

The CQC survey had responses from 12,139 individuals. The results showed that, when rating on a scale of 1–10 where 10 is 'I had a very good experience' and 1 is 'I had a very poor experience', 64% gave a score of 7 or above – this left 33% who rated their overall experience as 6 or below. Of the respondents, 26% felt that they did not get the crisis help they needed and a quarter stated that they had not seen mental health services enough to meet their needs over the preceding 12 months (this proportion rose from 21% in 2014 to 25% in 2017). Just under half of the respondents (42%) experienced changes in which professional they saw, and of those, only 47% said that this change had been completely explained to them; 31% stated that their care got worse after the change. Only 76% of respondents said that they had agreed with the treatment they would receive, leaving 24% who had not agreed; 61% (again, a fall from 65% in 2014) felt that they had 'definitely' had enough time to discuss their needs and treatment, leaving 39% who did not.

Most importantly in this survey, those patients with non-psychotic disorders reported worse than average experiences (those with psychotic disorders generally reported better than average experiences); those patients in the care cluster 'non-psychotic chaotic and challenging disorders' reported the worst experiences of all, with the exception of 'crisis' care, in which they reported better experiences than the average respondent.

The CQC (2017) concluded that locked rehabilitation hospitals were, in reality, long-stay wards, which did not employ staff with the right skills, and where patients were becoming institutionalised. It further concluded that the models of care in these wards were not appropriate for the type of patients that were accessing the service. An interesting point to note is that locked rehabilitation wards were much more likely to be operated by the independent sector, with the potential issues that brings for integration with other community services and pathways of care. In addition, this same report highlights the falling numbers of mental health nurses (a fall of 12% between 2010 and 2017). The report also outlined some very positive findings, such as:

> 'with very few exceptions (in core mental health services) staff formed relationships with their patients that were respectful and compassionate and treated patients with dignity and respect.'

In terms of leadership (one of the ten standards of an 'Enabling Environment', or EE: Centre for Quality Improvement, Royal College of Psychiatrists, 2012), the report stated that 39% of NHS trusts and 15% of the independent sector needed to improve; however the experience of staff with respect to support, team working and line management was generally better than for those working in acute services. That mental health services are tough to work in is not in dispute: a high proportion of mental health staff reported experiencing harassment, bullying, abuse or physical violence from patients, relatives or the public in the 12 months prior to the survey. The report appears to independently verify the ten EE standards by drawing out six themes that contributed to an outstanding or good rating on 'well-led': leadership, clear vision and values, culture of learning and improvement, good governance, quality assurance and engagement and involvement. This suggests that working toward or achieving EE status could be protective for both staff and patients, and the EE standards themselves are built on a relational underpinning of service delivery.

Other themes that emerged from the inspections were, in no particular order; some wards still had dormitory accommodation; the fabric of the buildings was old and dilapidated, with significant ligature point risks; staffing levels did not allow enough one-to-one time with patients; patients did not see their psychiatrist often enough; high use of agency and bank nurses (with an associated impact on consistency and continuity of care); insufficient induction and training of new staff; some wards had 'blanket restrictions' that were not based on assessed needs and thus contravened the requirement for care in the 'least restrictive' environment possible. A companion report from the CQC (2018) shows that locked rehabilitation wards are often a long way from people's families and friends, and that lengths of stay are often very long (on average 683 days when taking in a 'whole care episode' – transfer from or to another mental health service). Both of these issues are increased in the independent sector. All of these issues fundamentally undermine the ability to provide services, to ensure competent and confident staff and to provide a consistent relational environment that is evidence-based.

Lastly, staff training is a critical element in good service provision but is very often inadequate. This is coupled with a reluctance from some staff to work with 'personality disorder' due to a lack of confidence and understanding of the complex interactions they may encounter. Crawford (2007) identifies this as resulting from the previous universal opinion that 'personality disorder' is 'untreatable'.

Problems from an individual perspective

'Individuals with complex emotional needs struggle with interpersonal relationships and social relationships, so the task of navigating complex care pathways in order to receive care and understand the system is beyond their capabilities. This is difficult for professionals to do at times, let alone those who do not have the requisite skills to do so.' (Shields & Mullen, 2007)

The Consensus Statement for People with Complex Mental Health Difficulties who are diagnosed with a personality disorder (British Psychological Society, 2018) reported a survey that was conducted on social media by the National Survivor Network, on behalf of the consensus group. In total 281 service users responded, with the following expectations: that they have a consistent professional who listens in the right service setting; knowledgeable, competent and understanding staff; the ability to connect with other service users; collaboration across services; and the ability to choose interventions. These are also key expectations both in formal NHS specifications and in NICE guidance (2009a; 2009b) – they are not unreasonable, and further they are backed up by evidence (for example Wilson and Haigh, 2011) as being critical ingredients in successful services.

This consensus statement also drew together some shocking statistics, such as the increased likelihood of people diagnosed with 'personality disorder' suffering serious physical as well as other mental health co-morbidities. They concluded that men with such a diagnosis die on average 18 years before men without a diagnosis; for women it is 19 years. This statement goes on to clearly articulate that the traditional way of organising mental health services is not fit for purpose: everyone needs support at some time in their lives, and for some the range and depth of their problems is so pronounced, over a long period of time, that appointment-based short cycles of intervention, or medication, simply are not sufficient.

Further, people often experience services and the system in such a way as to exacerbate their underlying problems, with multiple rejections, a lack of understanding and a sometimes punitive approach to behaviour that is actually signalling distress.

Promising solutions

Individual level

A formulated, bio-psycho-social approach and new ways of thinking about diagnoses and how to understand an individual's narrative and life course, such as the Power Threat Meaning Framework (Johnstone & Boyle, 2018), allow direct engagement and mutual understanding between the expert by profession and expert by experience (EBE). Understanding problems from an individual's perspective allows a 'whole person' and 'whole life' narrative that ensures a trauma-informed, non-judgmental approach, which is co-owned and co-developed.

The NHS continues to embrace and develop service user involvement at every level in the organisation and there are increasing calls for the professionalisation of EBEs and peer supporters. In the prison and probation services, desistance theory and the Good Lives model (Maruna, 2001; Ward *et al*, 2007 respectively) are leading staff to stop referring to people as 'offenders', in the same way that labelling someone as 'personality disordered' can very often be stigmatising and damaging. The OPD pathway is pushing boundaries with involving service users not only in feedback on how they find services, but also in giving them equal say in key decisions about what happens regarding services across the pathway.

Lastly, there is a need to get in early and identify difficulties in childhood – there is now incontrovertible evidence that Adverse Childhood Experiences (ACEs) and trauma will lead to problems in adulthood. The Welsh government is trying to embed this understanding in policy; it has recently published its first 'resilience report', which describes a national study that found adults who had suffered four or more types of ACE were ten times more likely to have felt suicidal or self-harmed than those who had experienced none (Hughes *et al*, 2018). This is an approach from which other governments and governmental bodies (such as councils) could learn.

Service level

The emerging evidence clearly suggests that multi-modal interventions are required, which attend to structure, consistency, the environment and validating relationships. Attending to the workforce is obvious, but is often not well developed or protected at service level. Making it an explicit outcome of a strategy (as in the OPD pathway programme) acknowledges the criticality of workforce issues. In addition, there are some excellent models of good practice, such as the Leeds Managed Clinical Network and the Pathfinder services in the South West, that use a mixed model of consultancy, workforce development and direct services to patients. In the criminal justice system, the Rehabilitative Culture initiative in prisons is placing relationships and procedural justice (fairness) at the heart of its operational delivery and all probation approved premises have signed up to work towards the Enabling Environments set of ten standards (Centre for Quality Improvement, 2012). However, despite this seeming good practice, these initiatives are often not led from a whole-system strategic perspective and can still feel vulnerable to change and abandonment, to silo working and to geographic disparity across the country. The Consensus Statement reiterates issues around silo services that only deal with one type of diagnosis – particularly when providing services to children and young people, these should be focused on the problems and experiences of the person, not reliant on a diagnosis. As the consensus statement says: 'better outcomes may result if we stop waiting for people to get bad enough to receive a diagnosis, before we offer them any help' (British Psychological Society, 2018).

Systemic and policy initiatives

Person-centred care and care pathways need to drive system change in how services are organised both within agencies and across agencies; there needs to be increasing recognition that single agencies are not able to tackle the range and complexity of problems alone. The OPD pathway strategy binds the NHS and CJS together to deliver a joint programme, each recognising they are weaker without the other. Such partnership working is hard, and constant attention has to be paid to it, to ensure that it endures and can overcome cultural and boundary barriers. The NHS (particularly since the 2012 Health and Social Care Act) has entered into using competition to drive quality. However, system change requires collaboration with individual services working together both within and between agencies. Public health has a vital role to play in getting messages out there and is leading the ACE strategy work in Wales. New Care Model initiatives (increasingly being called provider collaboratives) in the NHS are a way of trying to deliver coherent pathways of care in a single locality by bringing providers together and creating such partnerships, allowing a provider to effectively commission the whole pathway. The *NHS Five Year Forward View* (2014) and the *Long Term Plan* (2019) make it clear that new investment is needed in community mental health services, and that restrictive secure hospitalisation should be used only when absolutely necessary (and the patient should be as close to home as possible). To that end there is a promise of new investment into mental health services in the community and a trialing of new service models which step away from the traditional and embrace flexibility and the need to work across other public services. Sustainability and Transformation Partnerships (STPs; NHS, 2016) see the NHS and local authorities come together in 44 areas covering all of England to establish 'integrated care systems', acknowledging that people have multiple and agency spanning needs. Whether these changes result in appropriate services for people diagnosed with 'personality disorder' remains to be seen, and there is still a concern that there isn't enough emphasis on services for the harder to reach, complex patients that have been or could be diagnosed with 'personality disorder'.

Final word

This chapter has highlighted the huge unmet (often serious) need in relation to 'personality disorder'. The prevalence and severity of need drives system anxiety, and encourages rejection and avoidance both at an interpersonal level and at a service level. Siloed service design means issues are split off and there is a failure to see the whole; diagnostic categories, often with little basis in empirical evidence, in part drive this unhelpful response.

However, the current policy and strategic context is potentially moving in the right direction, toward better integration of services and a better understanding of the critical ingredients at service level. Individual voices are being heard, and the expertise offered by service users is being recognised and embraced. More can be done; leadership is recognised as key, and another joined up strategy for personality disorder generally, such as the previous community programme that finished in 2011, would support and inform these new provider collaboratives and enable appropriate commissioning at the regional and local level.

It could be argued that increasing specialisation in services is compounding silo working and failure to respond to a person's whole experience. Can we put the whole person back at the centre of the way systems and services are organised? Using developmental formulations and co-producing service and pathway delivery and design would help to move away from very narrow service offers.

It would be ideal to organise services on a local to regional footprint; to abandon tiering, and offer a flexible service that can work with the person and stay with them adjusting the service offer depending on need. It is vital that we intervene earlier, given our increasing understanding of the impact of ACEs. We need to bridge those cliff edges that are inherent in the way systems are organised and commissioned.

Developing local partnerships with other agencies, such as local authorities, probation and housing, and offering consultancy across sectors helps to keep a shared understanding and develops 'joint responsibilities' to offer effective services. Learning can be shared using networks: consultancy and training can be offered to staff who need it, regardless of where their primary employment is located. Systems can be redesigned to be flexible and empowering.

It is vital to establish evidence of outcome in order to validate different approaches; this requires explicit resources to deliver research and evaluation strategies which will then inform future practice. It is critical that learning is not lost or overlooked, and that attention is paid to the evidence, from both a service and a commissioning perspective.

All systemic changes require clear strategic vision, explicit aims and leadership. There must be a will to work in partnership, and this must be enabled from the 'top'. True partnerships become multi-disciplinary co-operatives with a single set of goals, and with people (both experts by profession and experience and service users) who understand their role and expected contributions.

'There are pockets of excellent practice around the country we just need to galvanise and spread them throughout the UK. The aim … is to highlight the many issues surrounding "personality disorder" to raise awareness and to hopefully bring some help for people such as health checks which are given to people with psychosis, the right treatment at the right time, including helping people when they are young so the onward economic and personal cost of a life lived in services can be halted … People with "personality disorder" have been left in the wilderness for too long and it's about time the system as a whole, such as health, social care, housing, third sector and community initiatives come together to bring help and hope.'

(Sue Sibbald, peer specialist and co-chair, Personality Disorder Consensus Group, British Psychological Society, 2018)

References

Black DW, Blum N, Pfohl B & Hale N (2004). Suicidal behavior in borderline personality disorder: Prevalence, risk factors, prediction, and prevention. *Journal of Personality Disorder* **18** 226–239 doi: 10.1521/pedi.18.3.226.35445

The British Psychological Society (2018). 'Shining lights in dark corners of people's lives.' The Consensus Statement for people with complex mental health difficulties who are diagnosed with a personality disorder. Retrieved from https://www.mind.org.uk/media/21163353/consensus-statement-final.pdf

Brooker C, Sirdifield C, Blizard R, Denney D & Pluck G (2012) Probation and mental illness. *Journal of Forensic Psychiatry and Psychology* **23** (4) 522–537.

Care Quality Commission (2017) Community mental health survey: Statistical release. Retrieved from https://www.cqc.org.uk/sites/default/files/20180515_cmh17_statisticalrelease.pdf

Care Quality Commission (2018) Mental health rehabilitation inpatient services: Ward types, bed numbers and use by clinical commissioning groups and NHS trusts. Retrieved from https://www.cqc.org.uk/sites/default/files/20180301_mh_rehabilitation_briefing.pdf

Coid J, Yang M, Tyrer P, Roberts A & Ullrich S (2006) Prevalence and correlates of personality disorder in Great Britain. *British Journal of Psychiatry* **188** 423–431 DOI: 10.1192/bjp.188.5.423

Crawford M (2007) Learning the lessons: A multi-method evaluation of dedicated community based services for people with personality disorder. Retrieved from http://www.netscc.ac.uk/hsdr/files/project/SDO_FR_08-1404-083_V01.pdf

Department of Health and Home Office (1999) Managing Dangerous People with Severe Personality Disorder. London: Home Office.

Department of Health and Ministry of Justice (2011) Response to the offender personality disorder consultation. London: Department of Health. Retrieved from https://webarchive.nationalarchives.gov.uk/20130105010410/http://www.dh.gov.uk/prod_consum_dh/groups/dh_digitalassets/documents/digitalasset/dh_130701.pdf

Doyle M, While D, Mok PLH, Windfuhr K, Ashcroft DM, Kontopoantelis E, Chew-Graham CS, Appleby L, Shaw J & Webb RT (2016). Suicide risk in primary care patients diagnosed with a personality disorder: A nested case control study. *BMC Family Practice* **17** (106) DOI: 10.1186/s12875-016-0479-y

Ewbank L, Thompson J & McKenna H (2017, 29 September) NHS Hospital Bed Numbers. Retrieved from https://www.kingsfund.org.uk/publications/nhs-hospital-bed-numbers

Fazel S, Danesh J (2002) Mental disorders in prisoners. *The Lancet* **16:359** (9306) 545–50 DOI: 10.1016/ S0140-6736(02)07740-1.

Gilburt H (2016, 14 October). Trust finances raise concerns about the future of the mental health task force recommendations. Retrieved from https://www.kingsfund.org.uk/blog/2016/10/trust-finances-mental-health-taskforce

Grierson J (2018, 27 July). Private probation companies to have contracts ended early. Retrieved from https://www.theguardian.com/society/2018/jul/27/private-probation-companies-contracts-ended-early-justice

Haigh R (2007) New kids on the block! The government-funded English personality disorder services. *Therapeutic Communities* **28** (3) 300.

Healthcare Quality Improvement Partnership, University of Manchester (2017) Safer care for people with personality disorder. Retrieved from http://documents.manchester.ac.uk/display.aspx?DocID=37564

Heeks M, Reed S, Tafsiri M & Prince S (2018) *The Economic and Social Costs of Crime* (2nd edition). Research Report 99: Home Office.

Her Majesty's Government (2019) Strengthening probation, building confidence. Retrieved from https:// www.gov.uk/guidance/strengthening-probation-improving-confidence.

Her Majesty's Prison and Probation Service (2018) Population and capacity briefing. Retrieved from https://www.gov.uk/government/statistics/prison-population-figures-2018.

Huang Y, Kotov R, de Girolamo G, Preti A, Angermeyer M & Benjet C (2009) DSM–IV personality disorders in the WHO World Mental Health Surveys. *British Journal of Psychiatry* **195** 46–53.

Hughes K, Ford K, Davies AR, Homolova L & Bellis MA (2018) Sources of resilience and their moderating relationships with harms from adverse childhood experiences. Welsh Adverse Childhood Experiences (ACE) Resilience Study. Retrieved from http://www.wales.nhs.uk/sitesplus/documents/888/ACE%20&%20 Resilience%20Report%20(Eng_final2).pdf.

Kane E, Reader N, Keane K & Prince S (2016) A cost and economic evaluation of the Leeds personality disorder managed clinical network: A service and commissioning development initiative. *Personality and Mental Health* **10** DOI:10.1002.pmh.1329.

Knapp M & Iemmi V (2014) The economic case for better mental health. Retrieved from http://eprints. lse.ac.uk/59520/1/__lse.ac.uk_storage_LIBRARY_Secondary_libfile_shared_repository_Content_ Knapp%2C%20M_Economic%20case_Knapp_Economic%20case_2014.pdf

Johnstone L & Boyle M (2018) Power Threat Meaning Framework. Retrieved from https://www.bps.org.uk/sites/bps.org.uk/files/Policy/Policy%20-%20Files/PTM%20Framework%20 %28January%202018%29_0.pdf

Livesley WJ (2017) *Integrated Modular Treatment for Borderline Personality Disorder: A Practical Guide to Combining Effective Treatment Methods*. Cambridge: Cambridge University Press.

Maruna S (2001) *Making Good: How Ex-Convicts Reform and Rebuild Their Lives*. Washington DC: APA Books.

National Institute for Health and Clinical Excellence (2009a) *Antisocial Personality Disorder: Treatment, Management and Prevention*. London: NICE.

National Institute for Health and Clinical Excellence (2009b) *Borderline Personality Disorder: Treatment and Management*. London: NICE.

National Institute for Mental Health in England (2003a) Personality disorder: No longer a diagnosis of exclusion. Retrieved from http://personalitydisorder.org.uk/wp-content/uploads/2015/04/PD-No-longer-a-diagnosis-of-exclusion.pdf

National Institute for Mental Health in England (2003b) Breaking the cycle of rejection: The personality disorder capabilities framework. Retrieved from http://personalitydisorder.org.uk/wp-content/ uploads/2015/06/personalitydisorders-capabilities-framework.pdf

NHS England (2014) Five year forward view. Retrieved from
https://www.england.nhs.uk/wp-content/uploads/2014/10/5yfv-web.pdf

NHS England (2016) Sustainability and transformation partnerships. Retrieved from
https://www.england.nhs.uk/integratedcare/stps/

NHS (2018, July–Sept) Beds open overnight published statistics. Retrieved from https://www.england.
nhs.uk/statistics/statistical-wok-areas/bed-availability-and-occupancy/bed-data-overnight

NHS (2019) Long term plan. Retrieved from https://www.longtermplan.nhs.uk/online-version/

Office for National Statistics (2018a) Statistical bulletin: Population estimates for the UK,
England and Wales, Scotland and Northern Ireland. Retrieved from https://www.ons.gov.
uk/peoplepopulationandcommunity/populationandmigration/populationestimates/bulletins/
annualmidyearpopulationestimates/mid2017

Office for National Statistics (2018b) Ethnicity facts and figures. Retrieved from https://www.ethnicity-
facts-figures.service.gov.uk/british-population/demographics/age-groups/latest

Rendu A, Mora P, Patel A, Knapp M & Mann A (2002) Economic impact of personality disorders in UK
primary care attenders. *British Journal of Psychiatry* **181** (1) 62–66 DOI:10.1192/bjp.181.1.62.

Royal College of Psychiatrists, Centre for Quality Improvement (2012) Enabling Environments.
Retrieved from https://www.rcpsych.ac.uk/docs/default-source/improving-care/ccqi/quality-networks/
enabling-environments-ee/ee-standards-document-2015.pdf?sfvrsn=abdcca36_2

Safer Care for People with PD (2018) National confidential enquiry into suicide and homicide by people
with mental illness. Healthcare Quality Improvement Partnership. Retrieved from http://documents.
manchester.ac.uk/display.aspx?DocID=37564

Shields F & Mullen T (2007) Working across whole systems: Using managed clinical networks. *Mental
Health Review* **12** (4) 48–54.

Singleton N, Meltzer H, Gatward R, Coid J & Deasy D (1997) *Psychiatric Morbidity among Prisoners*.
London: Department of Health.

Skett S, Goode I & Barton S (2017) A Joint NHS and NOMS offender personality disorder pathway
strategy: A perspective from 5 years of operation. *Criminal Behaviour and Mental Health* **27** 214–221.
DOI: 10.1002/cbm.2026.

Skett S & Lewis C (2019) Development of the offender personality disorder pathway: A summary of the
underpinning evidence. *Probation Journal* **66** (1) 167–180.

Torgersen S, Kringlen E & Cramer V (2001) The prevalence of personality disorders in a community
sample. *Archives General Psychiatry* **58** 590–596.

Tyrer P, Reed GM & Crawford MJ (2015) Classification, assessment, prevalence, and effect of personality
disorder. *Lancet* **385** 717–726.

Ward T, Mann R & Gannon TA (2007) The good lives model of offender rehabilitation: Clinical
implications. *Aggression and Violent Behaviour* **12** 87–107 DOI: 10.1016/j.avb.2006.03.004

Wilson L & Haigh R (2011) Innovation in action. Review of the effectiveness of centrally commissioned
community personality disorder services. Retrieved from http://personalitydisorder.org.uk/wp-content/
uploads/2015/06/Innovation-in-Action.pdf.

Yang M, Coid J & Tyrer P (2010) Personality pathology recorded by severity: National survey. *The British
Journal of Psychiatry* **197** 193–199 doi: 10.1192/bjp.bp.110.078956

Chapter 4:

The Politics of Personality Disorder: A Critical Realist Account

David Pilgrim

Introduction

This chapter addresses some fundamental questions about the function or purpose of those parts of modern mental health services that respond to and manage incorrigible forms of conduct, codified medically as 'personality disorder' (PD). These actions reflect particular forms of rule transgression, defined by current societal norms, which may or may not implicate criminality. My argument essentially is that it is that conduct which is the driver for 'PD services'.

The core question we need to address is not 'does this patient suffer from a personality disorder?' but 'what particular risk does this particular patient's conduct pose, if any, for this particular society or in which ways do they fail to conduct themselves in ways expected by those socialised into a particular culture?' Not only is the first question conceptually problematic, for reasons I explain below, but it is also, in a sense, a diversion from the second more pertinent one, which is the real driver of mental health service activity. That second question requires no specialist training to understand and debate it, even if our preferred answers may vary markedly. It ensures we attend to the social context of risk and not merely risky people, whether or not they are assumed to be mentally abnormal.

And where considerations other than risk are evident, mental health professionals will support their clients but also expect them to take responsibility for their actions. This is both a psychological and a moral process, which applies to interactions with professionals and significant others. Either arena (professional or lay) might be the place of personal stasis or change, but the point is that it is relationality that must be our central focus – not the presence or absence of a particular diagnosis, which is a 'red herring'. Relationality inherently is about getting on with others in ways that are acceptable to all concerned. A PD diagnosis is a summary gloss on a range of ways in which the latter expectation has broken down. This implies a need to reflect on the moral and psychological dimensions to those failed expectations. Therefore relationality should be our psychological and moral point of constant critical reflection. As I explore below, a diagnosis of PD is a diversion from these wider moral and psychological questions about how we do and should relate to one another. Any critique of a PD diagnosis is not the end *but the beginning* of understanding patterns of conduct that are problematic to self and/or others in our daily life. A warranted critical rejection of diagnosis should prompt more, not less, professional interest in why some of us more than others are prone to dysfunctional relational styles and tendencies in our lives.

And for those receiving a diagnosis of personality disorder where risky conduct does not predominate, other value judgements emerge from others ('the lay arena of society') *prior to diagnosis*. Later I argue that if we delete the umbrella diagnoses offered by psychiatry, we are left with a very lengthy list of ordinary attributions of immaturity or unreasonableness. For example, those working in 'PD services' will note that patients may be 'chaotic' in their lifestyle or 'unstable' in their intimate relationships and have problems containing their emotions. Emotional lability is expected from children, not rational adults, who are mindful of their fellow adults – and so immaturity is implied, whether or not it is named. All of this implies a failure to move from childish to adult functioning during primary socialisation. (Later in my ommisive critique I will argue that this matter of reasonableness is an unfairly narrow focus, if we only consider it in relation to those with a PD diagnosis.)

These professional observations are a reiteration of what non-professionals will have already noted, which at times are acknowledged by identified patients and at times not. If attributions of personality disorder are to be de-medicalised, then we have a collective challenge about responding in alternative ways, which recognise the moral agency of identified patients, while appreciating their particular lives compassionately. Getting that judicious balance of expected adult moral agency and empathic listening 'right', case by case, is the challenge for professionals. Even if this uncertain balancing act does not always lead to an effective outcome, if attempted it will at least be more acceptable to those using services (Pilgrim, 2018).

A critical realist approach to personality disorder

I approach this exploration as a philosophical critical realist (Pilgrim, 2015). That is, I take seriously the actual conduct, in context, that for now in our culture seems to warrant medical descriptions. This then is an ontological matter: some people in society recurrently really do act in a risky or incorrigible way that threatens social order and triggers anxiety, and at times disdain, in those who are sane by common consent. This conduct is not a 'social construction' or a 'myth'; it really does occur. In response, third parties really do 'want something to be done'. Mental health professionals accordingly respond to that expectation. Risk assessment and risk management in non-punitive settings then emerge, as do risk-averse professional norms. Given that the penal system also deals with risky conduct, this invites another question about how 'PD services' in healthcare systems are different. I discuss this later after flagging some relevant assumptions of critical realism.

Critical realism is a philosophy that guides us in a middle way between positivism on one side and radical social constructivism on the other (Bhaskar, 2016). The psychiatric version of the former assumes that mental disorders are real and *present in all times and places*, a position manifest in the International Classification of Diseases (ICD) from the World Health Organization and the Diagnostic and Statistical Manual (DSM) of the American Psychiatric Association. By contrast, the radical constructivist position can be found in postmodern versions of psychology, which focus in the main on representations, discourses and texts and their deconstruction. This argues for situated realities and different perspectives; it opposes positivist claims of empirical invariance and dwells on epistemology (statements about knowledge), not ontology (statements about being or reality).

The middle way offered by critical realism has three main axioms or fundamental premises. The first of these is *ontological realism*: events and processes exist in the world independent of how we describe them. In the case of descriptions of people who are 'personality disordered', they do indeed episodically act in identifiable ways (such as becoming chaotic or intoxicated, or harming, or threatening to harm, themselves or others). This socially disruptive conduct, which distresses others, is a defining feature, though the distress of the identified patient also may come and go in its salience.

Immediately then a second premise of critical realism comes into play: *epistemological relativism*. The latter refers to the way in which we then attribute meaning to the conduct that we broadly agree exists. Is it a moral matter, that is, does the conduct reflect malice or weakness under the direct control of the patient? Alternatively, maybe the incipient patient is out of control because they are diseased, and so they cannot be held responsible at all for their actions (Horne, 2014). And if it is some variable mixture of these assumptions, then how do we ascertain the balance of each, case by case? And when we make our best formulation in this regard, how do we negotiate agreement about it with those around us? This then is about communication, language use and the negotiation of meaning.

The linguistic ambiguity about these possibilities creates moment-to-moment uncertainties for all parties. For example, remorseless sexual offending against children (which in some cases becomes codified as a form of 'anti-social personality disorder' or 'psychopathy') can evoke an ambivalent response of the sort 'he is a totally evil bastard', but also 'he must be sick to do that'. These ambiguities, and the ambivalence they evoke, reflect a lack of clear consensus in everyday psychology, as well as in the 'psy professions', about the relationship between structure and agency. The first of these implies antecedents, be they biological, psychological or social, which might be seen to put risky conduct on pre-determined tramlines. The second implies that the agents of risky conduct are just that: fully aware moral agents, who know exactly what they are doing and could opt to do something different. If we explore that interaction of structure and agency, as some mental health professionals do, then this is a complex challenge both as a task with the identified patient, and when negotiating the post-hoc formulations developed and communicated to third parties, such as relatives or review tribunals.

If mental health professionals are content merely to manage risky conduct (or even merely assess it) but at the same time hold their patients totally responsible for their actions, then this poses another political challenge. That scenario is one in which patients with a PD diagnosis have the worst of all worlds. They are held in an open-ended way with no estimated date of discharge *and* they are denied a specific form of compassion and medical paternalism commonly associated with the response to people with a diagnosis of 'severe mental illness'. At least prisoners exist in a less mystified world, in which society has held them responsible for their rule transgressions and they are being punished accordingly by their loss of liberty for a defined period of time. They have access to processes of redress in which their innocence and/or their future prospects of risk are considered.

Psychiatric patients, whatever their diagnosis, are dealt with by different rules, in which the uncertainties linked to their abnormality of mind afford much wider discretion on the part of agents of the state. This tends to lead to a false positive bias in decision making: a person detained for too long goes unnoticed, whereas one who is discharged and then acts out riskily becomes a focus for condemnation and might have career-limiting consequences for the staff involved. With that knowledge, the self-protective policy of professionals is understandable.

This then brings into play a third core premise of critical realism: *judgmental rationality*. This entails us making our best and honest judgement about what is true in this particular situation. Whereas strong social constructivist arguments offer us judgmental relativism and scorn truth claims (everything is just a different perspective and all stories are equally valid), and positivism offers us recurring truths across all contexts (in this case 'covering laws' about the 'nature' of personality disorder), critical realism adopts a middle way. It respects the context focus of the strong constructivists but rejects judgemental relativism. It also respects the empirical descriptions of the positivists, as an undeniable part of our current reality, but rejects these as stable descriptions across time and place. This is the unfounded assumption of 'empirical invariance' in the DSM (American Psychiatric Association, 2012) or ICD (World Health Organisation, 2018). Context is all important and positivism, with its 'covering laws', invalidly prescribes reality in advance. In our case this means dubiously describing personality disorder as a skin-encapsulated disorder that expresses itself in characteristic ways in all settings. As I will discuss later, this is patently not the case.

I extend these points now by considering the intellectual and policy diversions triggered by over-valuing the diagnosis of personality disorder. I will use three forms of critique derived from critical realism: immanent, explanatory and omissive. The first tests out the adequacy of the PD diagnosis on its own terms (i.e. is it a coherent medical diagnosis that enables us to understand aetiology, treatment decisions and prognosis?). The second provides an explanation for why, despite its inadequacies according to its own expected criteria, a PD diagnosis retains legitimacy today. The third offers some views about what is silenced by accepting that legitimacy without critical reflection. Between them, these three forms of critique illuminate the political contention that attends any discussion of personality disorder.

Immanent critique

For any medical diagnosis to be plausible and make a claim to being superior, in its explanatory and predictive capability, to lay opinion and guesswork, it should succeed according to its own criteria. If we test out the adequacy of a PD diagnosis by the criteria of an optimal medical diagnosis, then we find the following:

1. The concept of PD is *not readily distinguishable from normality* but is often merely a description of exaggerated normal features that then become dis-valued in some circumstances but over-valued in others. Successful politicians, business leaders and sports heroes come into the second grouping (Dutton, 2012). A medical diagnosis usually makes a clear distinction between what is abnormal and what

is normal. The PD diagnosis is not clear-cut in this regard at all; for example, should chronic shyness be described as 'anxious avoidant PD' (Lane, 2008)? This point also becomes clear when we look at acculturated norms. A woman acquiring the attribution of 'passive dependent PD' in the United States may be considered normal in some Asian cultures. Similarly, the dramatic presentation of a man in Norway that might attract the attribution of 'histrionic PD' might be completely unremarkable in Italy. Note how narcissistic PD has been connoted in US culture and so has been part of the lexicon of the DSM but missing from the ICD. A dramatic dissociative capacity might afford success on the stage in some contexts rather than attract a psychiatric diagnosis. Careful and tedious attention to detail makes for a good accountant and may have been an exaggerated portrayal of the conformist Victorian personality, when it was first invented in the nineteenth century (Berrios, 1985). Western psychiatry has implausibly made claims about the invariant existence of mental disorders across time and place – a point to be made about all its diagnoses, not just those of personality disorder (Watters, 2010).

2. A particular PD diagnosis is not clearly distinct from other PD diagnoses or wider descriptions of neurosis and psychosis. Thus it does *not have a clear concept validity*. The ICD explicitly distinguishes PD from mental illness but there has been an absence of agreement about this within psychiatry ever since 'psychopathic states' were introduced during the mid-twentieth century (Henderson, 1938; Cleckley, 1941; Kendell, 2002). Some diagnoses, such as paranoid PD, obsessive-compulsive PD, anxious-avoidant PD and histrionic PD, are merely the codification of chronic psychotic or neurotic symptom presentations. They say more about chronicity of functioning and therapeutic pessimism than any clear abiding features of a personality (see later).

3. The diagnosis of PD is not used consistently over time (*the expectation of test-retest reliability*) about a case, nor between clinicians (*the expectation of inter-rater reliability*). The first of these takes on a particular salience when considering the legitimacy of a PD diagnosis because 'ordered' personalities are supposed to be unchanging over time – after all, that is what makes them 'personalities'. If a person recovers from PD or the diagnosis is dropped in favour of a totally different one, then this undermines our expectation of the very meaning of a 'disordered' personality and its implications of an enduring set of features linked to a named individual (Cacciola *et al*, 1998; American Psychiatric Association, 2012). It seems that the test-retest reliability of specific habits ('single symptoms') of PD is fairly good, but not that of the diagnosis itself (Zanarini *et al*, 2002). This is not surprising; old habits, good or bad, die hard in human beings. No professional expertise is needed to recognise this common-sense wisdom.

4. A good medical diagnosis should point back to the conditions of its emergence (this is a form of inference called 'retroduction'). However, *the aetiology of PD is either unknown or contested*. We do know that adverse childhood experiences increase the probability of all forms of psycho-social presentations that might be codified with specific diagnoses, including those of PD (Cutajar *et al*, 2010; Spataro *et al*, 2004; Luntz, 1994; Ogata *et al*, 1990). Some have argued that we should abandon the diagnosis of 'borderline PD' and simply recognize it as a chronic post-traumatic existential state (Herman *et al*, 1989). However, this suggests a specifiable aetiology of one version of diagnosed PD. In my view, this is not a helpful critique because early neglect and trauma increase the probability of a *wide range* of mental health problems (Read & Bentall, 2012). Paradoxically, special pleading that one form of diagnosis can be explained by adverse childhood experiences legitimises psychiatric diagnosis in general. It also diverts our attention from the wider impact of those experiences.

5. The *empirical validity of a case of PD cannot be confirmed by external evidence* (measurable and observable somatic signs) but only by a form of tautology, where the diagnosis is constituted by its symptoms and vice versa. For example:

Q: Why does this man molest children without remorse?

A: Because he is a psychopath.

Q: How do we know that he is a psychopath?

A: Because he molests children without remorse.

This circularity is evident in relation to, say, 'borderline' patients:

Q: Why is this woman inconsistent in her attachments to others, is emotionally labile, drinks heavily and cuts herself routinely?

A: Because she is suffering from borderline personality disorder.

Q: How do we know she is suffering from this particular personality disorder and not another condition?

A: Because she is inconsistent in her attachments to others, is emotionally labile, drinks heavily and cuts herself routinely.

This tautological confirmation of a diagnosis proves nothing of the actual existence of a state called 'psychopathy' or 'borderline PD'. (The common misleading tendency to confuse the map with the territory or to reduce statements about being to statements about knowledge is called the 'epistemic fallacy' by critical realists.)

6. A good medical diagnosis *guides effective treatment*. This condition fails in relation to all functional psychiatric conditions, not just diagnoses of PD. Drugs and psychotherapeutic models all offer themselves as blunderbuss responses across diagnostic boundaries. Only a few models have been tested specifically on some diagnostic related groups, such as borderline PD, but this is not usual (cf. Linehan, 1993; Kleim *et al*, 2010). The additional problem for the diagnosis of PD is that it has been met often with therapeutic nihilism (Salekin, 2002), prompting governments to use special pleading for the inclusion rather than the rejection of such patients from mental health services (NIMHE, 2003). The poor evidence of effectiveness of treatment outcomes has contributed to this daily clinical nihilism (Dolan & Coid, 1993; Rice *et al*, 1992).

In turn this has triggered an ethical debate about treatability and the legitimacy of merely labelling and containing patients with a PD diagnosis, but offering no corrective intervention to reduce their distressed and distressing conduct. It is common for PD patients in high security settings to languish with little or no therapeutic input, but nonetheless denied discharge. (In the UK these patients were recorded legally as suffering from 'psychopathic disorder', a term abandoned with the 2007 Mental Health Act.) If patients cannot be treated then why are they ever detained under mental health law (so called)?

7. A good medical diagnosis should be *experienced as helpful to the patient*. Some patients embrace their psychiatric diagnosis but many do not and a whole social movement has grown up in the past 50 years to oppose biomedical diagnostic psychiatry (Crossley, 2006). Within that social movement, there have been specific campaigns from some PD diagnosed groups, which focus on discrimination, stigma and the absence of compassionate care. It is not surprising that those receiving a diagnosis of borderline PD have been salient in this regard (see e.g. Stobbe, E. (2006) http://brainblogger.com/2006/06/20/anti-stigmatization-psychiatry-discriminates-against-people-with-borderline-personality-disorder/). It goes without saying that few of us would queue up enthusiastically to receive a PD diagnosis, given that it implies that we are failed people. A trend of othering or dehumanisation is evident when psychiatric authorities on PD use offensive language very publicly about those with the diagnosis: see, for example, *Taming the Beast Within* (Tyrer, 2018).

If the diagnosis of personality disorder fails on all of the counts listed above, then why is it still used? To answer that question we must move from an immanent to an explanatory critique about why PD – like other discreditable psychiatric diagnoses, such as, say, 'schizophrenia' – survive (Pilgrim, 2007).

Explanatory critique

At the centre of any explanation for why we persist with the diagnosis of PD, despite its obvious and extensive shortcomings, is the role of psychiatric services in society. They exist to manage psychological deviance, which is expressed in terms of self-confessed distress and role failure and/or rule infractions which are distressing to others. This is a normative matter in which agents of surveillance and control for our moral order, who are typically state employees, tidy up that deviance by either correcting it (with effective treatments) or, failing that, managing its consequences by sequestration or tranquilisation.

What we generically call 'mental health problems' begins with common distress, where help is anxiously sought and gratefully received. But in addition (and this is why the word 'distress' favoured as an alternative by some critics of psychiatric diagnosis does not exhaust our conceptual exploration) these problems, in varying degrees, entail conduct that is troubling to others. Even in the case of 'common mental health problems', depressed or agoraphobic patients fail to comply with role expectations in daily life. Psychotic patients transgress the rule of mutual accountability. As a social species we expect others to follow rule expectations and to account for themselves when they do not. People who transgress rules and fail to account for this rationally and persuasively to others are unnerving; madness is frightening because of its unintelligibility and the apparent lack of concern or insight on the part of the transgressor.

By being unintelligible and then not accounting for this conduct, psychotic patients put themselves in a precarious state. Specialist services deal with that state by tranquilisation and sequestration, within an ethos of paternalism. Anyone who has worked in statutory mental health services or been a patient there will have witnessed this in staff–patient interactions, when the discourse of 'not being well' predominates. Expectations of the agency of the patient deemed to be mentally ill are low or non-existent. Psychotic patients are viewed as victims of a disease process out of their control.

In the very same setting, staff views of patients with a diagnosis of personality disorder are typically different. Suspicion and caution instead predominate. The staff expectations now of the human agency manifested by patients are high, not low, and so cynicism rather than paternalism is ushered in and maybe the word 'behaviour' is used by staff, not 'illness', to signal purposeful conduct. This is not a recent discursive trend but goes right back to the origins of criminal lunatic asylums, when moral insanity was distinguished from insanity proper. Those in the former group were seen as lacking conscience and marked by their risk to others (often proved by past conduct, not just assumed in the present), while having a clear insight into what they were doing.

Today this anti-social and criminal focus has expanded to include risky conduct on the part of people who are self-preoccupied and have long-term problems which have either not resolved quietly and disappeared or have not been changed by professional efforts. If neurosis, broadly conceived, is mainly about self-declared distress and psychosis, broadly conceived, is about episodic periods of acute unintelligibility, then PD, broadly conceived, is about a vast range of incorrigible forms of conduct. Some of these are about chronic neurotic or psychotic symptoms, whereas others shade more towards a selfish disregard for the rights of others. This really is a vast range and if this is doubted, see what happens if we disregard the superordinate and implausible categories of PD but simply list the real enough conduct that lies beneath the labels.

To demonstrate this point, I invite the reader to look at the following list taken as a good chunk of descriptions from DSM and ICD. Discount the diagnoses to the left but stay with the behavioural descriptions and subjective reports of patients in brackets on the right. These are ordinary language descriptions of conduct, or its commonly assumed motive or associated experience, which we all understand within our shared normative context. This becomes a long list and we might wonder on reading what point, if any, there is in re-codifying it in diagnoses at all.

- Paranoid (suspicious, mistrustful, resentful, grudge-bearing, jealous, self-important)
- Schizoid (emotionally cold, detached, aloof, lacking enjoyment, introspective)
- Schizotypal (socially anxious, eccentric, oddities of thought and perception)
- Borderline/emotionally unstable (chronic feelings of emptiness and fear of abandonment, recurrently suicidal and self-harming, unstable mood states)
- Dissocial/anti-social (callous to others, impulsive, lack of guilt and remorse, irresponsible, failure to take responsibility for actions)
- Anankastic/obsessive-compulsive (perfectionist, preoccupied by rules and details, over-conscientious, rigid and stubborn, pedantic, overly conventional)
- Histrionic (self-dramatising, shallow, attention-seeking, over-concern with physical attractiveness, suggestible)
- Anxious avoidant (fearful avoidance of others, fear of being criticised or humiliated)
- Dependent (compliant, lets others take responsibility, fear of being left to care for self, needs excessive help from others to make decisions).

By slicing away the unhelpful medical labels to the left, we are left with a long aggregating list of moral attributions and claims. These may be fair comment according to our shared norms. They are real enough aspects of our experience and behaviour that we might witness in ourselves or others. They certainly have more solidity to them as agreed forms of distressed or distressing habits, moral weaknesses or rule transgressions, than the reified diagnoses trying and failing to chunk them together meaningfully. Maybe some of them emerge more in some contexts and not others, but maybe some people really are more prone to express them: why should we rule that prospect out *a priori*? If we reframe them as psychological continua that might, though do not inevitably, fluctuate within individuals over time and place, then we begin to understand complexity rather than reduce people to the labels attached to them.

To conclude this section, then, we can mainly explain the retention of PD labels, which are neither scientific nor humanistic in character, by the elephant in the room of social control. PD services mainly exist to manage and ameliorate the *troubling consequences or risks to self and others* of a wide range of forms of conduct, which are listed beneath the discounted diagnostic labels discussed above. If interventions fail, which they often do, then the working rationale for services is still one of the containment and management of incorrigible conduct. This is the non-criminal deviance discussed as 'residual' by labelling theory sociology, and still relevant as a conceptual insight today (Scheff, 1966). If the risk focus is in doubt, then look at the core business of specialist PD services or forms of secure provision that contain non-psychotic patients. They deal in the main with risky conduct subsumed by the diagnoses of borderline PD and anti-social PD. They are not bulging with patients with a diagnosis of 'anxious avoidant' or 'anankastic PD'. That contrast is telling.

The risk focus is also revealed by the failure of the concept of 'psychopathy' (e.g. Hare, 1993) to die away in the professional and lay discourse, despite it being absent from both ICD and DSM. Hare's work centres on the range of troubling conduct that emerges when histrionic, narcissistic and anti-social forms of conduct intersect in various permutations and then are expressed in life by us all, to some degree. The latter is important: Hare is discussing an exaggerated expression of self-centredness that, to a degree, all humans are capable of. Those with high scores on his checklist are at one end of a distribution. A variant of this general human tendency argument emerged controversially with claims about the 'dark triad' (narcissism, Machiavellianism and psychopathy) and the extent to which these are overlapping or distinct psychological continua/concepts and how often they are manifest in our lives (Paulhus & Williams, 2002). Those at one end of this distribution would include remorseless sex offenders (in prisons or secure hospitals), mass murderers, authoritarian politicians and notorious business leaders.

But it is Hare who has had the most influence in secure mental health service philosophy. He is a psychologist and uses a continuum, not categories. The empirical and moral implications of this difference are clear. Some of us at one end of the continuum are benignly considerate of others and selfless much of the time (though extreme conditions such as warfare may bring out another side). Some of us are very selfish and inconsiderate of others, using them as a means to an end rather than respecting their needs and rights. Many of us live our lives across varying situations in which we slide between these existential states. This reflects our faltering performance of Kant's second categorical (moral) imperative, which refers to our lived humanity and our expected constant obligation to provide honest respect to others (Vardy & Grosch, 1999).

Consigning PD to the bin, which it probably deserves in the light of the immanent critique above, does not alter the reality of that fluxing existential reality and its moral character (Blackburn, 1988). Psychiatric rehabilitation, or expectations of recovery, are moral, not merely medical, matters and so it is not surprising that the therapeutic community's approach to personality disorder is the legacy of moral treatment in the nineteenth century (Lillehet, 2002). This reminds us that PD remains a code for moralisation, not just a psychological or psychiatric conundrum. Given that complexity, we might critically reflect on what we are missing when we cling too unimaginatively to the conceptual wreckage of the reified PD label.

Omissive critique

Having used an immanent critique to expose the lack of coherence of a medical–categorical approach to those diagnosed with a personality disorder and an explanatory critique to account for the maintenance of that scientifically implausible psychiatric authority, we could leave the matter there. This section can be ignored if required, but if the reader is interested in the wider social context of that long list of moral attributions subsumed by psychiatric diagnosis which I noted above, we can push on with our societal exploration. We can phrase this as a question: what is ignored about risk and incorrigibility in society if we limit our attention to their expression only in those with a PD label?

Risk and incorrigibility are widespread outside of the population that is recorded by psychiatric epidemiology as being 'personality disordered'. Take the example of human beings being 'chaotic'. In Britain in the past few years our government, and our political class more generally, has acted in a chaotic and exasperating way in its dealing with Brexit. Or take anti-social brutality: the bombing of innocent civilians and the profits of the arms industry (a mainstay of the UK economy) is accepted as realpolitik today. The issue then is not being risky or incorrigible, but the manner in which this is expressed in society.

I now enlarge on this with a number points, *viz*:

1. *Self-centred risk taking or incorrigibility may be socially accepted and may even be valued.* The controversy about whether President Trump suffers from narcissistic personality disorder (Caruso, 2017) highlights an important ambiguity. It confirms the worst fears of his opponents but is dismissed as an irrelevance by his adoring supporters. And there is the intriguing evidence about the measured 'psychopathy scores' of successful business leaders, which at times may exceed those detained in secure psychiatric facilities (Babiak & Hare, 2000; Board & Fritzon, 2005; Boddy *et al*, 2010). Less controversially, we accept some reckless sporting conduct and at times even turn it into heroism. Mountain climbers routinely die and are often of child-rearing age. Boxing is highly prized and televised regularly, even though it involves two people deliberately trying their best to beat the other to a pulp.

Thus those people who end up receiving a PD diagnosis are a subset of risky or incorrigible people in society. The boundary between the two is porous. For example, a person with a diagnosis of obsessive-compulsive personality disorder may be an unceasingly diligent accountant but their checking of details means that they have no time to sleep. The latter might then prompt service contact and an ensuing diagnosis. The melodramatic actress may only receive a diagnosis of histrionic personality disorder when her actions spill over into a disrupted personal life, when her significant others become alienated in exasperation and so she seeks therapy. My point here is that the same conduct can at times reflect either a job description or an attribution of personality disorder.

Keeping in mind that porosity reminds us not to split off the diagnosis of PD from human conduct in general. This does not legitimise the diagnosis of personality disorder but it does honestly acknowledge that risky and incorrigible conduct is part of being human and that we can and do describe that conduct, whether or not it is medically codified. This point is even acknowledged by those who do retain a commitment to the diagnosis of PD. For example, a psychiatrist who has dedicated his career to the topic, and whom I noted above, admits: 'no one really knows where personality disorder begins or where it ends' (Tyrer, 2018, pxiv).

This normative point is important as well in children receiving a diagnosis of 'conduct disorder' (Wakefield, 1992). Wakefield points out that although the American Psychiatric Association has always insisted that mental disorder should be differentiated clearly from social deviance, this is a futile and vacuous demand. All descriptions of mental disorder, including personality disorder, reflect social judgements about rule transgressions and role failures. The professional who points out that PD patients are chaotic and distressed but the wider group which I note here is not (making those patients in some sense distinct) is describing a contingency when those social judgments prompt a request for help, from the incipient patient or their significant others (or sometimes the judicial system). That contingent shift from patient to non-patient reflects the porous boundary between psychological normality and abnormality. This is why the work of psychologists such as Robert Hare, who argues for continua not categories, is important. We are all more or less psychopathic, and more generally we are all more or less childish and self-centred, for varying amounts of time in our daily lives.

2. *Risk is not treated in a consistent way in society* A legal curfew on all people under 30 from dusk on Friday to dawn on Monday would reduce violent and sexual offending, road traffic collisions, domestic violence, suicide, sexually transmitted infections, unwanted pregnancies and peaks in resource allocation to police forces and accident and emergency departments. Alcohol consumption is a much better predictor of risky conduct than psychiatric diagnosis and yet binge drinkers are ignored or, at worst, suffer a night sobering up in a police cell. Compare that to the use of legal powers to detain those who are deemed by others to be mentally disordered in private and public spaces. In another relevant example, despite the known health risks, there are no grounds for detaining and forcibly treating people who smoke tobacco. So too in the case of people who have unprotected sexual intercourse. We can elaborate a wide range of risky behaviours that invoke no state intervention at all. Psychiatric patients are thus treated in a discriminatory manner in modern societies. Moreover, they are not offered ensured humane and effective care in exchange for their loss of liberty without trial (Eastman, 1994). To be clear here, this is a wider point about mental health services being risk-driven (applying to patients across diagnostic boundaries). However, the point does apply to many with a diagnosis of personality disorder as well.

3. *Confusion over what we mean by personality*. This goes 'under the radar' when we consider 'personality disorder'. Academic psychologists tend to either dismiss the very notion of personality, post-modern style, as being about texts or situated identities (Gergen, 1992), or they adhere, positivist-style, to the 'Big Five' tradition (Eysenck, 1947; Cattell, 1943). These purported traits are: openness to experience, conscientiousness, extraversion, agreeableness and neuroticism. As taken-for-granted assumptions in modern psychology, they are traceable to late-Victorian eugenics, which generated the psychology of individual differences (Galton, 1884; Pearson, 1904). These differences were assumed to be mainly inherited; thus personality would mean the temperament or character with which we are born, and which is thus fairly immutable. Not only do psychologists disagree on the term 'personality', but the descriptions they prefer align poorly with what psychiatrists are discussing in relation to 'abnormal personality'. The only points of contact with the Big Five relate to 'conscientiousness' and 'neuroticism'. (Confusingly, Eysenck

(1991) added 'psychoticism' as a personality dimension, which adds a sixth if we accept its validity.) Moreover, psychiatry remains in a state of confusion about what is meant by personality disorder (Tyrer *et al*, 2007). In the run-up to the publication of DSM-5, two international authorities, John Livesley and Roel Verheul, resigned from the DSM committee deliberating on the personality disorder section, condemning the emerging taxonomy as confused and lacking in scientific credibility (Frances, 2012).

Thus psychologists do not agree on personality, psychiatrists do not agree on personality disorder and psychology and psychiatry consider personality in ways that only partially overlap. To add to the confusion, the revisions of DSM over the years have contained factional disputes between biological psychiatrists and psychoanalysts (Wilson, 1993). The former 'neo-Kraepelinian' group have dominated the agenda on re-defining existing forms of diagnostic category and creating new ones. In the case of personality disorder, against that trend, psychoanalysts introduced the 'borderline' diagnosis (Kernberg, 1984). (DSM-5 added many elaborations to the DSM-IV version, widening the net of those likely to be diagnosed with borderline PD.)

4. *A diagnosis focus closes down our imagination about alternatives*. The inconsistent and unfair way in which risk is dealt with in society, combined with the poor showing of the scientific and humanistic outcome when that risk is medicalised and codified as PD, invites new and preferred scenarios. This is not easy because of the moral complexity of the matters involved, the uncertain balance to be struck about the relationship between structure and agency (we are all both determined and determining beings) and the challenge of dealing with old habits that die hard. One path to explore is to reject diagnosis in favour of trauma-informed formulations built up between professionals and patients: this is the Power Threat Meaning Framework (Johnstone & Boyle, 2018). I was part of the group developing the latter framework and it basically proposes a service philosophy that should be guided by a different approach to assessment and intervention. These are based upon four sorts of question, *viz*: (i) What has happened to you? (how have different forms of power operated in your life?); (ii) How did it affect you? (what kind of threats did this pose?); (iii) What sense did you make of it? (what is the meaning of these experiences to you?); and (iv) What did you have to do to survive? (what kinds of threat response are you using that help you cope but might also pose a problem to you or others?). This is not a panacea; nor does it claim that all mental health problems are traceable to childhood adversity. It is, though, a substantial improvement on the diagnosis of PD and its associated therapeutic pessimism. However, the ultimate constraint on the development of such an alternative remains the next point.

5. The elephant in the room of social control is explained away by the myth of 'mental health law'. The latter term is a misnomer. Dedicated laws to remove some, but not all, people deemed to have an abnormality of mind are now considered to be a progressive feature of democratic societies. They are not about promoting mental health but rather controlling particular forms of risk linked to mental abnormality. The professional discourse of 'treating patients under the mental health act' is an accurate but highly limited social administrative description. It obscures the well-practised long-term tradition of psychiatry being about social control (Szasz, 1963; Scull, 1985; Bean, 1986). A matter-of-fact social administrative approach to describing the state's response to those with a diagnosis of personality disorder remains both common and challenged (DoH, 2000; cf. Corbett & Westwood, 2005). The expensive and legally complicated world of inpatient psychiatry largely contains those who are adjudged to be a risk to themselves or others. These tend to be a sub-group of patients with diagnostic labels of psychosis and/or personality disorder. This point also now applies in jurisdictions which contain community treatment orders (Fabris, 2011; Riley *et al*, 2018). The point here is that while diagnosis broadly predicts inpatient status, this is a code for risky actions in society inflected by low social class, race and gender (MHAC, 2009; Pilgrim, 2012). Psychiatry functions in part as a response on behalf of its host (and employing) society to control the threat this risky action poses to our social order. If this is in doubt we can reflect on why so many patients with a recorded and clear diagnosis of psychosis or personality disorder are still free citizens. It is not their *diagnosis* that determines coercive action on the part of agents of the state, but *the way that they act*. The controversies this triggers includes the human rights challenge of false positive decision-making (inpatients are not discharged when they should be) and the challenge of assessing risk in the closed system of inpatient contexts. By definition and intent, the latter are not open systems. The actual ecology of risk, including the risky settings of the poor neighbourhoods hosting many psychiatric patients, bears little or no relationship to the environmental conditions of inpatient wards (Silver *et al*, 1999; Stockdale *et al*, 2007). This is why penal control is so much easier to administer. Prisoners obtain their liberty at the end of an agreed period of detention, determined by their past conduct. 'Personality disordered patients' are being considered for discharge in relation to future risk (bearing in mind current and past conduct). Thus while both penal and healthcare contexts contain and manage risk, they do so according to different rules of decision-making (Pilgrim & Tomasini, 2012).

Conclusion

This chapter has used the resource of critical realism to appraise the limitations of the diagnosis of personality disorder. Immanent, explanatory and omissive critiques were deployed to examine the latter. The focus has been on the reality of specifiable forms of conduct that are considered to be risky or incorrigible and so are a threat to our social order and often unnerving or offensive to those who are sane by common consent. Those with a diagnosis of PD may also be distressed but, in the main, that still becomes of practical relevance only when, and if, it leads to risky action (i.e. self-harm or suicide risk).

Specialist services are mainly concerned with those who act out risk to self or others. They have less concern for other forms of conduct that merely reflect self-identified distress alone. For this reason, some forms of PD may be diagnosed but not typically responded to or prioritised by specialist services, especially when coercion and involuntary detention are involved. Thus the politics of risk and the way in which risk more generally is embedded in public policy (including but not only mental health policy) are important considerations, when reflecting on the future of 'PD services'. That critical reflection could start with the agenda set listed in the ommisive critique above.

The preceding immanent and explanatory critiques might help 'jobbing clinicians' to defend their rejection of a diagnostic approach, while retaining an honest appraisal of the social and existential challenges facing their clients. The latter have found themselves, for a range of varied contingent reasons, turning to mental health professionals for help. However, progress in their lives will only be made by them expanding their acknowledgment of their personal agency and then 'doing daily life differently'. The wide range of conduct subsumed by the PD diagnosis I described above implies a shift from incorrigibility to social conformance being in the spotlight for professional and client alike. I mentioned the Power Threat Meaning Framework as one point of reference to guide that task.

References

American Psychiatric Association (2012) DSM-5 Field Trials *Psychiatric News Alert*, **30 October**.

Babiak P & Hare RD (2007) *Snakes in Suits: When Psychopaths Go to Work*. New York: Harper Collins.

Bean P (1986) *Mental Disorder and Legal Control*. Cambridge: Cambridge University Press.

Berrios GE (1985) Obsessional disorders during the nineteenth century: Terminological and classificatory issues. In: WF Bynum, R Porter and M Shepherd (eds) *The Anatomy of Madness* (Volume 1). London: Tavistock.

Bhaskar R (2016) *Enlightened Common Sense: The Philosophy of Critical Realism*. London: Routledge.

Blackburn R (1988) On moral judgements and personality disorders: The myth of psychopathic disorder re-visited. *British Journal of Psychiatry* **153** 505–512.

Board BJ & Fritzon K (2005) Disordered personalities at work. *Psychology, Crime and Law* **11** (1) 17–32.

Boddy RP, Ladysjewsky R & Galvin PL (2010) Leaders without ethics in global business: Corporate psychopaths. *Journal of Public Affairs* **10** (1) 131–138.

Cacciola JS, Rutherford MJ, Alterman AI, McKay JR & Mulvaney FD (1998) Long-term test-retest reliability of personality disorder diagnoses in opiate dependent patients. *Journal of Personality Disorders* **12** (4) 32–37.

Caruso C (2017) Psychiatrists debate weighing in on Trump's mental health. *Scientific American* **15 February**.

Cattell RB (1943) The description of personality: Basic traits resolved into clusters. *Journal of Abnormal and Social Psychology* **38** (4) 476–506.

Cleckley H (1941) *The Mask of Sanity*. St Louis: C. V. Mosby.

Corbett K & Westwood T (2005) 'Dangerous and Severe Personality Disorder': A psychiatric manifestation of the risk society. *Critical Public Health* **15** (2) 121–133.

Crossley N (2006) *Contesting Psychiatry: Social Movements in Mental Health*. Abingdon: Routledge.

Cutajar MC, Mullen PE, Ogloff JRP, Thomas SD, Wells DL & Spataro J (2010) Psychopathology in a large cohort of sexually abused children followed up to 43 years. *Child Abuse & Neglect* **34** (11) 813–822.

Department of Health (2000) *Managing Dangerous People with Severe Personality Disorder*. London: DH.

Dolan B & Coid J (1993) *Psychopathic and Ann-social Personality Disorders: Treatment and Research Issues*. London: Gaskell.

Dutton K (2012) *The Wisdom of Psychopaths: What Saints, Spies and Serial Killers Can Teach Us about Success*. New York: Farrar, Straus and Giroux.

Eastman N (1994) Mental health law: Civil liberties and the principle of reciprocity. *British Medical Journal* **308** 43.

Eysenck HJ (1991) Dimensions of personality: 16, 5, or 3? Criteria for a taxonomic paradigm. *Personality and Individual Differences* **12** 773–790.

Eysenck HJ (1947) *Dimensions of Personality*. London: Routledge and Keegan Paul.

Fabris E (2011) *Tranquil Prisons: Chemical Incarceration under Community Treatment Orders*. Toronto: University of Toronto Press.

Frances AJ (2012) Two who resigned from DSM-5 explain why they spell out the defects in the personality section. *Psychology Today* **11 July**.

Galton F (1884) Measurement of character. *Fortnightly Review* **36** 179–185.

Gergen KJ (1992) The decline and fall of personality. *Psychology Today* **25** (6) 58–63.

Hare RD (1993) *Without Conscience: The Disturbing World of the Psychopaths among Us*. New York: Pocket.

Henderson DK (1938) *Psychopathic States*. London: Wiley.

Herman JL, Perry CJ & Van der Kolk BA (1989) Childhood trauma in borderline personality disorder. *American Journal of Psychiatry* **146** (4) 490–495.

Horne G (2014) Is borderline personality disorder a moral or clinical condition? Assessing Charland's argument from treatment. *Neuroethics* **7** (2) 215–226.

Johnstone L & Boyle M with Cromby J, Dillon J, Harper D, Kinderman P, Longden E, Pilgrim D & Read J (2018) *The Power Threat Meaning Framework: Towards the Identification of Patterns in Emotional Distress, Unusual Experiences and Troubled or Troubling Behaviour*. Leicester: British Psychological Society.

Kendell RE (2002) The distinction between personality disorder and mental illness. *British Journal of Psychiatry* **180** 110–115.

Kernberg OF (1984) *Severe Personality Disorders: Psychotherapeutic Strategies*. New Haven, CT: Yale University Press.

Kliem S, Kröger C & Kossfelder J (2010) Dialectical behavior therapy for borderline personality disorder: A meta-analysis using mixed-effects modeling. *Journal of Consulting and Clinical Psychology* **78** 936–951.

Lane C (2008) *Shyness: How Normal Behavior Became a Sickness*. New Haven: Yale.

Lillehet E (2002) Progress and power: Exploring the disciplinary connection between moral treatment and psychiatric rehabilitation. *Philosophy, Psychiatry and Psychology* **9** (2) 167–182.

Linehan MM (1993) *Cognitive Behaviour Therapy of Borderline Personality Disorder*. New York: Guilford Press.

Luntz BK (1994) Antisocial personality disorder in abused and neglected children grown up. *American Journal of Psychiatry* **151** 670–674.

MHAC (2009) *Coercion and Consent: Monitoring the Mental Health Act 2007–2009* (13th Biennial Report). London: Stationery Office.

NIMHE (2003) *Personality Disorder: No Longer A Diagnosis of Exclusion*. London: NIMHE.

Ogata SN, Silk KR, Goodrich S, Lohr NE, Westen D & Hill EM (1990) Childhood sexual and physical abuse in adult patients with borderline personality disorder. *American Journal of Psychiatry* **147** (8) 1008–1013.

Paulhus DL & Williams KM (2002) The dark triad of personality: Narcissism, Machiavellianism, and psychopathy. *Journal of Research in Personality* **36** (6) 556–563.

Pearson K (1904) On the inheritance of mental and moral characteristics in man. *Biometrika* IV, 265–303.

Pilgrim D (2007) The survival of psychiatric diagnosis. *Social Science & Medicine* **65** (3) 536–544.

Pilgrim D (2012) Final lessons from the Mental Health Act Commission for England and Wales: The limits of legalism-plus-safeguards. *Journal of Social Policy* **41** (1) 61–81.

Pilgrim D (2015) *Understanding Mental Health: A Critical Realist Exploration*. London: Routledge.

Pilgrim D (2018) Are kindly and efficacious mental health services possible? *Journal of Mental Health* **27** (4) 295–297.

Pilgrim D & Tomasini F (2012) On being unreasonable in modern society: Are mental health problems special? *Disability and Society* **27** (5) 631–646.

Read J & Bentall RP (2012) Negative childhood experiences and mental health: Theoretical, clinical and primary prevention implications. *British Journal of Psychiatry* 88-91.

Rice ME, Harris GT & Cormier CA (1992) Evaluation of a maximum security therapeutic community for psychopaths and other mentally disordered offenders. *Law and Human Behaviour* **16** 399–412.

Riley H, Fagerjord GL & Høyer G (2018) Community treatment orders – what are the views of decision makers? *Journal of Mental Health* 97–102.

Salekin RT (2002) Psychopathy and therapeutic pessimism. Clinical lore or clinical reality? *Clinical Psychology Review* **22** (1) 79–112.

Scheff TJ (1966) *Being Mentally Ill: A Sociological Theory*. Chicago: Chicago University Press.

Scull A (1985) Humanitarianism or control? Some observations on the historiography of Anglo-American psychiatry. In: S Cohen and A Scull (eds) *Social Control and the State*. Oxford: Basil Blackwell.

Silver E, Mulvey EP & Monahan J (1999) Assessing violence risk among discharged psychiatric patients: towards an ecological approach. *Law and Human Behavior* **23** 237–255.

Spataro J, Mullen PE, Burgess PM, Wells DL & Moss SA (2004) Impact of child sexual abuse on mental health: Prospective study in males and females. *British Journal of Psychiatry* **184** 416–421.

Stockdale SE, Wells KB, Tang L, Belin TR, Zhang L & Sherbourne CD (2007) The importance of social context: Neighbourhood stressors, stress buffering mechanisms and alcohol, drug and mental disorders. *Social Science & Medicine* **65** 1867–1881.

Szasz TS (1963) *Law, Liberty and Psychiatry*. New York: Macmillan.

Tyrer P (2018) *Taming the Beast Within*. London: Sheldon Press.

Tyrer P, Coombs N, Ibrahimi F, Mathilakath A, Bajaj P, Ranger M, Rao B & Din R (2007) Critical developments in the assessment of personality disorder. *British Journal of Psychiatry* **190** s51–s59.

Vardy P & Grosch P (1999) *The Puzzle of Ethics*. London: Fount.

Wakefield JC (1992) The concept of mental disorder: On the boundary between biological facts and social values. *American Psychologist* **47** 373–388.

Watters E (2010) *Crazy Like Us: The Globalization of the American Psyche*. New York: Free Press.

Wilson M (1993) DSM-III and the transformation of American psychiatry: A history. *American Journal of Psychiatry* **150** (3) 399–410.

Zanarini MC, Frankenburg FR & Vujanovic AA (2002) Inter-rater and test-retest reliability of the revised diagnostic interview for borderlines. *Journal of Personality Disorders* **16** (3) 270–276.

Chapter 5:
The Importance of Personal Meaning

Sharon Prince and Sue Ellis

Introduction

Debates about the utility of the 'personality disorder' diagnosis have raged for years and have preoccupied many of those using and delivering services. While this chapter advocates for a critique of the traditional biomedical approach, it also recognises the stultifying effect that these debates can have on service delivery. While these debates rage, Rome burns in many quarters, meaning that some services are free to dismiss criticisms and to maintain increasingly discredited and problematic treatment models focused on the alleviation of the symptoms of intra-psychic pathology. This book advocates for a universally better approach to working with people with personality difficulties or personality disorder and of the importance, therefore, of reconciling some of these arguments, so that polarised division can be less of an obstacle to achieving the ideals outlined in the *Consensus Statement For People With Complex Mental Health Difficulties Who Are Diagnosed With A Personality Disorder* (Personality Disorder Commission, 2018). The utility of personal meaning as a way of achieving this is proposed.

The loss of personal meaning

A historical and 'traditional' approach within psychiatric practice has been to inadvertently divest meaning from an individual's experiences. It indicates that experiences are caused by psychological phenomena outside of the individual's control, have a biological basis and can only be remedied or cured by a medical and chemically based intervention and, for a limited few, psychological therapy. Further understanding of an individual's behaviour and narrative in terms of meaning and communication is often lost because their experiences are seen as random symptoms of distress. Many authors argue that these 'pathology-focused' approaches are not only unhelpful but actually invalid when working with individuals diagnosed with 'personality disorder', and that they further compound distress and despair.

The position argued within this chapter is, broadly, that it is the development and understanding of personal meaning and narratives that contributes towards an individual leading a life that leaves them feeling healthy and fulfilled. This position has been informed first by many years working with, and alongside, individuals who have experienced childhood trauma and adversity, and have been diagnosed as having a personality disorder as a consequence. Second, it has been informed by working alongside practitioners who have felt frustrated and outraged by the experiences of individuals stigmatised by this label and who want to provide a different experience. The 'personality disorder' service with which we have been associated for many years has tried to work in a compassionate and authentic way with service users who have been described as presenting with a profile of significant risk to themselves and/or others and who are often 'hard to reach'. We would argue that these individuals are not necessarily 'hard to reach' or difficult to engage; instead we would propose that staff and service providers should adjust the lens through which they view the work, recognising the importance of trauma in distress, the operation of power between individuals and within systems, the capacity of services to compound suffering and ultimately the need to 'speak truth to power', if we are to provide meaningful services to improve outcomes for a group of people who have been marginalised for too long.

Psychiatric diagnoses and their role in obscuring personal meaning

The classification systems used by modern psychiatry are recorded by the Diagnostic and Statistical Manual of Mental Disorders, fifth edition (DSM 5) within the United States and by the World Health Organisation's (WHO) International Classification of Diseases (ICD 11) in the rest of the world. These systems have had a significant influence upon how personality disorder is clinically conceptualised and researched, and have evolved out of a need to find a common language and understanding about 'mental disorder' and distress. However, two similar but different paths have been pursued by these classification systems, which may be understood to reflect cultural and political factors within both wider society and the field of psychiatry and psychology. Understanding the development of these systems provides some insight into what some argue is the often arbitrary and morally suspect nature of psychiatric diagnosis (Widiger, 2012). The arbitrary nature of the classification systems refers to the fact that both are atheoretical and based on expert clinical consensus rather than empirical analysis; therefore any changes made within the system are essentially made by committee, with lobbying and voting, rather than predominantly determined by research and evidence.

Various revisions of the classification systems have led us to the diagnoses currently included in ICD 11 and DSM 5. However, both these systems are subject to significant criticism from both within and outside of psychiatry (Division of Clinical Psychology, 2013; The Critical Psychiatry Network, 2014; Johnstone, 2014). The main criticisms can be summarised as follows:

■ The vast majority of psychiatric problems have no biological basis. Therefore, using a 'medical model' to conceptualise psychological distress is fundamentally flawed as there is an absence of evidence for a 'disease process'. Johnstone (2014) argues that the criteria of psychiatric diagnoses, rather than being 'actually sensible or meaningful clusters of "symptoms", are just as likely to be a random set of experiences without a shared underlying cause'. Indeed, David Kupfer, Chair of the DSM 5 Task Force, noted that:

> 'In the future, we hope to be able to identify disorders using biological and genetic markers that provide precise diagnoses that can be delivered with complete reliability and validity. Yet this promise, which we have anticipated since the 1970s remains disappointingly distant. We've been telling patients for several decades that we are waiting for biomarkers. We're still waiting'
>
> (Kupfer, 2013 in Johnstone & Boyle, 2018).

■ Many psychiatric diagnoses lack an evidence base, and there is an absence of empirical support for reliability (that different professionals presented with the same 'symptoms' will provide the same diagnosis) and validity (validity has a number of different meanings but essentially the focus is on whether the phenomenon as described exists) of diagnosis (Widiger, 2012).

■ Some have argued that diagnostic criteria are no more than social judgements about how people, think, feel and behave (see Pilgrim, this volume). A personality disorder diagnosis is often made when behaviour falls outside cultural 'norms', but with norms diverging across time and cultures, the question has to be asked: who determines what is 'normal/abnormal'? One classic example of how concepts of mental disorder are socially constructed, informed and changed by social norms was the DSM classification of 'homosexuality' as a mental disorder. It was not completely removed from the DSM until 1987 and from the ICD-10 until 1992.

■ Finally, psychiatric diagnosis does not determine treatment. The deliberately atheoretical and descriptive nature of the criteria and levels of comorbidity mean that neither manual takes any stance on how best to address the problems that have been identified, thus having very little utility in clinical contexts.

Given that the system for psychiatric diagnosis is so fundamentally flawed, why does the practice persist? In the United States, Johnstone (2014) argues that psychiatrists' continued belief in a 'medical model' rests essentially with the idea that psychological/mental distress is an illness originating from the brain or body which can be treated like any other biological illness. Research grants are awarded to studies which use the diagnostic categories, insurance companies insist on patients receiving a diagnosis to fund care and there are significant links between big pharma and committee members (Cosgrove & Drimsky, 2012). Actuarial data is also used as a method for excluding individuals from acquiring insurance. All of which, it is argued, contributes to the continued reification of psychiatric diagnosis and its self-perpetuation.

In the United Kingdom, however, the national healthcare system is not insurance-based and so not solely reliant on psychiatric diagnosis; psychiatrists are able to choose to adopt a more 'biopsychosocial' rather than 'biomedical' model which moves away from stating that an individual's difficulties are based on genetics and/or biology but moves toward considering other influences. This is a position adopted by most 'mainstream' mental health services and cited in numerous clinical and policy documents. It could be argued that the biopsychosocial approach is an attempt to find a synthesis between a dominant biomedical model and a more psychosocially informed approach to understanding mental distress/disorder. However, Johnstone (2014, p20) argues that, with a few exceptions:

> 'there is no solid evidence at all that any psychiatric problems ... are the result of faulty genes, or biochemical imbalances, or any other identifiable causes in the brain or body. And indeed, the attempt to integrate the two is conceptually flawed.'

Despite all of the above, we should acknowledge that many service users find a diagnostic process helpful for enabling them to access appropriate services. The Consensus Statement (Personality Disorder Commission, 2018, p4) states:

> 'The label is controversial for good reasons: it is misleading, stigmatising and masks the nature of the problem it is supposed to address, adding to the challenges people experience. However, it has its advocates, not least among those for whom it has been the only passport to effective help.'

Definition of Personality Disorder (DSM 5)

■ An enduring pattern of emotional and cognitive difficulties which affect the way in which the person relates to others or understands themselves.

■ This pattern is pervasive and occurs across a broad range of social and personal situations

■ Is a longstanding difficulty which always appears in childhood or adolescence and continues into later life.

■ May lead to significant problems in occupational and social performance.

■ Is not attributable to another mental disorder, substance misuse or head injury.

Definition of Personality Disorder (ICD 11)

■ An enduring pattern of disturbance characterised by problems in functioning of aspects of the self and/or interpersonal dysfunction.

■ Is associated with substantial distress and significant impairment in a wide range of personal and social settings.

■ Has persisted over an extended period of time.

■ The disturbance is manifest in patterns of cognitions, emotional experience and expression, and behaviour.

■ Is not developmentally appropriate or explained by social or cultural factors, including socio-political conflict.

■ Is not attributable to another mental disorder, health condition or substance misuse.

Advances in thinking

Until recently the DSM was organised by a system of 'Axes', which were used to provide a holistic and comprehensive assessment of an individual's difficulties. Historically, 'personality disorder' did not have its own axis and different personality disorder presentations were considered to be extremes of other conditions. For example, borderline personality disorder was thought to be an extreme variant of a mood disorder and schizotypal personality disorder was linked to schizophrenia (Widiger, 2012). An axis solely focused on 'personality disorder' was created out of concern that psychiatrists would neglect this part of the assessment because of their focus on clinical disorders such as mood and eating disorders.

Recently in DSM V and ICD 11, a dimensional approach to the assessment and diagnosis of personality disorder has been incorporated. This change reflects criticisms that the categorical approach cannot be appropriately applied to the study of personality disorder, not least because the categories are overly focused on observable behaviours and not linked to theories of personality development (Eysenck, 1987; Costa & McCrae, 1990; Livesley, 1990; Mulder & Joyce, 1997; Sanderson & Clarkin, 2002; Clark, 2007; Tyrer *et al*, 2015). The dimensional model sees personality disorder as a continuum, with 'normal healthy functioning' at one extreme and what is called 'personality disorder' at the other. There is overwhelming empirical support for a dimensional representation of personality (Widiger & Frances, 1994; Livesley, 2007), with most models describing three (extraversion, neuroticism, psychoticism), four (emotional dysregulation, dissocial behaviour, inhibitedness, compulsivity) or five (neuroticism, extraversion agreeableness, openness and conscientiousness) dimensions as basic structures (Sarker & Duggan, 2012, p160).

Despite academic support, the dimensional system is still subject to criticism, being described as unreliable and unsatisfactory (Frances, 2010) and as upholding a distinction between abnormal and normal personality and, as a consequence, replicating the classification system by inherently failing to take context into account and privileging the importance of individual intra-psychic pathology.

In an attempt to situate 'personality disorder' more practically, and perhaps less judgementally, within the contexts within which people live, Livesley (2003) defines personality disorder 'as a failure to achieve adaptive solutions to life tasks'. Adaptive tasks involve one or more of the following:

- Achieving a coherent sense of self (intrapersonal).

- Developing intimacy in personal relationships (interpersonal).

- Behaving prosocially (social group).

'Failure' or 'deficits' in these areas are only indicative of personality disorder when they are enduring and can be traced to adolescence or early adulthood, and when they are not due to a pervasive mental state disorder. Of clinical significance is Livesley's use of personality traits organised into 'patterns of personality disorder'; for example:

> *'Emotional Dysregulation: The Borderline Pattern*
> *A general tendency towards instability in emotions, interpersonal relationships, cognitive functioning and sense of self. The pattern is organised around two core emotional traits: affective lability and anxiousness both of which are associated with cognitive dysregulation, a tendency towards confused and disorganised thinking especially around times of stress.'*
>
> Livesley (2003, p48)

Unlike traditional psychiatric diagnoses, this 'trait conceptualisation' indicates potential interventions, such as dialectical behaviour therapy (DBT) (Linehan, 1993) or systems training for emotional predictability and problem solving (STEPPs) (Blum *et al*, 2002), to address emotional dysregulation.

Whether professionals are proponents of a dimensional, categorical or 'hybrid' approach, the dominant narrative is one which supports a construct of 'personality disorder' as described in the best practice guidance published by the National Institute for Mental Health in England (NIMHE), *'Personality Disorder: No Longer a Diagnosis of Exclusion'*, in 2003; subsequent National Institute for Clinical Excellence (NICE, 2009a & b) guidance for borderline (BPD) and anti-social personality disorder (ASPD), and other policy and commissioning guidance. Service providers are guided in their approach towards the treatment of 'personality disorder' as inherently and irrevocably the result of core pathology.

Borderline and anti-social personality disorder are arguably the presentations which are most commonly described and referred to in clinical practice, and those which have received the most attention in terms of treatment innovations. However, these two personality disorder diagnoses, in particular, are also extremely controversial, with significant criticism from many corners, including service user groups and mental health professionals.

Many feminist writers argue that the diagnosis of borderline personality disorder is an invalid construct which pathologises women for their response to gender oppression and abuse. Shaw and Proctor (2005) argue that borderline personality disorder is located within 'gendered structures of power', which are used to minimise strategies that women use to survive and resist oppression and obscure the fact that many women with a diagnosis of borderline personality disorder have significant trauma histories. Wilkins and Warner (2001) state that the 'symptoms' which define borderline personality disorder can be better understood as reactions to early relational traumas rather than as a result of a 'disorder of personality that is solely defined as an internal deficit' (Wilkins & Warner, 2001, p292). These writers, along with an increasingly vocal and political service user movement – for example, 'Personality Disorder in the Bin' (@pdinthebin) and 'A Disorder 4 Everyone' – continue to challenge the construct, stating that the diagnosis is toxic, stigmatising and pejorative (Personality Disorder Commission, 2018).

Others have argued that the use of the psychiatric system to detain individuals described as having ASPD is a form of social control and should not be the business of mental health services. The incarceration of, predominantly men, in psychiatric hospitals for concerning and 'dangerous' behaviours (anticipated or actual) reached a pinnacle with the announcement of the 'Dangerous and Severe Personality

Disorder' Programme (DSPD). DSPD is not a clinical entity but was defined by the Department of Health as encompassing individuals over 18 'who have an identifiable personality disorder to a severe degree, who pose a high risk to other people because of serious antisocial behaviour resulting from their disorder' (Department of Health, Home Office & HM Prison Service, 2004). It could be argued that this medicalisation of antisocial behaviour enabled detention of individuals without the offer of evidence-based treatment. The programme was decommissioned with an understanding of its significant limitations and replaced by the Offender Personality Disorder Pathway Strategy (2012), with a removal of the emphasis on 'treatment' towards providing a psychologically informed understanding of offending and risk behaviours. Moncrieff writes that 'ideas about mental health and mental abnormality are intrinsically linked to the social and economic conditions in which they emerge' (The Occupied, March 2014). This was absolutely reflected in the DSPD programme, conceived following public outrage after a number of high-profile incidents in England.

What we know to be 'true' about 'personality disorder'

In seeking to find a way to reconcile many of the often intractable and furious debates about the nature of 'personality disorder' and how to define it, it is, perhaps, useful to return to what we know. Of particular importance is the relatively undisputed fact that the difficulties which underpin many of the interpersonal and intrapersonal aspects of – what is described as – borderline and antisocial personality disorder, have their roots in early adverse developmental experiences. One study found that 88% of people diagnosed with BPD had experienced abuse: for 80% this was childhood abuse and for 70% early sexual abuse (Castillo, 2000). Douglas *et al* (2011) reported that a history of adverse childhood events was a significant predictor of ASPD among a cohort of men who were dependent upon substances. Such is the importance of trauma, and especially the impact of childhood sexual abuse, on mental health and psychological well-being that a growing number of mental health professionals and survivors have argued for recognition of the diagnosis of 'complex post traumatic stress disorder' rather than the 'misdiagnosis' of borderline personality disorder. Complex PTSD is diagnosed in adults or children who have repeatedly experienced traumatic experiences such as violence, neglect or abuse. It is similar to the diagnosis of post traumatic stress disorder (PTSD), but can also include feelings of shame or guilt, difficulty controlling emotions, dissociation, relationship difficulties and self-destructive behaviours – 'symptoms' which overlap with borderline personality disorder.

We would hypothesise that this lobbying for wider recognition reflects a number of needs, including a need for survivors and professionals to distance themselves from the stigma and lack of compassion often shown to those with a diagnosis of personality disorder and a need for others to understand the individual's distress as a consequence of abuse, and not as a result of a 'flawed' or 'disordered' personality. Finally, there would also seem to be a need to elicit a more compassionate response from professionals and the wider community, a response which is often not afforded to those with a diagnosis of personality disorder: 'these are the patients psychiatrists dislike' (Lewis & Appleby, 1998; Bodner *et al*, 2015).

The experience of trauma is not unique to individuals diagnosed with BPD and ASPD. Studies have shown that trauma is a significant part of all our lives (Benjet *et al*, 2016). Trauma also disproportionately affects people from marginalised populations, with stressful events tending to be more frequently observed in individuals of 'low socioeconomic status', minority ethnic groups and young people (Hatch & Dohrenwend, 2007). There are also gender differences in the experience of trauma, with women more likely to experience physical and sexual abuse in the context of relationships (Briere & Jordan, 2004; Scott & McManus, 2016).

When these events occur in childhood, they can have negative and long-lasting effects on a child's health and well-being. These potentially traumatic events are described as 'adverse childhood experiences' (ACEs) and include sexual, emotional and physical abuse, neglect, parental divorce and parental mental illness (Felitti *et al*, 1998; Bellis *et al*, 2014). In the United Kingdom there has been increasing attention on the impact of ACEs on the health and psychological well-being of citizens, with this agenda becoming a focus for public health policy in both Scotland and Wales (NHS Scotland, 2017). And while there may be some criticism of this approach as reductionist and potentially simplistic – for example, in linking numbers of certain life events to the likelihood of psychological and physical health problems – the increasing discourse around ACEs has raised awareness of the impact of adversity on individual development and challenges policy-makers to think more creatively and innovatively about the communities within which individuals live, moving towards a more contextually and socially driven understanding of life experience and distress.

Given the prevalence of trauma and social adversity within our communities, and the associated psychological and social legacy, it is important to reflect upon how individuals come to the attention of services and how, too often, they and their distress become pathologised rather than their pain and behaviour being conceptualised as understandable and adaptive responses to their experiences. Boyle (2011) proffers compelling arguments with regard to the role of both psychiatry and clinical psychology in contributing towards the obfuscation of individual experience, and also the operation of power on maintaining the focus on the intrapsychic rather than the social context.

The conceptualisation of personality disorder, especially borderline and antisocial personality disorder, in our view is a perfect illustration of this denial, minimisation or avoidance of life experience and social context in the development of distress and troubled or troubling behaviour.

> Sandeep was referred to a specialist personality disorder service. She was a young Asian woman, who had fled a violent partner. After years of erratic behaviour from her partner, chaos and abuse; she was anxious, depressed and self-harming. The shame she experienced regarding her situation had led her to become isolated from her community. Since fleeing her partner she had remained homeless and vulnerable.

In the example above, the referral to the specialist personality disorder service obscured Sandeep's need for a more meaningful and compassionate response to provide safety and security. A diagnosis of personality disorder was unlikely to determine treatment or her social support needs. In this example we can see how the medicalisation of social problems can be a real and inherent risk with the diagnosis.

In response to frustration with the pathologising and increased medicalisation of distress, psychologists, in collaboration with a survivor activist, service users and carers, and supported by the British Psychological Society, have developed what they describe as an alternative psychosocial narrative framework to diagnostic categories (Johnstone & Boyle, 2018). The Power Threat Meaning Framework is an integrative framework which aims 'to aid the provisional identification of evidence-based patterns in distress, unusual experiences and troubled or troubling behaviour' (Johnstone & Boyle, 2018, p.10). They suggest that this framework can be used to conceptualise the experience of all of us, not just people who have been in contact with the mental health and criminal justice systems. It is a deliberate and political attempt to 'de-medicalise misery' (Rapley *et al*, 2011), helping people to create more hopeful stories about their lives and the difficulties that they may have faced or are still facing, instead of seeing themselves as blameworthy, weak, deficient or 'mentally ill'. It highlights the links between wider social factors such as poverty, discrimination and inequality, along with traumas such as abuse and violence, and the resulting longstanding distress and/or troubled behaviour. The main aspects of the framework are summarised in the following questions:

- What has happened to you? (How has Power operated in your life?)

- How did it affect you? (What kind of Threats does this pose?)

- What sense did you make of it? (What is the Meaning of these situations and experiences to you?)

- What did you have to do to survive? (What kind of Threat responses are you using?)

■ What are your strengths? (What access to Power resources do you have?)

■ What is your story? (How does all this fit together?)

This stance moves away from a position which ultimately locates difficulties within the individual and considers the impact of the economic and social contexts which have and continue to contribute to distress and pain. It is an approach which gives prominence to culture, power, social justice, context and the impact that these factors have on an individual's well-being. Distress, unusual experiences, troubled or troubling behaviour are conceptualised as 'patterns of embodied, meaning-based threat responses to the negative operation of power' (Johnstone & Boyle, 2018, p10).

The adoption of this framework is in its infancy and its developers are currently promoting the model in the hope that it will begin to influence service commissioning, design and delivery, therapeutic practice and research. One of the main purposes of the framework is to support the development of narratives, in their various versions, as an alternative to psychiatric diagnoses. Nonetheless, there has been criticism that the framework lacks evidence and denies the reality that diagnosis can be helpful (Salkovskis & Sutcliffe, 2018). Others have suggested that, despite the importance of the framework in bringing a 'more explicit, more radical and better articulated discussion of the role of power' (Ramsden, 2019) to our understanding of mental health, it nonetheless (and especially if clumsily applied) implicitly upholds a 'treatment' focus on core pathology. It is argued that it does this by being inherently therapy-driven, meaning that the role of trauma in an individual's ability to find therapeutic services meaningful will fail to be addressed. The capacity for services to blame, other and stigmatise traumatised service users for whom their therapy service is irrelevant is potentially maintained through the use of the framework, which does not, it is argued, pay enough explicit attention to the impact of trauma on systems, organisations and workers (Ramsden, 2019).

The importance of personal meaning

How then should we move forward to design and deliver meaningful services in a coherent and coordinated way, underpinned by agreement and consensus? How do we move away from intractable debates which, we would argue, do little to enable restorative wisdom? At present it would seem that those who occupy polarised positions are singularly failing service users by preventing discussion, agreement and compromise within and between teams.

Focusing on personal meaning is, we would argue, a principle to inform service delivery models that would 'cut through' much of which is currently problematic. This means grounding treatment, support and management of individuals in the personally held narratives they use to make sense of what they experience and to articulate what it is they need. This is a principle which is less about dictating to services how they should be (diagnosis driven or not), and more about encouraging those services to be as flexible and responsive to need, language and culture as possible.

> Sarah was meeting with John for the first time since his admission onto the low secure ward where she worked. As his key worker Sarah was keen to think with John about how they were going to describe his problems so that they could work out how best to help him. John said that he had an anti social personality disorder. Together they explored how well that term fitted John 's experience of himself and discussed whether he wanted to continue to use it as the best description of his problems. Together they agreed that they would describe his problems as being 'the things that make my head go.' John decided that when his ' head went' he had an anti social personality disorder.

The term 'formulation' is commonly used by mental health practitioners but can be conceptualised differently depending upon the professional discipline. Indeed, even within psychotherapy and psychology, approaches to formulation differ, if they are employed at all (Johnstone & Dallos, 2014; White, 2000). The use of formulation is increasingly seen as integral to good practice, but problems arise, as with all practices/concepts, when it is not well understood and is potentially used in a tyrannical way which serves to contain the anxieties of staff and organisations at the expense of service users. It has been our experience that formulation in itself does not guarantee a meaningful, sense-making process.

Formulation can be conceptualised as both an 'event' and 'a process' (Johnstone & Dallos, 2014, p4). The former is a more traditional stance where the formulation is written in the service user's notes, or in a letter to a general practitioner or to the service user themselves, and can thus be described as a tangible 'object' (Division of Clinical Psychology, 2011). However, formulation as a process (which is the approach that is advocated here) should be dynamic, hopeful, transparent, collaborative and open to regular revision, enabling the development of a reflective narrative of an individual's life, 'a process of collaborative sense-making' (Harper & Moss, 2003). However, Johnstone and Boyle (2018, p74) acknowledge that this written version of a narrative reflects a dominant Western approach and that other kinds of narrative expressed through art, music, theatre, poetry and dance can sometimes be more helpful and relevant.

Too often, in our clinical experience, this collaborative endeavour has proved challenging for both service user and staff, with formulations being developed with little or no involvement from the service user. This interpersonal process is challenging for a number of reasons. It can feel overwhelming due to the associated levels of distress, terror, hypervigilance, anger and powerlessness experienced by many individuals in need of support, and thus avoided by both service user and practitioner. For the service user who has or is experiencing trauma, construction of their personal narrative is not always a neutral and benign process (Ramsden, 2018). Because of their adverse experiences, service users often do not trust practitioners, expecting them to abuse, humiliate, shame or hurt them as perhaps other 'trusted' individuals have done before. Fonagy and Allison (2014) use the term 'epistemic mistrust' to describe the mistrust of knowledge offered by practitioners for service users who have experienced early trauma. This means that the information and insights shared by the worker may not be trusted by the service user, and at one extreme may be experienced as 'dangerous and disorienting' (Ramsden, 2018). Whichever psychotherapeutic modality is drawn upon, the development of trust is central to an effective intervention.

For professionals, being able to make sense of an individual's distress is dependent upon a number of factors, including the models and resources that the individual has available to them, both professional (psychological theory and models) and personal (internal working models which determine the quality and ability to develop and form relationships). The practitioner needs to be able to draw upon their theoretical and experiential knowledge, with regard to what we know about trauma and the impact upon psychological well-being. They also need to be reflective and reflexive, mindfully managing and attending to their own emotional responses to service users' disclosures and/or behaviours, thereby providing congruent, empathic and compassionate responses. This dynamic interpersonal exchange, often characterised by intense emotions, is a significant challenge for workers if a co-constructed narrative is to be developed, but being able to notice and speak about these challenges within the process is an important and valid part of the work.

Clare (psychologist) and Max (service user) had a difficult encounter during which Max thought that Clare was lying to him. The encounter ended badly with Max shouting at Clare and Clare ending the session early. Following some time out and supervision Clare got in touch with Max to talk about what happened. She started off by apologising – she hadn't meant to make Max feel that he was being lied to. She acknowledged that she had handled the whole thing badly and talked about how she felt angry and upset because it felt like Max had misunderstood her. Max said that was how he felt too. Eventually they could talk about how these feelings often occurred for Max and they acknowledged how easily he felt confused about what people meant. They noticed that Max readily assumed – when he felt confused – that he was being lied to.

We would argue that the development of meaning which considers, with the individual, the impact of trauma and other adversity, social and environmental factors, attachment and relationship histories is a worthwhile endeavour which is validating, authentic and compassionate and allows the individual to 're-story' (White, 1998) their past.

One of the challenges or risks with the formulation approach as described is its dependence upon language and being informed solely by a Western/European narrative about distress. We need to be open to including other cultural perspectives within our conversations with individuals and creatively consider how to develop meaning using other mediums. This is where creative therapies such as music and art come to the fore and should be considered more widely in our work with survivors of trauma.

This stance about formulation and its use is political and challenging for practitioners, as it embraces complexity and the need for complex responses in a way which is often not commensurate with the way in which traditional biomedical services are organised. It also suggests a challenge to the current neoliberal agenda and how we as a society understand the wider determinants of psychological well-being. Indeed, it requires practitioners along with service users to be courageous, to set aside the notion of 'personality disorder' with all its limitations and constraints, and to co-create a narrative which makes sense of an individual's experience in a highly supportive and containing way. This innovative way of working is one to which we aspire and which we attempt to uphold in our clinical practice. However, this often proves extremely challenging in a system which operates in a more 'traditional' manner, obscuring personal meaning, failing to acknowledge power differentials within systems of care and failing also to acknowledge the impact of the work on 'its' own capacity to think.

Personal meaning within systems of care

The majority of individuals with a diagnosis of personality disorder are not in receipt of individual therapy, so priority needs to be given to understanding how systems of care around the individual can function more effectively and not act iatrogenically. Holding personal meaning within systems of care means that services need to be trauma-informed and aware of the operation of power. The importance of trauma-informed care has grown in prominence over the last few years (Sweeney *et al*, 2018), with this approach recognising the need to provide services which do not, through their processes and structures, inadvertently re-enact and thus re-traumatise service users.

Of particular importance is the fact that a trauma-informed approach involves recognising the impact that trauma has on a service user's ability to use the service which is offered. This highlights the importance of an organisation's capacity to find and use personal meaning even when the service user is 'disengaged' or 'absent'.

It is a central theme of this book that the very nature of work with other human beings renders organisations anxious and potentially ineffective (Menzies Lyth, 1960). It is common that services blame individuals for not using what it is that they provide, using phrases such as 'disengaged' or 'lacks motivation'. A focus on organisational anxiety helps us to understand that blaming service users potentially protects the organisation from the anxiety associated with their absence and, in this way, we highlight two key things. First, we stress that services working with individuals with 'personality disorder' using a trauma-informed approach need to search for personal meaning not just in stories of trauma but in absences and 'disengagement'. Second, we highlight the importance of meaning for the organisation in helping workers to understand the impact of working with this service user group on their capacity to think and to remain compassionate.

Searching for personal meaning for organisations means potentially seeking to understand a range of behaviours which, to service users, are likely to appear oppressive and potentially abusive. Too often when service users present with significant risks to self, including life-threatening behaviours, the pull is to become more restrictive with the care that is provided. This often reflects an understandable level of organisational anxiety about the potential death of a service user within their care, and the associated emotional devastation for family, carers and staff at this loss, but also the scrutiny, criticism and potential liability that this will incur for the organisation. This anxiety, however, has the potential to stifle any meaningful therapeutic endeavour, with teams responding to the risk by engaging in ever increasing restrictive attempts, including restriction of leave, eyesight observations and/or transfer of care to a 'locked environment' so as to prevent the service user from engaging in life-threatening behaviours. There is often a real dilemma for the team with regard to 'therapeutic risk taking' or 'positive risk management'. We would argue that these considerations are extremely difficult in the absence of an attempt to understand the personal meaning associated with whatever is challenging. This is not to suggest that this process is an exact science and infallible, but of importance is that it is grounded in the context of someone's life experiences and can be held in mind by staff and used as a thread which keeps them connected to service users when in the storm of a 'crisis'.

Summary

To work in the field of personality disorder is to be all too aware of the debates and hotly contested discussions about the diagnosis. This chapter has suggested that these debates can distract us from the important work of delivering meaningful services. Searching for personal meaning, for narratives, stories, links, explanations to help us define and explain an individual's suffering, seems to us to constitute a helpful solution that transcends intractable polarising debates.

In addition, the search for personal meaning is likely to be inherently therapeutic; many service users with a diagnosis of personality disorder present to services with an incoherent and fragmented sense of self as a direct consequence of the trauma that they have experienced. They are unable to provide a story of their life from childhood to date. They find it difficult to articulate their experiences, which they have tried to eradicate, often unsuccessfully, because of the continued experience of intrusive flashbacks, nightmares or voices. Beginning to gently co-construct a story of a person's life is the beginning of a validating experience of self- healing, acceptance and resurgence.

References

American Psychiatric Association (2013) *Diagnostic and Statistical Manual of Mental Disorders* (5th Edition). Arlington, VA: APA.

Bellis MA, Lowey H, Leckenby N, Hughes K & Harrison D (2014) Adverse childhood experiences: retrospective study to determine their impact on adult health behaviours and health outcomes in a UK population. *Journal of Public Health* **36** (1) 81–91.

Benjet C, Bromet E, Karam EG, Kessler RC, McLaughlin KA, Ruscio AM, Shahly V, Stein DJ, Petukhova M, Hill, E & Alonso J (2016) The epidemiology of traumatic event exposure worldwide: Results from the World Mental Health Survey Consortium. *Psychology Medicine* **46** (2) 327–343.

Blum N, Pfohl B, St. John D, Monhan P & Black DW (2002) STEPPS: A cognitive-behavioural systems-based group treatment for outpatient clients with borderline personality disorder. A preliminary report. *Comprehensive Psychiatry* **43** 301–310.

Boyle M (2011) Making the world go away, and how psychology and psychiatry benefit. In: M Rapley, J Moncrieff and J Dillon (eds) *De-Medicalising Misery: Psychiatry, Psychology and the Human Condition*. London: Palgrave Macmillan.

Briere J & Jordan CE (2004) Violence against women: Outcome complexity and implications for assessment and treatment. *Journal of Interpersonal Violence* **19** (11) 1252–1276.

Castillo H, Allen L & Warner K (2000) Crossing the borderline. *Openmind* **106** (Nov/Dec) 20–21.

Clark LA (2007) Assessment and diagnosis of personality disorder: perennial issues and an emerging reconceptualization. *Annual Review of Psychology* **58** 227–257.

Cosgrove L & Drimsky, L (2012) A comparison of DSM-IV and DSM-5 panel members' financial association with industry: A pernicious problem persists. *PLOS Medicine* **9** (3) 1–5.

Costa PT & McCrae RTR (1990) Personality disorders and the five factor model of personality. *Journal of Personality Disorders* **4** 362–371.

Critical Psychiatry Network (2014) Alternatives to western psychiatry: Recognising and supporting alternatives to western psychiatry (Statement to All Parliamentary Group on global mental health). Retrieved from http:www.criticalpsychiatry.co.uk/index.php/articles/35-documents/395-alternatives-to-western-psychiatry-statement-to-appg

Department of Health, Home Office & HM Prison Service (2004) *Dangerous and Severe Personality Disorder (DSPD) High Security Service: Planning and Delivery Guide*. London: Home Office.

Division of Clinical Psychology (2011) *Good Practice Guidelines on the Use of Psychological Formulation*. London: British Psychological Society.

Division of Clinical Psychology (2013) *Classification of Behaviour and Experience in Relation to Functional Psychiatric Diagnosis: Time for a Paradigm Shift*. London: British Psychological Society.

Douglas K, Chan G, Gelernter J, Arias AJ, Anton RF, Poling J & Kranzler HR (2011) 5-HTTLPR as a potential moderator of the effects of adverse childhood experiences on risk of antisocial personality disorder. *Psychiatric Genetics* **21** 240–248.

Eysenck HJ (1987) The definition of personality disorders and the criteria appropriate for their description. *Journal of Personality Disorder* **1** 211–219.

Felitti VJ, Anda RF, Nordenberg D, Williamson DF, Spitz AM, Edwards V & Koss MP (1998) Relationship of childhood abuse and household dysfunction to many of the leading causes of death in adults: The Adverse Childhood Experiences (ACE) study. *American Journal of Preventative Medicine* **14** 245–258.

Fonagy P & Allison E (2014) The role of mentalising and epistemic trust in the therapeutic relationship. *Psychotherapy* **51** (3) 372–380.

Frances A (2010, 22 March) DSM 5 and dimensional diagnosis – biting off more than it can chew. Psychiatric Times.com

Hatch SL & Dohrenwend BP (2007) Distribution of traumatic and other stressful life events by race/ *ethnicity, gender, SES and age: A review of the research*. American Journal of Community Psychology **40** (3–4) 313–332.

Harper D & Moss D (2003) A different kind of chemistry? Reformulating 'formulation'. *Clinical Psychology* **25** 6–10.

Johnstone L (2016) *A Straight-Talking Introduction to Psychiatric Diagnosis*. Monmouth: PCCS Books.

Johnstone L, Boyle M, with Cromby J, Dillon J, Harper D, Kinderman P & Read J (2018) The Power Threat Meaning Framework: Towards the Identification of Patterns in Emotional Distress, Unusual Experiences and Troubled or Troubling Behaviour, as an Alternative to Functional Psychiatric Diagnosis. Leicester, UK: British Psychological Society.

Johnstone L and Dallos R (2016) *Formulation in Psychology and Psychotherapy: Making Sense of People's Problems*. London: Routledge.

Lewis G & Appleby L (1998) Personality disorder: The patients psychiatrists dislike. *The British Journal of Psychiatry* **153** (1) 44–49.

Linehan MM (1993) *Cognitive-Behavioural Treatment of Borderline Personality Disorder*. London: Guilford Press.

Livesley WJ (1990) Dimensional Assessment of Personality Pathology: Basic Questionnaire (DAPP-BQ). University of British Columbia.

Livesley WJ (2003) *Practical Management of Personality Disorder*. London: Guilford Press.

Livesley WJ (2007) A framework for integrating dimensional and categorical classifications of personality disorder. *Journal of Personality Disorders* **21** 199–224.

Menzies Lyth I (1960) Social systems as a defence against anxiety: An empirical study of the nursing service of a general hospital. In: E Trist and H Murray (eds) (1990) *The Social Engagement of Social Science volume 1: The Socio-Psychological Perspective*. London: Free Association Books.

Moncrieff J (2014) The psychological is political. Retrieved from htpss://the occupiedtimes.org/?p=12763

Mulder RT & Joyce PR (1997) Temperament and the structure of personality disorder symptoms. *Psychological Medicine* **27** (1) 99-106.

National Institute for Health and Care Excellence (2009a) *Borderline Personality Disorder: Recognition and Management* (Clinical Guideline CG78). London: NICE.

National Institute for Health and Care Excellence (2009b) *Antisocial Personality Disorder: Recognition and Management* (Clinical Guideline CG77). London: NICE.

NHS Scotland (2017) Transforming psychological trauma: A knowledge and skills framework for the Scottish workforce. Retrieved from https:www.nes.scot.nhs.uk/media/3971582/nationaltraumatrainingframework.pdf

Personality Disorder Commission (2018) The consensus statement for people with complex mental health difficulties who are diagnosed with a personality disorder. Retrieved from https//www.mind.org.uk>media>consensus-statement-final

Ramsden J (2018) 'Are you calling me a liar'? Clinical interviewing more for trust than knowledge with high-risk men with antisocial personality disorder. *International Journal of Forensic Mental Health* **17** (4) 351–361.

Ramsden J (2019) Editorial: The Power Threat Meaning Framework and forensic mental health settings. *Criminal Behaviour and Mental Health* **29** (3) 131–133.

Rapley M, Moncrieff J & Dillon J (2011) *De-Medicalising Misery: Psychiatry, Psychology and the Human Condition*. London: Palgrave Macmillan.

Salkovskis P & Sutcliffe I (2018) Power Threat Meaning Framework: Innovative and important? [Blog post] Retrieved from https://www.nationalelfservice.net/mental-health/power-threat-meaning-framework-innovative-and-important-ptmframework/

Sanderson C & Clarkin JF (2002) Further use of the NEO-PI-R personality dimensions in differential treatment planning. In: PT Costa and TA Widiger (eds) *Personality Disorders and the Five Factor Model of Personality* (2nd edition). American Psychological Association Books.

Sarkar J & Duggan, C (2012) Diagnosis and classification of personality disorder: Difficulties, their resolution and implications for practice. In: J Sarkar and G Adshead (eds) *Clinical Topics in Personality Disorder*. London: Royal College of Psychiatrists.

Scott S & McManus S (2016) Hidden hurt: Violence, abuse and disadvantage in the lives of women Retrieved from https//weareagenda.org.wp-content/uploads/2015/11/Hidden-Hurt-full-report1.pdf

Shaw C & Proctor G (2005) Women at the margins: A critique of the diagnosis of borderline personality disorder. *Feminism & Psychology* **15** (4) 483–490.

Sweeney A, Filson B, Kennedy A, Collinson L & Gillard S (2018) A paradigm shift: Relationships in trauma-informed mental health services. *British Journal of Psychiatric Advances* **24** 319–333.

Tyrer P, Reed GM & Crawford MJ (2015) Classification, assessment, prevalence, and effect of personality disorder. *Lancet* **385** 717–726.

White M (1998) The externalising of the problem and the reauthoring of lives and relationships. In: M White, *Selected Papers*. Adelaide: Dulwich Centre Publications

White M (2000) *Reflections on Narrative Practice: Essays and Interviews*. Adelaide: Dulwich Centre Publications.

Widiger TA (2012) *The Oxford Handbook of Personality Disorders*. Oxford: Oxford University Press.

Widiger TA & Frances AJ (1994) Toward a dimensional model for the personality disorders. In: PT Costa and TA Widiger, *Personality Disorders and the Five-Factor Model of Personality*. American Psychiatric Association.

Wilkins T & Warner S (2000) Understanding the therapeutic relationship – women diagnosed as personality disordered. *The British Journal of Forensic Practice* **2** (3) 30–7.

World Health Organisation (2018) International Classification of Diseases and Related Health Problems (11th edition). Retrieved from https//icd.who.int/browse11/l-m/en

Chapter 6:

The Organisation and Its Discontents: In Search of the Fallible and 'Good Enough' Care Enterprise

Jina Barrett

Introduction

From the point of view of the individual seeking help with the part of themselves which is attempting to manage relational and psychic struggles associated with living, the service organisation can be a crucible through which to pass: potentially an extremely difficult experience, at best offering the possibility of understanding and managing oneself differently; at worst, causing extreme harm.

On the one hand, in the individual, there may be hope for refuge from intolerable psychic strain. On the other hand, there may be a 'pathway' to the door evidencing attempts at fulfilling a profound wish for an ordinary life, one 'worth living', regarded by the individual as failures rather than as experiences in need of being understood.

In between, and far beyond the individual's aspirations and experience, lie myriad facets to the organisation. Deeply prosaic preoccupations of bureaucracy and finance mix with critical existential concerns on a daily basis in human services. There are conversations that can never get started because of the language and cultural differences of disciplines, departments and sectors. There are conflicts which never end because one or another project or clique gets stuck in grievance. There are risks to sanity in attempting to make sense of resource constraints in relation to commissioning demands. There are extreme provocations to the will to live in the neoliberal marketisation of public sector services, with, in some instances, completely unrealistic and deeply punitive inspection frameworks and performance indicators designed to identify successes and failures based on instruments which are inappropriate for human service evaluation. The discontents are legion.

And yet, and yet...
The readers of and contributors to this book, its editors, commissioners, managers and staff of services, users of services, carers – all of these people continue to try to create decent environments, treatments, pathways.

So what keeps us going? What are the organisational conditions that promote developmental services, and enable the crucible to be, in one sense of its meaning, a laboratory container for users and staff? And what might the search for these conditions, and discovery, teach us about how we might describe that which we collectively, even now in the twenty-first century, inappropriately refer to as 'personality disorder'?

In science, 'crucible' describes a container in which materials can be combined, affected or otherwise transformed by processes subjected to heat. It seems a useful metaphor from both individual and organisational points of view. It is often when things get difficult, or 'hot', that change occurs: in organisational life, when anxiety occurs, relationships intensify and the 'emotional heat' (Adshead, 2012, p97) or 'hot spots' created can either force people into action, for example, by getting rid of something or somebody considered the source of 'trouble', or else into a state of paralysis or 'stuckness', like a broken record. If the meaning of anxiety remains unexplored, its effects impact upon the capacity of the entity to be of use to those using its services.

This chapter offers an organisational perspective on the task of providing services for individuals whose journey of development has left them alienated in an essential or existential sense, with the consequence of reliance on strategies which are potentially harmful to themselves and/or others – communicating, if we can just listen for, see and hear, the alienation and harm at the core of their way of being.

It is divided into three sections. The first offers a psychoanalytic perspective on human development; the second describes an 'open systems' approach to organisations and the third considers the idea of designing organisations on the basis of an emergent or provisional understanding of what it means to be of use to individuals whose way of being in their world represents 'a solution to an existential dilemma of living' (Stokoe, 2020, p129). There is no distinction drawn between services in custodial settings and those in the community: the requirements are the same, though the environmental challenges may differ.

The core theme of the chapter is the need to think about the organisational context in which people are living and working. The conditions necessary for attending to and learning from experience, and being curious enough to wish to do so, are predicated on relational foundations which provide containment of the anxieties inherent in acknowledging difficult or threatening realities. In human services, supporting learning from experience requires systems of containment designed specifically for the task of attending to the anxieties, and co-existing defences against anxiety, of staff teams. Such anxieties and defences are both a representation of service user anxieties and a reflection of the ordinary anxieties of collaboration with others in organisations.

i   Individual development as social process

A consideration of human development viewed through a psychoanalytic lens offers a foundation for understanding the essentially relational, or social, nature of psychological and emotional growth. Implicit in this journey is the challenge that anxiety, and defences against anxiety, pose in development, and the paradoxical reality that one's emotional capacity to face anxiety is a part of learning from experience.

There are many ways to offer a perspective on what psychoanalytic theory has given us in terms of understanding individual development, drawn, as it is, from over a century of work. Here I have chosen to describe the journey of development of the human mind through relationships with others in psychoanalytic terms which have a bearing on the task of this chapter – to set out an organisational framework for work with people whose capacities of mind have been compromised in development. It is a necessarily brief and circumscribed rendering of an extensive, complex and continually developing field. For a fuller understanding, see Alvarez, 1992; Waddell 2002; Yakeley 2010.

Psychoanalytic theory does not have the term 'personality disorder' as part of its lexicon: the approach requires more experiential descriptors. Psychoanalysis does however suggest ways to understand aspects of what came to be known in psychiatric diagnostic terms as 'personality disorder', but in doing so describes universal developmental challenges, locating problematic experiences and their working through in the context of relationships.

Early life

At birth, an infant arrives into the world outside the womb, with experience of intrauterine growth 'imprinted' but not yet 'known', and without a mind as we might construe it – with an as yet undeveloped capacity to 'mentalise' experience.

The earliest experiences after birth are characterised by bodily adaptations to life outside the womb, the biological imperative of the search for food to take in and the beginnings of a cycle of taking things into, and pushing things out of, the body – the result of the first negotiations between the infant and their environment. Experiencing the world through the senses and the body in this way, before understanding about what is happening is available, means the body becomes the first template for apprehending the world.

Psychoanalytic theory suggests the infant is driven to seek comfort, or 'pleasure', and to avoid discomfort, or 'unpleasure'. The main activity consists of ensuring physical comfort: for example, when feeling the sensations of hunger, seeking the satisfaction of that need, vocalising and moving the body, if the need is satisfied and food is found or given, comfort is achieved. If not, the vocalisations and bodily movements increase, communicating a state of discomfort, but also fear. The infant does not have a way to understand what is happening and, in the absence of something to take away the discomfort or pain of the hunger, can only feel assailed by feelings. The infant, feeling overwhelmed is driven to divide or split the experience of the moment into good (pleasurable) and bad (unpleasurable), and seek to push away or get rid of the 'bad' feeling.

Defensive operations

Melanie Klein offered a description of this early stage of development which uses the idea of splitting as a response to fear: she called it the paranoid-schizoid position (Klein, 1975, p252). The idea is that the experience of anxiety or fear leads to the defensive 'action' of the need to divide or split that experience, but the attempt to push away (or 'project') the unwanted or fearful aspects does not actually make them disappear: it results in increased fear, an experience of the failed projection as a further threat. Under these conditions, the development of a mechanism which seeks to deny aspects of the experience of reality helps counter the escalation of anxiety into terror. Denial as a defensive solution is a version of closing the eyes to what is happening.

Klein also posited the existence of a drive from early in life to make sense of experience (she called this the 'epistemophilic impulse'): in the paranoid-schizoid position, with a very limited range of experience to draw upon, the threat arising from the failure of the attempt to be rid of the 'bad' feeling is not seen for what it is, but replaced by an idea or a 'phantasy' of something coming from somewhere else, such is the force of the wish to disown the feeling.

This paranoid-schizoid 'position' is a primitive state, characterised by profound extremes – not just feeling bad or good, but extreme states of terror or bliss.

The infant is trying to control the world as experienced, like an orchestra leader, trying to make things happen, with what might be described as omnipotence. Action and reaction are central: 'doing to' and 'being done to' in dramatic and survival-oriented terms. There are no whole objects, only awareness of others as part objects and a narcissistic assumption that all good comes from the self, with no real appreciation of the real sources outside the self.

Where there is no response to the infant's communication, it becomes an action without a response; the infant is repeatedly thrown back on what is known – and what is known is the attempt to divide experience into good and bad, and get rid of the bad: a default defensive manoeuvre to manage anxiety. An idealised version of the carer develops as a defence against fear: the greater the terror, the more the idealisation. This idealised part object has magical qualities, is omnipotent and can become the basis for a belief system or a talisman – an illusion or phantasy that can be wielded in the face of evidence of powerlessness, but also a vital means of psychic survival.

In circumstances of ordinary, good enough care, it is only the repetition of the experience of needs being met that allows the infant to develop a capacity to pause, to wait before reacting and becoming overwhelmed by frustration, and eventually, with help, modulate the extremes of feeling. When the infant attempts to be rid of or 'projects' unwanted feelings, an attentive carer picks up the cues. Attending to the infant's 'projection' as a form of communication without words, the carer (using their own capacity to pause) notices the infant's state, takes it in, figures out what it is, thinks about what to do about it and then acts to resolve the situation.

Containment

Wilfred Bion described the carer's capability to receive the communications of the infant as being able to 'contain', that is, to take in and metabolise and then give it back in a manageable form to the infant, at the same time conveying that this process is possible (Bion, 1962a; 1962b). Additionally, the carer adds a name for the feeling, suggesting it is/things are nameable, which becomes part of symbolising experience. In this way, over time, as well as having experiences understood and made manageable, the capacity to do so is also taken in, or 'introjected'. This is the basis of thinking, a process of conversion of raw feelings into manageable thoughts, which can be used to make sense of experience, to make links and join things together in the mind, and to contribute to learning from experience. This is different from the splitting tendency of the paranoid-schizoid position, and is predicated on the availability of an attentive 'other' as a part of a relationship. In this way, ordinary, 'good enough' care develops the infant's world, inside as well as out, creating the potential for anxieties to be faced and understood rather than defended against.

For the infant, the repeated experience of containment of experience and satisfaction of need allows the development of an illusion of need being met (and, later, memory of need being met) which helps to contain need momentarily and for long enough to recognise that need satisfaction comes not from the self but from another. The pause this engenders forces a recognition of dependency on this other for sustenance, and a recognition that the source comes and goes. Then the infant worries about causing the carer to stay away, or not return, through 'phantasies of' damage done by the demands and rages and frustration when being made to wait.

The provision of ordinary, good enough, ongoing care provides reassurance that damage has not been done, and a capacity for concern begins to emerge, which tempers the way frustration is expressed (Winnicott, 1953). The infant can feel gratitude for needs being met, for the meaning of communications being understood, and feel validated by an actual response that meets actual need.

Equally, however, there may be feelings of envy of both the resources of the carer, and their capacity to actually give and share those resources.

Developing complexity

This is a problematic moment in development because it faces the infant with more complex anxieties – about not being in control of, or being the source of, sustenance, and having to recognise dependency and separateness simultaneously. At the same time, because the carer comes to be recognised as both the source of sustenance and the source of bad feelings when needs are not being met, the power of earlier defences of splitting and projection reduces, resulting in less protection against the associated anxieties.

The implications of this reality include having to survive the loss of being able to defend against terror and anxiety by using the defence of the idealised magical object, and the loss of sole ownership of the carer. Mourning these losses becomes a developmental task in this movement towards what Klein described as the 'depressive position' (Klein, 1975, p254). This position is characterised by an ability to acknowledge reality, which has both good and bad aspects.

In addition, the infant has to face the reality that, having been in receipt of resources and help from the carer – that is, having been dependent – this model of existence of a relationship with a 'helpful other' must also apply to the carer, who must be in a similar relation to someone else.

Third position

If the infant can acknowledge and tolerate discoveries made as a result of what curiosity about the carer's relationship reveals, there is a possibility of occupying a third position. This is a situation where significant others can be observed in interaction with each other, and the infant's own relation to others can also be observed (Britton, 1989).

If there is enough toleration of anxieties about exclusion and difference, of smallness and of not being the centre of the world, then curiosity becomes a tool to be enjoyed and used (the component of the epistemophilic instinct which seeks knowledge, as distinct from beliefs), creating a foundation for learning from experience in ways that promote psychological growth and development of the mind (Britton, 1998).

This stage of development is never fully attained by anyone, and is revisited again and again in life. Neither is the development of the mind linear or emphatic: adults move between depressive and paranoid-schizoid states of mind, the latter being a default position when faced with anxiety. Where development cannot proceed, the individual may come to rely on an in-between world of their own making, or a 'psychic retreat' (Steiner, 1993).

Relational rupture of personality development: adaptation of personality to adverse circumstances

Where there is insufficient, absent or inconsistent containment in early stages of life, the development of 'mind', or the capacity to 'mentalise' experience, is compromised, and with it the infant's capacities to manage anxieties. Instead, reliance grows on early mechanisms of defence – splitting, projection and denial of reality. Projective identification is used as the predominant means of either managing or communicating in the absence of moderated or 'digested' experience. The defence of idealisation, and identification with an idealised (often magical) object, can protect the individual against the hopelessness and depression that would accompany giving up the illusion or belief in an extremely good object. The problem with idealisation is its close association with denigration, born of the inevitable failure of idealised solutions or persons.

The absence of integrative experience of containment creates difficulty in learning from experience. The challenge of modulating experience results in, at times, inhabiting a world of extremes and extreme motility between these extremes. There is a feeling of being unable to go forward when caught in this 'borderland' between wished-for merger and enough separation to facilitate independent action; this results in oscillation between extremes of dependency and self-sufficiency. This can create an aggrieved state, where it risks too much to mourn the loss of the idealised magical object. Repeated disappointment and the absence of trust creates the potential for a very punitive internal world moral arbiter. These are, in fact, universal challenges in development.

Where the continuum of experience becomes neglect (whether benign or malign), the ground for trauma or abuse is created, which intrudes or impinges upon the 'going-on-being' (Winnicott, 1960) of the child and profoundly alters, or ruptures, the child's relationship to the world, with consequences for psychic development and therefore for the trajectory of the organisation of personality into adult life. Put another way, if the development of a relatively integrated personality is dependent upon a fairly consistent loving and attentive environmental mediator (parent or carer), then the absence of this kind of relationship, for whatever reason, becomes the absence of a mind that 'sees' and 'knows' the infant and will leave the infant without the means to incrementally discover a sense of self, vulnerable to being used as a receptacle for the projections of others – such as a carer's own needs – or harmed by disturbed and disturbing figures encountered in unprotected environments. There are internal world corollaries – the infant's experience of an absent primary carer before an internal representation is secure is the experience of a mother whose lack of presence is felt to be dangerous, as it conjures sometimes unmanageable fears about survival of the feelings created.

A scaffolding-like structure, or internal psychic organisation, of defensive operations is built to cope with the absence of an 'other' on whom to be able to rely consistently, designed to survive, or at least keep at bay defensively the effects of, impingements and intrusions, both physical and psychological. Unmodulated innate aggression and destructive impulses become part of the defensive structure.

Application of the term 'personality disorder' to the adult for whom such experiences have been formational seems rather simplistic and critical: it might be more accurate to describe the situation, or experience, as relational rupture of personality development, offering an explanatory framework and the potential for discovery of the self. Such a framing as 'relational rupture' allows for the paradoxical and confusing admixture of profound need and 'deep alienation' (Hinshelwood, 2002) which interferes with the development of helping relationships.

ii   Organisations as 'open systems'

In using the term 'organisational perspective', the invitation is to think of organisations as entities: groupings of people coming together to transform something, some raw materials or inputs, into a finished product/state or outputs, through some kind of conversion process.

Take a university, for instance, whose enterprise is to take individuals wishing to learn, specialise or achieve a qualification. The university outputs, if it is doing its job, are students with a certificate to confirm they have learned all there is to know about a subject to the specified level of that degree. The conversion process of the university enterprise, therefore, involves educators providing a containing space for learners to let go of previous ways of understanding and take in new ways.

Open systems theory suggests a frame for the study of organisations that draws attention to the processes which underpin its existence:

input -----> throughput (conversion) -----> output

'Input' captures the types and nature of materials required for particular kinds of output, which in turn shape or structure the conversion process. The conversion process (essentially a superordinate system governing subsystems of activities) is created in part by the requirements of output, in part by the nature of the materials available, but also by the quality of the structures used to contain the throughput. The idea of 'containing' the throughput draws attention to boundaries which require management:

(i) between inside and outside domains;
(ii) at entry and exit specifically; and
(iii) between internal functions, or parts.

This way of thinking about organisations emerged from the application to human systems of discoveries associated with cell biology which demonstrate that the membrane unit of the living cell requires permeability to substances available for nourishment, and excretion of unwanted products, while at the same time being strong enough to 'hold' the contents together. If the boundary were to become impermeable, that is, if it closed up, the cell would die.

The application of these ideas to human systems (Lewin, 1947) was extended to the study of organisations by social scientists at the Tavistock Institute of Human Relations in the 1950s, offering the possibility of studying the whole organisation in relation to its parts and to its environmental context.

Open systems and complex needs

Using an open systems perspective, starting at the end of an organisational process, the 'output' of a complex needs service, whether in the community or in custodial settings, could be characterised as individuals who have enough understanding and acceptance of themselves to be able to acknowledge their emotional and mental states to help manage a life in which their own emotional and physical safety and the safety of others matters.

If we take seriously the idea of an individual's psychic organisation as having been forged in a relational context to protect against knowing about certain intolerable, sometimes unspeakable or unthinkable, realities and ruptures, we have to acknowledge that efforts to understand the self may lead to psychic breakdown or externally expressed violence, and that the very attempt to understand is unwanted, a persecutory intrusion or an attack on that which holds the self together.

If we also take seriously the implications of the need for emotional containment in the development of thinking – the idea that arriving at even a provisional understanding of the self involves repeated experience of having one's communications, whether psychic or physical, noticed, acknowledged, metabolised and returned in digestible form – we have to see that such human connectedness requires profound reserves of tolerance and skill, as well as the requisite organisational structures to make this feasible.

The 'outputs', then, of a 'personality disorder' service cannot be set out in advance, because the nature of an individual's difficulties plus the effect of 'help' will be unknowable. However, intended outputs can be aspirational and provisional, and will be supported by offering the possibility of being involved in one's own discovery processes and development, rather than being treated as a passive recipient of a 'treatment' (Turner et al, 2011). The use of the term 'recovery' constitutes a fundamental misunderstanding of human development in these terms.

The 'conversion process' under these circumstances, using the model offered by the open systems perspective, will require specific organisational structures so that the inevitable anxieties, defences and apparent failures in organisational functioning can be not only survived, but predicted in order to survive. It will be a process where managed work is taking place at both conscious and unconscious levels, requiring systems which constantly attend to, and seek to make sense of, information arising from relations and communications between individuals with different tasks and roles.

Task

Eric Miller and Kenneth Rice particularly, on the basis of studies which they and colleagues were undertaking at the Tavistock Institute, suggested that survival in relation to the demands of an external environment is supported by organisational clarity about its primary task. Their definition of primary task is 'the task which has to be achieved in order to survive' (Miller & Rice, 1967). They offered it as a heuristic concept, or a tool, to be used in establishing the parameters of an enterprise, which could in turn define and help manage coherent activity systems. They also suggested that there are different kinds of primary task in subsystems designed to achieve an overall primary task, pointing to the need to monitor and manage the interplay and interdependency of these subsystems. Inadequate task definition is often the source of institutional difficulties, yet even where there is adequate and transparent task definition, there are times when anti-task activity can emerge, suggesting that it helps organisational functionality to constantly monitor the primary task activity.

Role

Attending to this inter-relational aspect of organisational life brings into view the concept of role. Role as a concept is helpful in defining facets of individual (and departmental) responsibility, accountability, relationships, resources and attitudes which enable task performance.

The idea of role is where the human aspect of systems comes more sharply into view, and where questions of control require consideration, because where certain machine functions can be replicated in, say, a factory setting to ensure similar products are made, individual staff members differ from each other, and differ in the way they take up their roles: the idea of role definition helps create terms of engagement in relation to task, while leaving some room for autonomy and creativity, moderated according to level in the hierarchy, or in relation to networked activities. Defining limits of accountability and responsibility contributes to clarity of role, which supports both activity in role and inter-role relating.

Boundaries

Tavistock Institute research over 60 years, based on consultation projects in organisations and on Group Relations conferences, demonstrated the importance of identifying the boundary of an enterprise, to demarcate activities inside from those outside.

Identified boundaries support attention inwards to the task of the enterprise, while giving managers the job of monitoring the boundary to ensure adequate flows of necessary information and resources for the task, as well as protecting task continuity from unnecessary interference.

Eric Miller and Ken Rice distinguished between task and sentient boundaries, and in doing so drew attention to the importance of a sense of belonging to a work group or team, and being identified with its aims. They demonstrated how the boundary of the task differs from the sentient boundary, each contributing differently to the achievement of task (Miller & Rice, 1967).

At the point of writing, there are no stand-alone services for people with 'personality disorder': all services are situated within, or in a specific relation to, other kinds of services, whether in health, social care or criminal justice, across public, private and third sectors. This means 'personality disorder' services are constantly having to manage boundary relations with other services which exist for a different purpose. This characteristic inter-relating aspect of organisation functioning is an important part of the field of study, because in requiring active monitoring and management, inter-relating resonates with a key challenge of living with and working with relational rupture.

Environment

The organisational studies undertaken by the Tavistock Institute suggested that the environment of the organisation has to be taken into account and monitored constantly, usually by individuals with boundary management roles, both for the purposes of exchange of materials and information, and to protect the internal workings of the organisation from the impingements of environmental turbulence. This suggests requirements of both flexibility and firmness in both individuals in boundary roles and in the policies they develop or adopt, in this vital function of leadership and management.

Not all organisations are equal, however, and human service organisations in particular have to take into account societal shifts, both political and social, as they affect attitudes towards social groupings. This is an area where environmental impingement can have acute repercussions for organisations. For example, the emergence of an attitudinal shift in government policy after the 2008 financial crash towards recipients of welfare, in being characterised as 'scroungers and skivers', accompanied critical reductions in public spending, silencing any outrage about the resulting privations by promoting guilt and shame as the only position to inhabit in relation to being in need (e.g. *New Statesman*, 2012).

Beyond and underlying the effects of societal events, however, there are conscious and unconscious roles assigned to social institutions. For example, one could regard prisons as having to survive the confusion of society's competing perspectives – the wish for rehabilitation of 'offenders', as against the requirement to punish and to hide its inmates from view.

Contemporary environmental turbulence

Organisations exist in turbulent environments which take many forms. In the contemporary world of public sector services, there are myriad pressures to operate as if we are not human, that is, as if we are not possessed of a mind with which to think, and as if we should only act in ways which are instrumental and 'countable' (in terms of saving money and counting, e.g., bed-days or tick boxes) rather than as being accountable to our service users.

The bureaucracy associated with healthcare, for instance, is strikingly risk-averse in its operations, designed to demonstrate that every possible governance arrangement has been predicated on defensibility in case of 'critical incidents'. Paradoxically, this approach interferes with real learning from the experience, potentially contributing to repeated rather than reduced instances of such events.

The importation of the market into the operations of public services has progressively changed the focus from 'provision of service', to 'value for money in the provision of service', to 'valuation of service' (commodification), placing financial considerations ahead of human need. One of the more insidiously destructive recent developments of a services market dominated by accountancy principles, in our thoroughly 'neoliberalised' world, is the practice of hiving off units of activity and commissioning these separately, or 'putting them out to tender'. Part-system commissioning or competitive tendering fragments public services, diverting attention from care principles, and requiring repeated attempts to re-draw and re-establish boundaries to enable task performance throughout the systems where tendering has changed its functioning.

Inspections and audits of public services operate from a neoliberal mindset (rational, individualistic and 'consumer'-oriented (Pratt, 2006 in Stokoe, 2019, p15)). Most are designed from, and therefore promote a state of mind akin to, the paranoid-schizoid position, that is, a primitive state of mind, where the form the anxiety takes is of the persecutory kind – a simplistic but damagingly moralistic and punitive world of 'good' and 'bad', or 'outstanding' and 'failing', with no help given (ever).

As David Bell attests in his important propositional work 'Neoliberalism is bad for your mental health':

> 'Attacks on the Welfare State (i.e. attacks on awareness of human need and vulnerability), coupled with the idealisation of the market, powerfully support the delusion of the autonomous individual, bring profound alienation, denial of the role of social values and contempt for ordinary human vulnerability. [The] hated dependency is projected elsewhere – onto those on benefits, refugees, "welfare tourists", and so on.' (Bell, 2019)

I believe we are grieving the Welfare State, changed beyond recognition, forcing those reliant on the state for benefits and care into situations where survival is a challenge. However, we are behaving as if we cannot afford to allow our mourning its full expression as it might force us to face a reality in which the conditions we believe necessary for decent work no longer exist. We risk being stuck in an aggrieved state, and becoming melancholic.

Our co-existing guilt about not being able to change the system from its current inhumane trajectory makes it difficult to think – we put our heads down, we work, we try to protect our ideals. We create maverick or, sometimes, rogue operations, like professionals working alone or in small groups to provide ungoverned services quietly, or as a rebuttal of the prevailing ideology and potentially our shared despondency.

Recognising and acknowledging the reality of the environment matters, including grieving the damage done, because it is only in doing so that the political nature of social, health and criminal care will be clear, and with it our responsibility to make good work, together.

iii   Designing for containment

Group and organisation defences against anxiety

Such unhealthy environmental conditions require that we design and interpose healthy services between these conditions and those who would make use of our services. However, contemporary environmental conditions notwithstanding, staff within organisations also face collusive dynamics in responding to anxiety and associated defences. The discontents of the title are thus not just environmental, but, inevitably, internal, and are the source of fallibility in the human enterprise.

Social defences systems in organisations

A core theme of a psychoanalytic perspective on individual life is that of the challenges of attending to and processing or defending against anxiety – and so it is with organisations. Isabel Menzies Lyth, in her study of a general nursing teaching hospital (Menzies Lyth, 1960), found institutionally structured social defences against the anxieties generated in and by 'interaction with the "human throughput" of patients' (Miller, 1993b, p29).

Essentially, the study found that encountering the difficult realities associated with illness and physical contact, and the uncertainties and emotional distress of patients and their families, caused the nurses stress and anxiety. Nursing staff at all levels were found to have evolved a complex system of defensive strategies, essentially a 'superstructure' of socially acceptable ways of organising work, designed to protect nurses from having to manage or take responsibility for the whole picture of a patient's situation. For instance, detachment was promoted by moving staff around, to prevent development of attachments to patients, and implicit attitudes and unspoken rules sought to curb distress and keep disturbing emotions in check. Although it was obvious the socially sanctioned defensive structures didn't actually work, junior and senior nurses colluded in preventing discussion of these experiences and thereby created the conditions for this shared social defence system to continue.

The defences used to effect these complex collusive psychological and emotional manoeuvres were unconscious mechanisms of denial, splitting and projection: strategies designed to relieve individuals of unwanted feelings and attributes, but here sanctioned by what Menzies Lyth referred to as the 'structure, culture and mode of functioning' of the hospital. She also noted that not only did these 'social' defences not relieve the anxieties, but they created more anxiety, both in and of themselves and because of the conscious reactions to the defences.

A contemporary exploration of the paradigm finds social defence systems alive and well across a range of organisations: the editors of the collected evidence suggest that, 'while social defences are unlikely to be helpful to an institution or to its members in achieving their primary goals or outputs, they may nevertheless perversely contribute to their psychic survival' (Armstrong & Rustin, 2015, p14). My own view is that social defences are necessary for psychic survival in settings where the predominant anxieties are concerned with survival, and, as such, have to be brought into awareness again and again, where change is sought.

Gwen Adshead has noted the Menzies Lyth study as 'important work … because it shows how individual defences can become mirrored and intensified in group situations in institutions, ultimately becoming mirrored and enacted in institutional policy and procedures' (Adshead, 2012, p104). She also thought the study 'demonstrated how the care of the sick is stressful and distressing, and how impossible it is for staff not to have negative feelings about their patients from time to time' (Adshead, 2012, p104).

The paradigm of social defences against anxiety is a particularly humane framework for the study of organisations (including organisation self-study by members), because it attends to the unavoidable reality of anxiety in the workplace, identifies attempts to manage task-characteristic anxieties and offers a template for an organisation's understanding of itself, in all its fallibility.

Teams as work groups

The team, or specialised work group, is where staff and service user experience can be at its most visible, as it is here that the organisation meets the unconscious functioning of the individual. I believe that the construction of teams as specialized work groups is the optimum means to design a service that stands a chance of care-giving (Kahn, 2005). I'm referring to a social unit providing opportunities for more transparent or at least 'observable' functioning.

Wilfrid Bion provided a way of observing how groups adopt what he called 'basic assumption' ways of functioning to manage the two-fold anxiety of group life: the anxiety about being part of a group and the anxiety associated with the task of the group. These basic assumptions influence group members' adoption of anti-task activity in favour of comfort, in other words, in the direction of an activity designed to manage or defend against anxiety, rather than face and work with it (Bion, 1961). He described how the group can 'find' the individual with the right valency for the 'as if' task, because the unconscious group, without the constraints of organisation behaviours, much more straightforwardly propels individuals into action on behalf of the group.

The main basic assumptions he identified were dependency, fight/flight and pairing. Similar key mechanisms of defence against anxiety are in operation in the group as in the individual: splitting off unwanted experiences such as anxiety, denying its existence, projecting it elsewhere. The social mechanism which pushes the group into action is projective identification: in basic assumption dependency, the group finds the member most likely to want to be depended upon to save the group from its fears, who in turn identifies with the need to be depended upon to the extent that he acts to save the group from its worries – thus taking the group off task.

In fight/flight, the group will usually identify an enemy outside of the group with whom to either enter into conflict, or take flight from. In basic assumption pairing the group behaves as if the emergence and coming together of two of its members will create something new, usually represented by a future solution, rather than tackling current problems.

As well as this, the greatest challenge is that the team will take in, and be affected by, the struggles of the service user group in a way which interferes with work. In Francesca Cardona's paper 'The Team as Sponge', she says 'the term sponge describes the striking way in which the team absorbs and soaks up the central dynamics which operate within its [service user, or client] group' (Cardona, 1999).

These realities of the group life of teams are what make the design of formally structured thinking spaces within clear organisational management structures necessary: unconscious anxieties and defences against anxiety functioning at individual, team and organisational levels are thus a resource for development.

Healthy organisations: the relation of thinking capacity to structure

Eric Miller referred to the process of building healthy organisations as 'creating a holding environment [that influences the] psychological security of the organisation's members' (Miller, 1993a):

'Let me spell out a little more fully the provision that is necessary for the staff member to make for the client. First the staff member has to provide psychological safety through total reliable attention. Secondly the relationship must be felt to be meaningful in that it deals with the really relevant issues of the client. In other words it requires total involvement and identification. At the same time thirdly, however, it has to be an empowering relationship which enables the client to take charge of his or her own life. If staff are to provide that relationship I argue that this has implications for organization design, for management and also for supervision. Corresponding to the requirement on the staff member the organization needs to be designed in a way that provides safety for the staff member through clear role boundaries, a meaningful definition of the task attached to the role, and thirdly authority to enable the staff member to use discretion and initiative. The requirement on the role of the manager is comparable. The manager should provide attention – in other words treating the staff member as a whole person – to the real concerns of the staff member in a meaningful way, and at the same time should be enabling in terms of providing the boundary conditions within which the staff member can exercise his or her own authority to get on with the job. In other words the

manager / staff member relationship needs to reflect the desired staff / client relationship. As for supervision, here too it must be safe to bring up the real difficulties that the individual staff member is facing.

Essentially I am putting forward here two inter-connected propositions:

1. The quality of the holding environment of staff is the main determinant of the quality of the holding environment that they can provide for clients.

2. The quality of the holding environment of staff is mainly created by the form of organization and by the process of management.'

(Miller, 1993a)

Philip Stokoe developed an accessible synthesis of the findings of the Tavistock Institute of Human Relations studies, offering a framework for organisational functioning which he refers to as 'a model for a healthy organisation'. This is not as simple as it sounds, as there is no such thing as a healthy organisation, only the aspiration to be one. He contends that healthy functioning is supported by having shared clarity about:

(i) primary task;
(ii) operational principles;
(iii) structure of roles and responsibilities; and, because in human services people have an impact on each other, there needs to be:
(iv) a regular thinking space, aimed at discovering a layer of organisational information which may not be available in the form of language (Stokoe, 2011).

This idea of a 'space to think' might translate in the reader's mind to a phrase in wide currency in human service organisations: 'reflective practice'. However, in using this latter descriptor, it is useful to stress the variance in how this term is used, as not all reflective practice forums provide space to think.

Let me come at it through the work of another organisational consultant, Angela Foster, whose paper *'The Duty to Care and the Need to Split'* describes how in the course of daily work with people struggling with how their mind is functioning at a given time, staff (who have a duty to care) are having to split off their awareness of psychic impacts in order to continue to function and to be available to the next person. Splitting off awareness of the psychological and emotional impact of work in this way is an ordinary self-protective mechanism. In the kind of thinking space I'm describing here, the staff member can allow the split-off experiences to return to awareness with the conditions in place to support team/workgroup attempts to understand their meaning (Foster, 2001).

I was interested, a few years back, to discover a slideshow as part of a training course about the model for a healthy organisation, which suggested that thinking space is for solution finding. It is not: solution finding is a form of taking action, not thinking. However, solution finding-type activity may sometimes be a substitute for thinking, where, because thinking is hated, this proves to be the only possible group work under some circumstances.

The invitation of this chapter is to consider designing the organisational conditions of a psychoanalytic-systems 'laboratory' in which the crucible of the interactions of service user–service provider can be explored and contained. The relationship between worker and service user, in all its feeling states, needs laboratory conditions designed for the study of the repeated encounters in the service of learning in the service of learning, not because such work is experimental but because it is provisional and relational work takes time - for failures of containment and crises to be survived and thought about, for understanding to grow. The laboratory would be the place where curiosity about social defences against anxiety would be noticed, and basic assumption and work group activity monitored, to promote the kind of resilience born of facing the worst of one's fears in a containing structure, in the interests of development and sustainability (Barrett, 2011).

The risk of not paying attention to staff experience is of sanctioning harmful treatment, both by ignoring evidence of acting out of countertransference, and of colluding with projection of staff difficulties into service users. The 'laboratory' would be helped by including service users in design and delivery as projection of staff difficulties is reduced by meaningful involvement structures.

Such an approach would also mitigate the risk that work in personality disorder services is reduced to interpersonal skill work, individually supervised – vulnerable to the seduction of locus of control, the marketisation of validated manualised interventions, in resonance with a culture of 'methodological individualism' (Pratt, 2006 in Stokoe, 2019).

Conclusion

In public sector human services, I continually encounter individuals who are beleaguered and troubled by their work, which I take as a sign of health (I worry much more about people who have no problems at all). These workers and their managers, in health and criminal justice, in probation and prisons, in social care, are, on their good days, curious, driven to help, appropriately anxious, aware of boundaries – and most of all courageous.

They already know what makes for healthy organisational functioning, the value of a shared purpose, clear principles and role structures. Their capacity for concern, ordinary reparative instincts and a keen sense of curiosity form the ground of the 'good enough' care enterprise. They get it wrong, things go wrong, they consider their part in it, they learn. They know they are fallible; their knowledge of their fallibility is their strength. Importantly, they take up authority for authentic work and, in doing so, demonstrate political responsibility.

Alongside a dependable structure; a clear, shared statement of purpose, or primary task; and transparent working principles, a healthy respect for the defences of the individual and the dangers of omnipotence will help contain most existential problems. And we know, though we repeatedly fail to remember, that learning from experience helps us grow, and that failing and 'not knowing' support learning (French & Simpson, 2000).

Acknowledgements:
- I am grateful to the British and Irish Group for the Study of Personality Disorder for their permission to develop my 2019 conference contribution for publication.

- Emergence was a national service user organisation in the UK, which closed in 2016: the field is poorer for its absence. This organisation's ability to hold us all to account for our instances of unthinking differentiation is responsible for fundamental shifts in the field paradigm.

- The approach to service delivery outlined in this chapter underpinned the organisational aspect of the Personality Disorder Knowledge and Understanding Framework (the 'PD KUF'). The Programme ran in the UK from 2009 to 2018.

- I support the Consensus Statement (2018) and the aims of the working group that produced it (Personality Disorder Consensus Statement, 2018).

References

Adshead G (2012) *'Mirror, Mirror': Parallel Processes in Forensic Institutions in The Therapeutic Milieu Under Fire: Security and Insecurity in Forensic Mental Health*. Forensic Focus 34. London: Jessica Kingsley Publishers.

Armstrong D & Rustin M (2015) *Introduction: Revisiting the Paradigm in Social Defences against Anxiety: Explorations in a Paradigm*. London: Karnac.

Barrett J (2011) Sustainable organizations in health and social care: Developing a team mind. In: A Rubitel and D Reiss (eds) *Containment in the Community: Supportive Frameworks for Thinking about Antisocial Behavior and Mental Health*. London: Karnac.

Bell D (2019) Neoliberalism is bad for your mental health. In: D Morgan (ed) *The Unconscious in Social and Political Life. The Political Mind Series*. Oxfordshire: Phoenix Publishing House.

Bion WR (1961) *Experiences in Groups*. London: Tavistock; reprinted Routledge, 1989.

Bion WR (1962a) A theory of thinking. *International Journal of Psychoanalysis* **43** 306–310; reprint in Bion WR (1967) Second Thoughts. London: Heinemann.

Bion WR (1962b) *Learning from Experience*. London: Heinemann.

Britton, R (1989) The missing link: parental sexuality in the Oedipus Complex. In R. Britton, M. Feldman, & E. O'Shaughnessy (eds) *The Oedipus Complex Today: Clinical Implications*. London: Karnac.

Britton R (1998) *Belief and Imagination: Explorations in Psychoanalysis* (London: Routledge, in association with the Institute of Psychoanalysis).

Cardona F (1999) The team as sponge: How the nature of the task effects the behaviour and mental life of a team. In: R French and R Vince (eds) *Group Relations, Management and Organization*. Oxford: Oxford University Press.

Foster A (2001) The duty to care and the need to split. *Journal of Social Work Practice* **15** (1) 81–90.

French R & Simpson P (2000) Learning at the edges between knowing and not knowing: Translating Bion. *Organisational and Social Dynamics* **1** 54–77.

Hinshelwood RD (2002) Abusive help – helping abuse: the psychodynamic impact of severe personality disorder on caring institutions. *Criminal Behaviour and Mental Health* **12** S20–S30.

Kahn WA (1992) To be fully there: Psychological presence at work. *Human Relations* **45** 321–350.

Kahn WA (2005) Teams, real and imaginary. In: WA Kahn, *Holding Fast: The Struggle to Create Resilient Caregiving Organizations*. Hove and New York: Brunner-Routledge.

Klein M (1975) *Envy and Gratitude and Other Works 1946–1963*. London: The Hogarth Press.

Klein M (1985) Our adult world and its roots in infancy. In: AD Colman and MH Geller (eds) *Group Relations Reader 2*. Washington, A. K. Rice Institute.

Lewin K (1947) *Field Theory in Social Science*. New York: Harper & Row.

Menzies Lyth I (1960) Social systems as a defence against anxiety: An empirical study of the nursing service of a general hospital. In: E Trist and H Murray (eds) (1990) *The Social Engagement of Social Science Volume 1: The Socio-Psychological Perspective*. London: Free Association Books.

Miller EJ (1993a) The healthy organization. Creating a holding environment: conditions for psychological security. Based on a talk given at the Clinical Psychology and Organizational Consultancy conference on 'What makes a healthy organization – models for intervention', 27 April 1993. Retrieved from https://www.johnwhitwell.co.uk/child-care-general-archive/the-healthy-organization-by-eric-miller/

Miller EJ (1993b) Introduction to Part Two: Three studies of 'people-processing' institutions. In: *From Dependency to Autonomy: Studies in Organization and Change*. London: Free Association Books.

Miller EJ & Rice AK (1967) *Systems of Organization*. London: Tavistock Publications.

Personality Disorder Consensus Statement (2018). Retrieved from https://www.mind.org.uk › media › consensus-statement-final

The New Statesman (2012) Scroungers, fraudsters and parasites: How media coverage affects our view of benefit claimants. Retrieved from https://www.newstatesman.com/economics/2012/11/scroungers-fraudsters-and-parasites-how-media-coverage-affects-our-view-benefit-cl

Steiner J (1993) *Pathological Organizations in Psychotic, Neurotic and Borderline Patients*. London: Routledge in association with the Institute of Psychoanalysis.

Stokoe P (2011) The healthy and the unhealthy organization: How can we help teams to remain effective? In: A Rubitel and D Reiss (eds) *Containment in the Community: Supportive Frameworks for Thinking about Antisocial Behavior and Mental Health*. London: Karnac.

Stokoe P (2019) Where have all the adults gone? In: D Morgan (ed) *The Unconscious in Social and Political Life. The Political Mind Series*. Oxfordshire: Phoenix Publishing House.

Stokoe P (2020) *The Curiosity Drive: Our Need for Inquisitive Thinking*. Oxfordshire: Phoenix Publishing House.

Turner K, Lovell K & Brooker A (2011) '... and they all lived happily ever after': 'Recovery' or discovery of the self in personality disorder? *Psychodynamic Practice* **17** (3) 341–346.

Winnicott, D. (1953). Transitional objects and transitional phenomena, *International Journal of Psychoanalysis*, **34**:89-97

Winnicott DW (1960) The theory of the parent-infant relationship. *Int. J. Psycho-Anal.* **41** 585–595.

Part 2

Governance Principles: Supporting Services to Enact Contemporary and Critical Perspectives

Chapter 7:

Access to Services: Moving beyond Specialist Provision while Applying the Learning

Jo Ramsden

Governance principles:

■ Assessments should be based around trying to ascertain if the service can provide what the individual needs (rather than whether the individual can access what they provide).

■ Specialist services should offer support to other generic systems and services which work with high numbers of people who would meet the diagnosis for a 'personality disorder'. This support should focus on enabling systems to manage anxious responses to the work.

■ Services should look to establish partnerships to enable them to increase access and capacity and to work with 'personality disorder' in a way that is more socially focused.

Introduction

This chapter is concerned with how we best ensure that people who have the problems associated with a 'personality disorder' diagnosis get fair and equitable access to services which are relevant and meaningful for them.

To consider how best to achieve this, this chapter will consider some of the current barriers to access and will argue that our best attempts to facilitate entry to services have, in reality, become part of the problem.

In keeping with the theme that organisational anxiety is problematic for service users, the barriers which have unconsciously emerged as we have attempted to widen and enable access over the past 16 years will be framed as the products of organisational attempts to manage ambivalence and disquiet associated with the work. A number of principles will then be outlined regarding how best to ensure that services which can provide appropriate help are as widely available as possible to those who need them. In addition, these principles will seek to ensure that all relevant services work collaboratively and supportively to develop the workforce and increase capacity for working with those in extreme distress.

While there are important arguments for fundamental changes to the way in which we plan and commission services for people who experience the difficulties associated with 'personality disorder' (see Skett & Barlow, this edition), there is also a need to work pragmatically and with the reality of service provision as it is currently commissioned. As a consequence, this chapter makes recommendations for practice based on our current service delivery models. It is hoped that, over time, the application of the principles outlined here will lead to a greater appreciation of the overlapping needs of different groups using a variety of services which may or may not be described at present as specialist personality disorder services. In addition, it is hoped that adoption of these principles will lead to a widening of provision and of the offer which, currently, is located almost exclusively within specialist services.

No longer a diagnosis of exclusion

In 2003, and based on surveys which indicated that only 17% of English mental health trusts had some provision for people with 'personality disorder', the seminal paper 'No Longer a Diagnosis of Exclusion' (NIMHE, 2003) was published. This landmark document sought to increase access to 'appropriate clinical care and management from specialist mental health services' for people with a 'personality disorder' diagnosis and to ensure that the workforce was developed for working with this client group.

To support the ambitions of the paper, the National Institute for Mental Health (NIMHE) developed the personality capabilities framework (NIMHE, 2003), which was intended to 'break the cycle of rejection' by equipping the workforce at all levels, and in every type of service, with the capabilities for working with this client group. With an increasing awareness of the stigmatisation that came with exclusion from services, the Knowledge and Skills Framework (KUF) initiative ('personality disorder knowledge and understanding framework', 2019) which originated in 2007 sought to deliver what was outlined in the capabilities document by providing training programmes on 'personality disorder' from basic awareness to masters level. The training package was co-produced, with lived experience practitioners fully involved in its development. Co-production was a central pillar of the KUF training offer and all programmes were co-delivered by practitioners with both registered professional and lived experience, thereby directly challenging perceptions of 'personality disorder'.

Around the same time, changes to the Mental Health Act (1983, amended in 2007) attempted to offer treatment more equitably to people with 'personality disorder' by replacing restrictive diagnostic criteria (e.g. 'psychopathy') with the more generic term 'mental disorder' as a prerequisite for detention. In addition, the 2007 revisions replaced the requirement for people to have problems that were assessed as 'treatable' (the 'treatability test') with a more inclusive requirement that appropriate treatment is available. What constitutes appropriate treatment was also more widely defined. Previously, 'personality disorder' was considered not amenable to 'treatment' and people with the diagnosis were largely excluded from secure inpatient services. Dale *et al* (2017) suggest that the revisions to the MHA fundamentally changed the culture in mental health services towards 'personality disorder' as mainstream mental health business.

The National Institute for Health and Care Excellence (NICE) Guidelines on Borderline Personality Disorder: Treatment and Management and Antisocial Personality Disorder; Treatment, Management and Prevention were published in 2009 and provided a number of recommendations for the NHS. Again, these aimed to address continued shortcomings in the recognition, management and treatment of personality disorder and highlighted the importance of specialist services. NICE supported training of all mental health staff members by personality disorder-specific teams based in mental health trusts and detailed a range of preventative interventions for children and young people at risk of developing anti-social personality disorder (ASPD).

Without doubt, all these initiatives were driven by a growing awareness not only of the scale of need within a 'personality disorder' population but also, in some cases, of the potential for damaging, stigmatising or even re-traumatising service responses to individuals. These initiatives were bold and well-intentioned and have brought with them a raft of positive benefits. KUF training, for example, is thought to increase levels of staff understanding and decrease negative attitudes (Davies *et al*, 2014). The impact of 'No Longer a Diagnosis' is, reportedly, that there are now five times more dedicated 'personality disorder' services than was the case prior to its publication (Dale *et al*, 2017). According to these authors, the proliferation of specialist services has brought with it increased training and research activity and a greater depth of service user involvement.

It is, therefore, tempting to believe that we are on a positive trajectory toward fair and equitable provision of high-quality specialist services. While there is more work to do, the ambitions of the 2003 NIMHE publication and NICE guidance are, it would seem, gradually being realised.

It is, however, debatable whether the reported proliferation of services actually meets the needs of individuals with 'personality disorder'. There is, for example, no agreed specification for these specialist services, and some indications that they are inadequate (Tetley *et al*, 2012). Dale *et al* (2017) also acknowledge that exclusion, variability in practice and inconsistencies remain.

Undoubtedly, problems also remain regarding hospital treatment of individuals diagnosed with 'personality disorder'. Estimates place the prevalence of 'personality disorder' at around 70% of the patient population within secure services (Dale *et al*, 2017) and these services have proliferated in recent years, with a massive growth in expenditure (Centre for Mental Health, 2011). Arguably, changes to the MHA have led to growth in the very services that have the potential to do the most iatrogenic harm: the revised MHA offers compulsory treatment for people with or without capacity, meaning that even those who have capacity to decide upon treatment in hospital often find their needs overridden once admitted. It is beyond the scope of this chapter to explore (as other authors have) the fundamental flaws inherent in an approach focused on the treatment of intra-psychic pathology and the organisational anxiety that stems from our inability to 'cure' people. Suffice to say that, once detained, people diagnosed with 'personality disorder' are frequently exposed to a variety of restrictive interventions that they do not agree with, want or need. This leads to further distress, understandable anger and lack of cooperation, which then compounds problematic organisational responses. While revisions to it were intended to widen access to supportive and therapeutic help, use of the MHA is nearly always counterproductive for this group of people.

The problem of inclusion/exclusion

When we examine the growth in services dedicated to working with 'personality disorder', we can see that other problems also exist. One fundamental issue is the capacity for specialist services to apply reasonably strict exclusion criteria. Evidently, this potentially leads to services working with a sample of people that may not represent the larger, heterogeneous population. In one study, Crawford *et al* (2009) found that 60.1% of referrals were accepted by ten specialist services, with 23% of that number dropping out before an episode of care had been completed. These authors concluded that specialist services are able to work with the majority of people who are referred to them. Whether or not an exclusion rate of 40% is acceptable, the reality remains that specialist services are in a position to be able to select who is eligible for their treatment.

Some of the most common reasons for excluding people are to do with assessed level of 'risk'. At one end of the scale, acute hospital admission is frequently used to contain risk which is not manageable in the community. At the other end, many individuals are excluded from specialist services if they do not reach the required 'high risk' threshold. This latter position leads us to a situation where people who may present with a lower level of risk (and who may, in some cases, be helped to avoid engaging in even riskier behaviour) may not be able to access help. The message in these instances could be interpreted as: 'to access our service you need to hurt yourself or someone else more seriously.' As one prominent critic has observed:

> 'if someone finds themselves in an area that has a 'pd' specialist service ... The current clustering system for entry into this service is often so high that many people, despite having had a label of "PD" applied to them are denied help in these services. One of the inclusion criteria for "PD" severity is aligned to risk, which of course is aligned with suicidality. It doesn't take a genius to work out that the more suicidal you appear then the more at risk you seem and therefore you might have a slim chance of finding a service that offers something remotely helpful.'

(PD In The Bin, 2017)

Other common exclusion criteria are to do with levels of motivation to change or for engagement with therapy. To require demonstrable levels of engagement is often to require the individual to be able to manage the very emotional and interpersonal challenges that characterise their 'personality disorder'. Murphy and McVey (2010) describe the assumption that people with 'personality disorder' 'have both the desire and ability to suppress symptoms ... in order to receive care' (p105) as a 'logical error'. For these authors, errors such as these 'contribute to the difficulties that people ... have experienced in accessing treatment' (p105).

Using the growing number of specialist services as a measure of our success in working with people with 'personality disorder' is, therefore, potentially misguided, in that it allows us to ignore how and where the needs of those who fail the service requirements are met. Some of us working within clinical services speculate that the rise in 'locked rehabilitation' wards has occurred as a consequence of mainstream and specialist services not being able to meet these needs. While 'locked rehabilitation' wards are sometimes described as 'specialist personality disorder' services, these long-stay wards (mainly provided by the independent sector and usually requiring people to move far away from home) tend to generally cater for individuals with complex presentations who would otherwise be classified as having a 'personality disorder'. The defining characteristic of many of the people on these (often profit-making) wards is likely to be the incapacity of specialist and other mainstream services to safely and effectively care for and manage them. Similarly, many of those who make frequent use of emergency, crisis and acute services are also those who have the problems associated with a 'personality disorder' diagnosis but who are unable to access specialist 'treatment'.

It is in these more mainstream services (the services that are unable to apply strict exclusion criteria) that the majority of damaging or unhealthy interactions tend to take place. For example, the Consensus Statement for People with Complex Mental Health Difficulties who are Diagnosed with a Personality Disorder (e.g. MIND, 2018) provides a direct challenge to a prevailing narrative that specialist services are developing, growing in number and meeting the needs of the client group. This consensus statement argues that the mental health system, which makes use of standard psychological treatment alongside detention, seclusion, restraint and medication, does not work effectively to meet the varied and complex needs of traumatised individuals. Where people are cared for by mainstream services, there are many testimonies to suggest that, despite efforts to develop the workforce, compassion and understanding are rare:

> *'Once identified as local A&Es most frequent attender, Child 2 became a joke, a time waster, to be seen & despatched as fast as possible. As staff became more obviously irritated, she attended less, not because the need was reduced but she was humiliated, too ashamed, embarrassed.'*
>
> (Justamum, 2019, Twitter post retrieved from https://twitter.com/AFjustamum/status/1088404758929522693)

> *'The grim reality is many MH professionals collude with this targeting of people with mental ill health by changing diagnoses to a PD label and subsequently utilising that to justify discharge as part of the person's treatment (to prevent dependency).'*
>
> (PDIntheBin, 2019, Twitter post retrieved from: https://twitter.com/pddxinthebin?lang=en)

Specialist provision as a product of organisational anxiety

An overarching theme of this book is that working with human beings is inherently stressful and emotional for workers and organisations. It is also a central assertion that practices emerge as a result of this emotional reaction to the work, which reduces anxiety at the worker and organisational level at the expense of providing what service users need. These practices (termed 'social defences' in the literature) are all the more problematic by being organisationally sanctioned and by being experienced by workers as professional, responsible and mature (Menzies Lyth, 1960; Obholzer & Zagier-Roberts, 1994).

Specialist 'personality disorder' services, viewed by the policy documents outlined earlier as the answer to the problem of access to services for people with 'personality disorder', are arguably now part of the same problem, and it is interesting therefore to consider whether our appreciation of them constitutes a response to the work which is driven less by service user need than by a need to reduce organisational stress. These often high-quality services are potentially increasingly rarefied as they choose who to work with, leaving many distressed and troubling individuals to be picked up by mainstream services which lack the resources and the frameworks for working effectively with them.

This exclusivity is, arguably, further reinforced through commissioning using a biomedical definition of the problem ('personality disorder'). Implicitly, therefore, specialist 'personality disorder' services uphold a situation which maintains high-status 'expert' professional roles and concomitant 'patient' roles associated with ill health, incapacity and the need for treatment. While many services work creatively within these frameworks and are only lightly informed by a biomedical model, the situating of services in this way nonetheless has the potential to create an illogical state regarding access to services: while worker/organisational anxiety in specialist services is better managed through being defined as teams of expert professionals who can select who is eligible for treatment, generic services (by definition less expert in this field) are left to work with those who are not selected but who are nonetheless desperate, distressed and disturbing – and in many cases diagnosed with the very problem that should allow them access to the specialist service which operates as a treatment for this problem.

Rather than working to develop and improve the skills and capacity of the generic workforce, it could be argued that these specialist services work instead (unconsciously perhaps) to continually prevent change: specialist services provide a hoped-for referral route for those in generic services. According to Stokes (1994), this collective and unconscious belief that a future event (referral accepted by specialist services) will solve current problems is a defence against the difficulties of the present. It could be argued, therefore, that a collusive interdependence between generic and specialist services exists whereby specialist services foster hope and dependence from generic services while ensuring that those using more mainstream services are the least 'attractive' from a treatment point of view.

Left to care for and manage those individuals who lack the characteristics which would make them eligible for specialist treatment, generic services work, with few resources, on managing highly stressful and distressing presentations. It is perhaps not surprising that, under these circumstances, mainstream services tend to rely on more brutal, less humane coping mechanisms.

What is good access anyway?

What constitutes healthy engagement and access to services is unclear. A level of what might be termed 'emotional intimacy' is required for most psychologically based treatments or interventions, meaning that individuals are usually expected to be able to talk about their past and, to some degree, to be able to reflect on their current functioning. On either side of this optimum level of engagement would appear to be ways of accessing services that are disturbing for the workforce. Too much engagement tends to be thought of as dependency/infatuation and too little as lack of motivation, and either may lead to exclusion from services.

Evidently, someone who has had traumatic or otherwise problematic early attachment relationships is likely to find it challenging to be able to function interpersonally at the optimum level described, meaning that 'access to services' is frequently obstructed by the very 'personality disorder' symptoms that those services are supposed to help with.

> 'Do not admire or pin any hope to a professional who appears to understand the social context of your distress (this is idealisation…)
> … Your mental health team believes in its adequacy, despite all the evidence. Do not do or say anything that threatens professionals' fixed delusional beliefs, they may decompensate, becoming either coldly punitive and violent or weirdly smiley and dissociative, forcing you to have too much "service" and then none at all.'
>
> (PD In the Bin, 2017, blog post)

Once again, exclusion on the basis of how well individuals are able to make use of the services ('effective use' being something which is usually defined by workers) could be conceptualised as a social defence. Where those using our services are highly engaged and attached to workers, this can be threatening for the worker. The threat may come from worries about infatuation, about being stalked or metaphorically suffocated, about never being able to fulfil expectations or being the only person who might be able to rescue the other from despair. Where there is a lack of interest, being dismissed can feel as if we (the workers) are not valued or lack skills. Dismissiveness can make us feel incompetent or self-conscious, or relieved that we are not wanted by someone dangerous, boring or hateful. Excluding, therefore, on the basis of 'overdependence' or 'lack of engagement' becomes a way of managing the emotional impact on the workforce of either one of these extremes of attachment style.

In addition, clarifying expectations of service users (as needing to demonstrate an optimal level of engagement with our service) enables us to avoid asking what it is that we should be doing. All too frequently assessments of levels of engagement and risk serve to exclude people rather than include.

The problem of assessment

During a telephone conference it quickly became clear that John was assessed as unsuitable for both the specialist hospital services that he had been referred to. He was too risky for the low secure hospital service and not risky enough for the medium secure hospital service. Meanwhile, his offender supervisor in prison had good knowledge about John's current period of stability and how it had been achieved. Despite his best attempts the offender supervisor could not convince either assessor to consider whether what he knew about John could help them in thinking about whether their service could meet his needs.

Assessment processes are understood to be the preferred mechanism whereby services ensure that access is enabled to only those who are most appropriate. Arguably, however, the assessment process is deeply flawed when it comes to assessing 'personality disorder'. Once again, the process tends to be based on biomedical assumptions about distress equalling stable states of health. Risk is typically conflated and, as in the example above, it also often categorised in a way that ignores the fact that it is highly context-specific. Once assessments are established as expert gatekeeping judgements they are then frequently contested and, as in the example above, can lead to blocked pathways and intractable professional disagreements.

To work differently with barriers created by assessments, services would need to approach the issue about whether they can meet need from an entirely different perspective. The Offender Personality Disorder (OPD) strategy (e.g. Joseph & Benefield, 2012) constitutes a good attempt to do things differently. Based on a recognition that it is difficult to evidence that treatment needs have been met when working with people described as having 'dangerous and severe personality disorders' (e.g. Vollm & Konappa, 2012), the OPD strategy aims to establish a more creative approach. The OPD pathway not only mandates that individuals should be screened for the problems associated with 'personality disorder' (rather than diagnosed), but also aims to enable frictionless pathways between services based on narratives (formulations) which seek to understand the psychological and emotional foundations of distress and associated risk. Despite this ambition, specialist 'treatment' services commissioned on the pathway also engage in assessment processes and apply strict exclusion criteria.

In keeping with the focus on 'social defences', it is arguable that assessment processes requiring expert professional judgements constitute organisational attempts to manage anxiety. The biomedical assumptions which underpin the majority of our interventions mean that the offer from services is usually one which requires reflection on intra-psychic processes and a willingness to change the self. Service delivery is, therefore, inherently linked to professional anxiety about a worker's ability to change people, to make them safer, better and happier. Seeking to eliminate those who are less likely to alleviate our anxiety or who might exacerbate a sense of failure or incompetence within the service is, therefore, an understandable response. Nonetheless, an assessment process – as it is traditionally conducted – ill serves the needs of a heterogenous client group who are defined less by their 'pathology' and more by idiosyncratic trauma narratives.

Principles

While it has been argued that a drive towards specialist provision has, in itself, brought with it a number of barriers, it should also be noted that the proliferation of these services has brought with it a unique opportunity to learn. Specialist services have had a number of years to better understand not only the needs of the client group but also a great deal about how they themselves respond helpfully and unhelpfully to the work. Networks have been established (e.g. BIGSPD community of practice) which allow for this learning to be shared and developed.

The climate is right, therefore, to think about how the learning from these services can be applied more effectively, not necessarily or exclusively to individual clinical interventions, but more widely to overcome the barriers created by specialist provision itself. The general principle supported here is one which upholds the ambitions of the Consensus Statement (e.g. MIND, 2018), which argues for a whole systems approach. In other words, the goal for specialist services should be to share learning and collaborate with partnership organisations to create networks of consistent, mindful support.

Services should ask 'can we provide what you need?' rather than 'can you access what we provide?'

Given the above, it is the ambition of this chapter to outline what might constitute a reasonably radical departure from traditional assessment-based barriers to services. Broadly speaking, it is recommended that, upon referral, services seek to understand what best helps an individual to be calmer, happier, less risky, less distressed, etc. On this basis, services should then assess whether they can offer what the individual needs, rather than whether the individual can access what they provide. The assessment becomes one of the service rather than the client. This is not intended to be a naïve approach where all the service user's wishes are fulfilled! Instead, it is intended to re-orientate workers towards a strengths-focused, needs-led assessment that draws on the understanding held within the system about what a person's situation means to them; about what hurts and what helps. It is also intended to re-orientate workers towards the utilisation of a wider set of resources than is often thought to be available.

In some respects this process would be reasonably straightforward to instigate. For example, assessment templates can be changed to focus on periods of stability or low risk and whatever it was that enabled them. Seeking narratives from other services where the individual is known and where there might be an opinion about what has helped would become another focus and would appropriately direct the knowledge-gathering process away from expert professional judgements about intra-psychic pathology. However, it should also be acknowledged that traditional practice has served an important purpose. We do things in the way we do them for good reason and our current, assessment-based gatekeeping practice enables us to clearly define what is provided by clinical services that are purchased with public money. Diagnostically driven access routes permit some level of assurance to commissioners that expensive resources are being allocated appropriately. It would be disingenuous to ignore the importance of clarity where accountability is necessary. With that in mind, the approach advocated here would require a different way of thinking about how this reassurance is given and how clinical teams are held accountable.

Undoubtedly, more creative thinking is required about how work is defined should bio-medically driven, 'treatment'-based descriptions become less applicable when services seek to provide whatever it is that people need. Recent guidance for intensive intervention risk management (IIRM) services which are currently commissioned under the OPD pathway do, perhaps, provide one example of how we might seek to define ourselves differently as we work to exclude fewer people and to meet the broadest need (see text box). These guiding principles outline a more flexible service delivery model which utilises a 'case management' framework within which to exercise a level of service adaptability to different needs and changing circumstances.

To maximise accessibility of the service, barriers to entry, and options for rejection need to be removed from the referral and engagement procedures. Joint case work becomes the assessment phase and the transition point. (IIRMs referral and entry criteria principle 2.1)

It is the duty of the IIRMS to engage the service user with the offer of a service that is meaningful and of relevance; the offering therefore needs to be responsive and flexible (IIRMs delivery principle 3.1)

…the primary task of the IIRMS (is to deliver) a psychosocially informed case management approach to individual offenders that is based on the four domains of the model of care, and includes a focus on relational engagement for all incomers,

The (standard) IIRMs offer is:

1. A high intensity outreach service offered (probably at least twice a week) to offenders over a relatively brief period of time (3-6 months) to manage transitions, achieve some stability, and build structure and meaning into the week.

2. A moderate intensity intervention service (probably 6-12 months, at least once a week) to deliver psycho-educational work and skills development in either group or individual modalities.

3. A low intensity maintenance service that is offered to offenders who are engaged but find higher intensity interventions intolerable, or to those who have progressed and are ready to maintain links with the IIRMS at arms length (including contact at the offender's instigation and/or 'drop in' services).Low intensity monthly interventions will also be appropriate for those waiting for medium intensity interventions (see section on Governance).

(Taken from Offender Personality Disorder Pathway guidance, September 2018)

As part of an approach which seeks to move beyond contested assessments of mental health and risk, services should also look to form networks with other services so that learning about individuals can be shared and thought about. Wherever possible, the processes that underpin these collaborations should be co-produced. What these look like is not known and, once again, creativity is invited.

Specialist services should work more proactively to support other systems and services that work with people who present in a way consistent with a 'personality disorder' diagnosis

In line with an approach to 'personality disorder' that has been prevalent in specialist services for many years, there is a general move within mental health services towards 'trauma-informed' care. A literature search on this subject, however, suggests that what this means has various definitions and may be interpreted in different ways. The recently published Power Threat Meaning Framework (PTMF, Johnstone & Boyle, 2018), for example, describes a trauma-informed approach to all varieties of mental health conditions. The PTMF describes how symptoms of mental ill health might be better understood as intelligible responses to the misuse of power, and offers four key questions (e.g. 'what happened to you?') to help formulate how power has operated problematically within people's lives. While the authors of this document are keen to emphasise the applicability of the document to systems and organisations, there is nonetheless the potential to mistake trauma-informed for trauma-focused, especially when there is a steer to ask 'what has happened to you?'

Specialist personality disorder services understand, perhaps better than generic mental health services, that a trauma-focused approach such as this has the potential to be problematic for individuals and systems (Ramsden, 2019). For example, it is likely to be aversive for many individuals to remember and discuss traumatic incidents, and specialist personality disorder services tend to have a good understanding of how speech and memory (and behaviour) function protectively – and often counter-intuitively or confusingly – to manage emotional reactions to what are often constant traumatic triggers in the environment. The theoretical frameworks and models employed by specialist personality disorder services tend to assist them to hold a compassionate frame towards reactions to trauma that are otherwise baffling, exhausting or overwhelming for workers.

Despite lengthy psychological therapy and intensive, trauma-informed care co-ordination and safeguarding involvement, Sally's clinical team came to recognise that she was never going to leave the husband who was violent towards her. Although Sally talked movingly about the domestic abuse she witnessed and suffered as a child, the clinical team realised that being in an unsafe environment was familiar to her. Knowing that Sally had a level of physical safety (her husband was ill, in pain and unable to hurt her badly), the clinical team worked on supporting her and helping her in ways that were meaningful to her. They held an understanding that her domestic situation allowed her to manage her trauma by being able to relive it in a way that was more predictable and where she was more powerful. In holding this understanding the service focused on supporting workers who had invested much in their relationships with Sally and who, despite having established trusting, therapeutic attachments with her, nevertheless had to witness the impact of the violence she suffered. It was important that the impact of this trauma on the workers was recognised and that they were helped to maintain authentic and compassionate hope for Sally, even though the outcome of their involvement with her was not what any of them had wanted for her.

In addition, much has been learned over the past ten years or so within specialist 'personality disorder' services about the impact of trauma not only on the lives of service users but on organisations trying to work with them (see **Chapters 6 and 12**). These services are exceptionally well-equipped to help others work effectively with deeply distressed individuals who often present with disturbing behaviour and deeply troubling histories.

While it is not suggested that specialist 'personality disorder' services can claim clinical expertise for other services working with individuals who could otherwise be diagnosed with a 'personality disorder' (e.g. expertise in eating disorder), these services may nonetheless claim some expertise in working with trauma, especially at an organisational level. It is suggested, therefore, that these specialist services can assist others who manage high caseloads of individuals who present with 'personality disorder' diagnoses or high levels of incidents associated with the diagnosis (e.g. self-harm) to maintain a healthy, compassionate approach.

This principle is in keeping with an understanding that the focus of any work with 'personality disorder' should be on relationships, rather than a clinical intervention-based emphasis on intra-psychic change. Helping workers and services in general to 'hold their minds' when the invitation with the work is to do the opposite (to behave emotionally) is a good use of specialist expertise.

Services should use partnerships to broaden the application of their expertise beyond what is prescribed by a biomedical, diagnostic framework

At the current time, most services that work with 'personality disorder' are – fundamentally – informed by a dominant diagnostic, medical framework. Even psychological approaches tend to be focused on working with intra-psychic phenomena, meaning that so many of the important, mainly social, factors involved are overlooked. As has been noted by other authors (e.g. Skett & Barlow, this edition), the needs of people who fit diagnostic 'personality disorder' patterns are so varied that multiple services are needed to collaborate and create whole systems around people.

Partnership working is essential if services are going to ensure that their learning and understanding can be applied to other, often more socially focused, agendas. Partnership working is dealt with in another chapter (Harvey & Tuohy, this edition), so won't be dwelled upon in any more detail here. Suffice it to say that access to services can be broadened when services work collaboratively with others and in a way that augments and enhances the work of both partners.

Tom gave one day a month of his time to a housing provider which worked with a number of individuals who would have fitted a 'personality disorder' diagnosis. As a specialist worker with 'personality disorder', Tom was able to help the housing workers provide more stable accommodation to these service users. Jack was one such service user, who, after a period of detention in hospital following a transfer from prison, was keen to reassure everyone that he was able to manage on his own. Hospital staff confirmed that he had many domestic skills and had done well in their less supported environment before being considered for discharge. His probation officer was worried, however, about how much he had self-harmed when in prison.

Tom helped the housing workers consider the possibility that Jack's confidence and assuredness may be part of an interpersonal pattern which helped him feel safe – rather than a direct representation of an internal state. Housing support workers approached Jack and talked about his worry that he might be viewed negatively if he admitted to needing a higher level of support in the community. Jack admitted that he was profoundly afraid of living alone but didn't want people to think him incompetent/worthless. A higher support package was put in place for Jack, who used this to help him to adjust slowly to community living. More importantly, a dialogue was now in place for Jack and his workers to talk about how Jack might mask his own needs so as to seek immediate affiliation with those around him.

Given the role of early trauma in the lives of people with 'personality disorder', these partnerships and collaborations should include services which work with young people and, in particular, families and mothers and infants. Specialist services work with people who have been in distress and emotional pain for years, with very little focus on what might be done not to manage these problems, but to eradicate them. It is, perhaps, another social defence that so much provision is given to services working with adults when the root of those problems lie much earlier in life. Arguably, working mainly with adults (and older children) allows services to avoid confronting the limits of their effectiveness with the most distressed, disturbing, dangerous and chaotic families.

Summary

This chapter has focused on how services can better ensure fair and equitable access for people who have been – or who could be – diagnosed with a 'personality disorder'. It has been argued that the best way to improve access is to work on disseminating and sharing some of the expertise and the knowledge about what works that is currently, typically, held in specialist 'personality disorder' services. It has also been argued that the current situation perpetuates an unhealthy state in which specialist services provide hope for generic services while (unconsciously) simultaneously creating a dependency that both legitimises their rarefied status and disempowers the services that tend to work with the most challenging individuals – a situation which undoubtedly ill serves individuals who may rely on generic services that are under stress partly because they perceive themselves to be lacking in the necessary expertise.

Governance of services is key if they are to be moved away from relying on some of the things that tend to create barriers. This chapter has outlined three key principles which, it is hoped, would enable services to work more flexibly and to face outward to ensure that more people get what they need. Undoubtedly, this is just a start. It is hoped that this chapter provides enough food for thought to stimulate innovation and creativity in finding ways to shift the current situation. It is also just part of a movement which is already underway in many specialist services who provide consultation and training and who work in partnership with third sector and other services. What many of these services lack is the resources to do more of this work and to explore the impact. In addition, there is the lack of a commissioning infrastructure which is supportive of a different way of entering a service (what do you commission if this is no longer a service for people with 'borderline personality disorder' but instead for anyone who is likely to find the service meaningful?)? In keeping with a theme that there is a need for a 'paradigm shift' in how we work with people who manage the day-to-day stress/distress that we call 'personality disorder', this chapter would, ultimately, argue for a new way of commissioning. The OPD pathway provides a contemporary example of how we might start to do this. Hopefully other examples are on the horizon.

Acknowledgements: With thanks to Mark Naylor, Tom Mullen and Jamie Scott

References

Centre for Mental Health (2011) Pathways to unlocking secure mental health care. Retrieved from www.centreformentalhealth.org.uk

Crawford MJ, Price K, Gordon F, Josson M, Taylor B, Bateman A, Fonagy P, Tyrer P, Moran P (2009) Engagement and retention in specialist services for people with personality disorder. *Acta Psychiatrica Scandinavica* **119** (4) 304–311.

Dale O, Sethi F, Stanton C, Evans S, Barnicot K, Sedgwick R, Goldsack S, Doran M, Shoolbred L, Samele C, Urquia N, Haigh R & Moran P (2017) Personality disorder services in England: Findings from a national survey. *British Journal of Psychiatry Bulletin* **41** 247–253.

Davies J, Sampson M, Beesley F, Smith D & Baldwin V (2014) An evaluation of Knowledge and Understanding Framework personality disorder awareness training: Can a co-production model be effective in a local NHS mental health trust? *Personality and Mental Health* **8** (2) 161–168.

Joseph N & Benefield N (2012) A joint offender personality disorder pathway strategy: An outline summary. *Criminal Behaviour and Mental Health* **22** (3) 210–217.

Menzies-Lyth I (1960) A case study in the functioning of social systems as a defence against anxiety: A report on the study of the nursing service of a general hospital. *British Psycho-Analytical Society* **13** (2) 95–121.

MIND (2018) 'Shining lights in dark corners of people's lives': The Consensus Statement for people with complex mental health difficulties who are diagnosed with a personality disorder. Retrieved from MIND.org.uk

Murphy N & McVey D (2010) *Treating Personality Disorder: Creating Robust Services for People with Complex Mental Health Needs*. London/New York: Routledge.

National Institute for Mental Health in England (2003) *Personality Disorder: No Longer a Diagnosis of Exclusion*. London: Department of Health.

National Institute for Mental Health in England (2003) *Breaking the Cycle of Rejection: The Personality Disorder Capabilities Framework*. Leeds: NIMHE.

National Institute for Health and Care Excellence (2009) *Borderline Personality Disorder: Recognition and Management* (Clinical Guideline CG78). London: NICE.

National Institute for Health and Care Excellence (2009) *Antisocial Personality Disorder: Recognition and Management* (Clinical Guideline CG77). London: NICE.

Obholzer A & Zagier-Roberts V (eds) (1994) *The Unconscious at Work: Individual and Organisational Stress in the Human Services*. London/New York: Routledge.

Personality Disorder Knowledge and Understanding Framework (2019). Retrieved from https://kufpersonalitydisorder.org.uk/

PD In The Bin (2017) Systemic oppression, 'PD' and suicidality [blog post]. Retrieved from: https://personalitydisorderinthebin.wordpress.com/2017/01/05/systemic-oppression-pd-and-suicidality/

PD In The Bin (2019) A simple guide to avoid receiving a diagnosis of 'personality disorder' UPDATE [blog post]. Retrieved from https://personalitydisorderinthebin.wordpress.com/2017/02/10/a-simple-guide-to-avoid-receiving-a-diagnosis-of-personality-disorder-update/

Ramsden J (2019) Editorial: The power threat meaning framework and forensic mental health settings. *Criminal Behaviour and Mental Health* 1–3. https://doi.org/10.1002/cbm.2118

Stokes J (1994) The unconscious at work in groups and teams: Contributions from the work of Wilfred Bion. In: A Obholzer & V Zagier-Roberts (eds) *The Unconscious at Work: Individual and Organisational Stress in the Human Services*. London/New York: Routledge.

Tetley A, Jinks M, Howells K, Duggan C, McMurran M, Huband N (2012) A preliminary investigation of services for people with personality disorder in the East Midlands region of England. *Personality and Mental Health* **6** (1) 33–44.

Vollm B & Konappa N (2012) The dangerous and severe personality disorder experiment: Review of empirical research. *Criminal Behaviour and Mental Health* **22** (3) 165–180.

Chapter 8:

Reimagining Interventions

Alan Hirons and Ruth Sutherland

Governance principles:

Interventions should seek to:

- ■ Develop epistemic trust
- ■ Be attuned to individual needs. Be consciously, deliberately focused upon meaningful change
- ■ Be relationally focused
- ■ Be a collective endeavour

Introduction

Interventions provided by services for people with personality disorder are an active representation of how services conceptualise the experience of personality disorder and what they understand their role to be in working with service users.

We have written this chapter based upon learning from our work designing and delivering services since 2004 in Leeds Personality Disorder Services, and our contributions to innovative and contemporary work in the wider personality disorder 'community of practice'. Leeds Personality Disorder Services currently provides a range of interventions across health and criminal justice settings, working with service users and the people and organisations charged with working with them (**Table 8.1**). This chapter illustrates our experience of engaging with the evidence bases and theoretical narratives in the design and delivery of interventions which aspire to be attuned to and effective in meeting service users' needs. This overview is subjective and qualitative in nature, reflecting our own interpretation of the journey of the past 15 or so years.

The requirement for 'up-to-date' and future-orientated thinking about the experience of personality disorder and what constitutes an effective response is the setting for this book. This chapter's specific contribution is a focus primarily upon the realm of direct intervention with service users, and commences with identifying the challenges. It then moves on to providing an overview of the current evidence-based interventions and their limitations. Other sources of theoretical knowledge and practice which usefully inform the design and delivery of interventions are identified and a range of case studies are presented which illustrate the use of these sources. Finally, the chapter states a number of principles which we propose can guide the development and delivery of interventions for people with personality disorder.

Table 8.1: Intervention in Leeds Personality Disorder Services

Personality Disorder Managed Clinical Network –

Care Co-ordination – Care Co-ordination is provided for people with significant risk to self and multiple complex needs who live in the community and includes input from occupational therapy, psychology, psychotherapy and accommodation support.

Dialectical Behaviour Therapy skills training group programme – DBT skills training groups 'teach' people skills to help themselves when they feel suicidal or want to use self-harming or life threatening behaviours to cope with intense emotional distress.

Journey Occupational Therapy group programme – an Occupational Therapy and Psychology informed group programme, with a focus upon assisting people to develop understanding of the form and function of their time use and to engage in activity which challenges early maladaptive schemata.

Personalities in Action service-user involvement group – meets to work on service evaluation, service development and a range of project work. This group recently developed animated films about the service, guidance on using self-help, developing and co-facilitating staff training and co-producing local conferences.

Cygnus Carer Education and Support Group – a psycho-educational course for carers, providing information about personality difficulties from a trauma-informed perspective.

Pathway Development Service –

Pathway planning and review – Provide psychologically informed opinion to assist with pathway planning for service users in Tier 4 and forensic services.

continued ➜

Yorkshire and Humber Personality Disorder Service –

Core Offender Management (OM) service – psychologists and psychotherapists work directly with Offender Managers who are managing offenders on the national Offender Personality Disorder Pathway. The aim is to ensure that risk management is psychologically informed.

Discovery Intensive Intervention and Risk Management Service (IIRMs) – psychologically informed therapeutic intervention with offenders, which focuses upon facilitating the experience of adaptive working relationships, the learning that arises from these and its potential impact to inform experience of well-being and risk reduction.

Mentalisation Based Therapy (MBT) – Weekly therapy group for men on the Offender Personality Disorder pathway who are identified as having problems consistent with an anti social personality disorder diagnosis.

Personality Disorder Knowledge and Understanding Framework (KUF) training – delivery of the range of PDKUF training to staff across the health, voluntary and criminal justice settings.

The current challenges

From our experience we agree with the observation that developments in the past two decades in service provision for people with personality disorder are 'one of the unheralded successes of contemporary mental health' (Livesley, 2017, p. iv). We need to remember that only two decades ago, personality disorder was regarded as untreatable, and that therapeutic pessimism was the norm (Lewis & Appleby, 1988). The personality disorder field has moved from generally prejudicial thinking and limited provision (with notable exceptions: see e.g. Campling & Haigh, 1999 re therapeutic communities), to having a range of theoretical narratives informing a variety of manualised therapies and promoting effective organisational and systems thinking for working with the experience of personality disorder.

We qualify this success with the proposition that that these successes have created some knowledge and some confidence for services to engage with and provide intervention with some service users, some of the time. Personality disorder services have developed and adopted an arguably 'comfortable' position whereby they provide interventions which are meaningful to themselves and certain groups of service users. There is still 'continued exclusion, variability of practice and inconsistencies in the availability of services' (Dale *et al*, 2017, p252), and where the diagnosis or description of personality disorder is 'highly stigmatising but is not necessarily experienced as a starting point for acceptable and effective forms of help' (Pilgrim, 2017, p389). Many individuals with personality disorder are not able to access specialist personality disorder services. Criteria to be accepted into such services typically exclude large numbers of individuals whose difficulties are considered insufficiently severe or complex for a specialist service, or who are excluded by virtue of receiving a diagnosis such as anti-social personality disorder. Even where specialist help may be available, the stigma of the diagnosis may deter people from seeking/accepting help from a 'personality disorder service'. Others may not perceive that they have a need for help and so do not seek treatment from mental health services (NIHCE, 2009a), or only do so at times of crisis. As such, many who experience high levels of distress (and, in many cases, who may also cause distress and harm to others) receive their care or management predominantly from non-specialist services such as GPs, accident & emergency departments, social services, voluntary sector organisations, housing services and/or the criminal justice system.

As a consequence of the above, we face two challenges when we seek to intervene to help people who may be identified as having a 'personality disorder':

- Our understanding of what works is limited, as it is based upon our work with people who find formally defined 'treatment'-focused services meaningful.

- We do not know the extent and nature of people's needs, as the majority of people are excluded or rejected from services.

Overall, we propose that this limited access to intervention is promoted and maintained by existing conceptualisations of personality disorder and interventions as having an often sole emphasis upon service user intra-psychic change, primarily through talking therapy. We suggest this emphasis promotes a view that 'something is to be fixed' in a linear fashion of a *doing to* process which limits our capacity to engage effectively in particular with excluded individuals. We suggest that this focus upon intra-psychic change through 'formal' therapeutic processes (although effective for some people) is by itself ultimately a limiting lens through which to view how to engage with and work with people with personality disorder.

However, the developing knowledge base, in particular around mentalisation (Fonagy & Allison, 2012) and the processes of epistemic trust and social learning (Fonagy & Allison, 2014), provides clues as to how services can consolidate and develop their current interventions, and, most importantly, begin to more effectively engage with the people excluded from services.

We need, therefore, to enhance, broaden and make more sophisticated our conceptualisation of what it is to intervene – the process of taking 'action ... to intentionally become involved in a difficult situation in order to improve it or prevent it from getting worse' (Cambridge Dictionary, 2019). We propose that, to do this, we need to 're-imagine' interventions. We assert that engagement in formal manualised therapeutic intervention should not be seen as a goal in its own right, with a sole emphasis on effecting intra-psychic change in service users. Rather, the extensive range of thinking and practices employed should inform intervention processes that are focused upon facilitating individualised, flexible and attuned communication and interaction between workers and service users, with the ultimate aims of adaptive engagement with the wider world of 'social learning' (Fonagy *et al*, 2015) and the development of individual 'personal niches' (Livesley, 2017). We propose that this 're-imagining' facilitates more effective intervention by expanding what is considered to be intervention into social and occupational arenas.

We define interventions as *all deliberate and conscious activities which have the potential to 'create' evidence and experience for service users of the efficacy and utility of engaging safely with other people in the service of immediate survival, emotional regulation and the development and maintenance of quality of life.*

Evidence-based interventions for personality disorder

The past two decades have seen a concerted effort to develop evidence-based psychological treatments for personality disorder.

Borderline/emotionally unstable personality disorder

A number of structured manualised psychological therapeutic approaches have been developed specifically for working with people experiencing the problems associated with a borderline personality disorder diagnosis (see **Table 8.2**). All of these approaches have demonstrated some evidence in randomised controlled trials of being more effective than treatment as usual (TAU) or treatment by experts (that is, psychiatrists or psychotherapists with expertise in BPD but not using a structured therapeutic approach) for reducing symptoms such as self-harm and suicidality (Koons *et al*, 2001; Doering *et al*, 2010; Linehan *et al*, 2006; Verheul *et al*, 2003; Budge *et al*, 2014; Clarke *et al*, 2013; Davidson *et al*, 2006; Grenyer *et al*, 2018).

Dialectical behaviour therapy has the largest evidence base (Stoffers-Winterling *et al*, 2012) and is the only psychological therapy currently recommended in NICE guidance, specifically 'for women with borderline personality disorder for whom reducing recurrent self-harm is a priority' (NICE, 2009b, p208).

However, a number of comparative randomised controlled trials (RCTs) (Bartak *et al*, 2001; Giesen-Bloo *et al*, 2006), systematic reviews and meta-analyses (Leichsenring & Leibing, 2003; Leichsenring *et al*, 2011; Budge *et al*, 2014; Cristea *et al*, 2017) have consistently concluded that none of these therapies is more effective than any other. Additionally, further RCTs have found both supportive psychotherapy (Clarkin *et al*, 2007; Jorgensen *et al*, 2013) and structured psychiatric management (Bateman & Fonagy, 2009; McMain *et al*, 2009; Chanen *et al*, 2008) to be as effective as manualised psychological therapies for reducing self-harm, suicidality, hospitalisation and depression and improving social adjustment.

Table 8.2: Psychological Therapies for Borderline Personality Disorder

- Cognitive analytic therapy (CAT; Ryle, 1997)
- Cognitive behavioural therapies (CBT; Beck & Freeman, 1990; CBT-PD; Davidson, 2007)
- Dialectical behaviour therapy (DBT; Linehan, 1993)
- Mentalization-based therapy (MBT; Bateman & Fonagy, 2004)
- Schema-focused therapy (SFT; Young, 2003)
- Systems training for emotional predictability and problem solving (STEPPS; Blum *et al*, 2002)
- Stepped care (Paris, 2013)
- Transference-focused therapy (TFT; Clarkin *et al*, 1999)

Another intervention approach is the therapeutic community (TC) (Campling & Haigh, 1999), which includes both residential and day unit communities in community and custodial settings and incorporates a wide range of therapeutic approaches (Haigh & Lees, 2008). Capone *et al*'s (2016) systematic review of the quantitative research on TCs identified the limitations of TC research and concluded there is insufficient evidence to determine interpersonal and offending risk outcomes following TC treatment.

Anti-social/dissocial personality disorder

A small number of systematic reviews (Duggan *et al*, 2007; Gibbon *et al*, 2010) have consistently concluded that the current evidence remains insufficient to make clear recommendations about psychological interventions for anti-social personality disorder (ASPD). Cognitive and behavioural approaches have demonstrated the most consistent effectiveness, particularly for offenders and those with comorbid substance misuse difficulties (Duggan *et al*, 2007; Gibbon *et al*, 2010); however, there is less evidence that such interventions lead to significant changes in other specific behaviours associated with ASPD, such as aggression or impulsivity (NICE, 2009a).

A number of other therapeutic approaches are demonstrating some promising initial findings, including mentalisation-based therapy (MBT) for reducing aggression (McGauley *et al*, 2011), cognitive behavioural therapy (CBT) for reducing physical aggression and improving social functioning (Davidson *et al*, 2009) and schema-focused therapy (SFT) for reducing re-offending (Bernstein *et al*, 2012). There is, however, insufficient evidence to make clear recommendations for any of these interventions at this time.

As such, at this time NICE guidance for ASPD only specifically recommends group-based cognitive and behavioural interventions which predominantly focus on substance misuse and/or reducing re-offending (e.g. 'Reasoning and Rehabilitation', Cann *et al*, 2003; 'Enhanced Thinking Skills', Friendship *et al*, 2002), for individuals in both community and institutional settings. Since the publication of the NICE guidance, two further RCTs have demonstrated initial findings for MBT (Bateman *et al*, 2016) and STEPPS (Black *et al*, 2016) for individuals who had received diagnoses of both BPD and ASPD, demonstrating clinically significant improvements across a range of symptoms associated with both diagnoses.

Other personality disorders

Bateman *et al* (2015) note that while there are protocols for cognitive behavioural therapy (e.g. Beck & Freeman, 1990) for schizoid, schizotypal and paranoid personality disorders (DSM 'Cluster A'), there have been no RCTs for any psychological approaches with individuals with these diagnoses.

There has also been limited research activity exploring the effectiveness of psychological approaches for avoidant, dependent, and obsessive-compulsive personality disorders (DSM 'Cluster C'). A small number of RCTs suggest that both psychodynamic (Winston *et al*, 1994) and cognitive behavioural therapies (Svartberg *et al*, 2004; Emmelkamp *et al*, 2006) have been demonstrated to be more effective than TAU in reducing distress, although it is not clear whether one therapy is more effective than another or whether any diagnostic group benefits more than another from intervention (Simon, 2009).

Pharmacotherapy

There is very limited evidence for any benefits of pharmacotherapy for any personality disorder other than for the short-term management of crisis. NICE guidance (NICE, 2009b) states that pharmacotherapy is not to be used for the treatment of personality disorder except for the management of co-morbid mental health difficulties, which should then be prescribed in line with the relevant guidance.

Evaluating the evidence

The current research evidence provides some reasons to be optimistic about interventions for personality disorder. It is encouraging that there has been an increase in the amount of published research since 'No Longer a Diagnosis of Exclusion' (NIMHE, 2003) many with positive findings, particularly for reducing suicide attempts, self-harm, aggression and depression, and for improving general functioning. However, while such interventions appear to be highly effective for some individuals, there remain significant issues with the quality of the research evidence and with the accessibility of such interventions for many people with personality disorder.

The overall evidence base for interventions is poor relative to those for other mental health diagnoses, such as depression (NICE, 2009c) or psychosis (NICE, 2009d). There are relatively few studies, many of which have significant methodological limitations, including small participant numbers, short or no follow-up and potential researcher biases (Cristea *et al*, 2017).

In addition, the changes (as measured by the relevant outcome measure) are relatively small (Cristea *et al*, 2017) and outcomes have often been unstable at the point of follow-up. The use of a wide range of outcomes measures makes comparisons between studies difficult; however, the focus has tended to be mainly symptomatic and behavioural (for example, reduction in self-harm), rather than measuring change of 'core aspects' of the personality difficulties experienced by service users (Bateman *et al*, 2015). Furthermore, many individuals continue to experience significant impairments in functioning, social adjustment and quality of life (McMain *et al*, 2009; Kröger *et al*, 2013) after the end of therapy. Reported drop-out rates are high, at an average of 37% (McMurran *et al*, 2010), although this is lower than the reported general psychotherapy drop-out rate of 47% (Wierzbicki & Pekarik, 1993).

Studies have used different diagnostic criteria and conceptualisations of personality disorder, making comparisons difficult; even where the same DSM or ICD criteria have been cited, the heterogeneity of the diagnostic categories means that the trials may be too 'all inclusive' (NICE, 2009b, p205) and so difficult to generalise to populations presenting with particular difficulties, symptoms or behaviours. The studies focusing on people diagnosed with ASPD in particular have tended to focus on treatment of individuals in prison rather than those in the community. This is likely to reflect issues around engagement in treatment; however, this means that it may be difficult to generalise outcomes to those living in the community (Bateman *et al*, 2015).

Reviews and meta-analyses repeatedly conclude that more, better designed studies are required in order to make stronger recommendations about interventions for personality disorder (e.g. Bateman *et al*, 2015; Cristea *et al*, 2017).

Other frameworks for approaching intervention

In our experience, the utility of the evidence-based manualised interventions in meeting the needs of service users in the 'real life' circumstances of everyday service delivery has been limited. While they meet the needs of the small group of people who find meaning in these approaches, they have had limited utility in informing our ability to engage with the needs of the majority of service users. The background theory and ideas of the manualised interventions have provided information about how we think about people and their needs, but the danger has been and is that these interventions become in our minds the 'gold standard' of intervening and that our resources, efforts and expectations in our work with service users become narrowed to moving people into these therapies with the expected 'intra-psychic' change. Service users' engagement in the therapies becomes the goal of services, rather than being 'but one moment' in a process of assisting people to make change. If, as we argue, evidence-based manualised therapies have their place but provide only a limited lens by which to view personality disorder and intervention, how else can we conceptualise and create the circumstances for the consolidation and the development of interventions? As noted earlier, there have been a number of key developments in recent years which we find useful for informing our own conceptualisation of intervention in this area.

Epistemic trust

Epistemic trust is defined as 'trust in the authenticity and personal relevance of interpersonally transmitted knowledge' (Fonagy & Allison, 2014, p5). These authors propose that epistemic trust is an evolutionary system which facilitates learning from the social environment. They propose that personality disorder can be 'characterised by temporary or permanent disruption of epistemic trust and the social learning processes it enables' (2014, p7) and as 'a failure of communication arising from a breakdown in the capacity to forge learning relationships' (2017a, p3).

Of importance here is that the concept of epistemic trust (and the epistemic vigilance which results from its disruption) may help us understand why research has failed to find any meaningful differences in the effectiveness of the various therapies listed above, given that increases in epistemic trust are assumed to underpin any effective therapeutic approach. To put this another way, all effective therapies facilitate epistemic trust in people who 'struggle to relax their epistemic vigilance in … ordinary social situations' (Fonagy *et al*, 2014, p10).

At this point we should acknowledge the importance of understanding high levels of epistemic vigilance as adaptive, given that people have typically experienced an interpersonal world which is traumatic, abusive and invalidating. It is not our intention to replace one framework which positions the problems that people encounter as the result of core pathology (biomedical, diagnostic) with another (epistemic mistrust). In line with the Power Threat Meaning Framework (Johnstone & Boyle, 2018: see below) we understand high levels of epistemic vigilance to constitute an intelligible response to the experiences that individuals have encountered, which, typically, have involved the misuse of power.

With this in mind it is important to view Fonagy *et al*'s (2017b) proposal – that effective interventions occur in relatively benign environments via three 'communication systems' – as promoting the importance of therapeutic approaches which are responsive to early experiences of disempowerment, trauma and abuse.

The first of these communication systems highlights the importance of providing credible models to explain people's difficulties and to communicate the sense that the workers have knowledge that may be of use to the service user. Our understanding of this would be that effective therapies utilise a shared explanatory language which has personal relevance for the service user.

The second communication system provides a focus on facilitating mentalisation. The service user's agency is acknowledged and their experiences validated. This experience 'invites' the service user to step back from their epistemic isolation and utilise their own mentalising skills, with a view to engaging with and learning from the social environment. Once again, our understanding of this would be that an approach is advocated which seeks to learn from the service user, to understand their mind while also remaining congruent so that other minds can be experienced and thought about. The invitation here is for workers to be safe and authentic enough to be experienced as having something meaningful, relevant and interesting to offer. Notably, Fonagy *et al* (2017a) identify that effective interventions may well require more than a focus upon cognitive processes (that is, talking) to help people to be less inhibited and to promote mentalising. They identify that mentalising is an embodied process, and propose there is a role for physical activity and the development of potential future interventions may lie in this area.

The third communication system offers the possibility that learning may extend beyond this therapeutic relationship to the wider world. The aim is for the service user, in the context of increasing epistemic trust, to be better able to apply their learning in different contexts, to be increasingly resilient. Our understanding is that this is a communication system which characterises interventions which are essentially hopeful for the individual – which are outward-facing, flexible and continually looking to understand the application of what is learned to other situations and different contexts.

The literature on epistemic trust shifts our thinking about what constitutes effective intervention with people experiencing the difficulties associated with personality disorder. It suggests that there is a requirement to focus more on the interpersonal realm and the social world, with less focus upon intra-psychic change (Ramsden, 2018). The role of attachment in the therapeutic processes needs to be repositioned in order for intervention 'to accommodate the imperatives of the wider social environment within which the dyadic relationship is located' (Fonagy *et al*, 2017b, p5). In essence, the attachment relationship between the worker and the service user needs to be 'held' with a conscious acknowledgement of the wider environment and its expectations, and with a view that change ultimately occurs in the context of active engagement with the social learning opportunities of the wider world.

Integrated modular treatment

Livesley's (2017) approach provides an essential review, consolidation and development of the manualised therapies. He has created a clear and structured context and framework by which services can effectively engage with the offerings of the manualised therapies in a way which is congruent with and meaningful to people's and services' needs to work together in flexible and yet boundaried ways.

Livesley (2017) identifies that the research evidence for the manualised therapies indicates that the therapies do not differ in effectiveness; nor do they produce better outcomes than dedicated clinical care and supportive therapy. He identifies that there is an inherent challenge – when only using one approach – of how to effectively work with the heterogeneity of experiences and needs within a population defined as having 'personality disorder'. He further asserts that the focus for future intervention development should be upon combining the effective theoretical ideas and processes of all the therapies, and proposes a 'unified trans-theoretical … trans-diagnostic model that [can] be used for treating all forms of personality disorder' (2017, p. x).

Livesley (2017) identifies that the goal of intervention is to assist people to develop a 'personal niche … a coherent sense of self and an environment that supports the changes they have made and provides opportunities for further growth' (2017, p255). His framework emphasises the importance of the therapeutic relationship and identifies that the therapeutic relationship is the work of personality disorder services. He identifies a range of defined therapeutic strategies: *structure, treatment relationship, consistency, validation, self-reflection and motivation,* alongside several phases of intervention: *safety, containment and engagement; emotional regulation and modulation; exploration and change; and constructing an adaptive sense of self.* Specific techniques from the different manualised therapies are located within the different phases of intervention, with the therapeutic strategies providing the overall framework for the processes of intervention.

Logical errors

The concept of logical errors originally articulated by Murphy and McVey (2010) and further developed by Ramsden and Lowton (2014) offers another useful framework for engaging with the complexity of working with people with personality disorder. The concept asserts that the utilisation of automatic basic assumptions to help us make sense of an ambiguous social world leads to the possibility of a number of errors (misinterpretations). When those basic assumptions stem from very different attachment and other interpersonal experiences, the potential for miscommunication and error is increased leading to the potential for interpersonal rupture and potentially to iatrogenic interventions. Synthesising the logical worlds of service users and those working with them is advocated as being the ultimate aim of any intervention (Murphy & McVey, 2010).

Power Threat Meaning Framework

The Power Threat Meaning Framework (Johnstone & Boyle, 2018) clearly sets out much of what we intuitively know but have struggled to formally and comprehensively articulate: that effective interventions require workers to consciously engage with the knowledge that service users 'are where they are' because of early adverse circumstances related to the misuse of power. The framework articulates how behavioural and emotional responses associated with a 'personality disorder' diagnosis are actually attempts to survive and accommodate those early disempowerments.

The Power Threat Meaning Framework was developed in response to the lack of utility of the DSM and ICD diagnosis systems in facilitating effective understanding of and consequently effective intervention, creating instead a framework to understand and engage with mental health experience from 'a multi-factorial and contextual approach, which incorporates social, psychological and biological factors' (BPS, 2018, p7). The framework proposes a replacement of the biomedical question posed by DSM and ICD systems of diagnosis, of 'what is wrong with you?', with questions to facilitate understanding of an individual's mental health experience in the contexts of the experience of *power*, *threat*, *meaning*, *threat responses* and *life narrative* (e.g. 'what has happened to you?').

Re-imagining interventions

Contemporary challenges for those seeking to helpfully intervene in the lives of people identified as having a 'personality disorder' are very different from those in 2004, when the developments outlined in this chapter began. Critically, we now have a sense of what works for some people, and a sense of the limits of that knowledge. We also have new ways of conceptualising the experience of personality disorder. Our tasks now are to: (i) integrate and consolidate existing interventions within the context of new conceptualisations of personality disorder; and (ii) bring to the fore the 'new and emerging' knowledge and ideas to help structure and facilitate interventions with those currently excluded from or poorly served by our current interventions.

We illustrate our thinking by identifying four key principles which encapsulate our engagement with the above challenges. Our hope is that these principles provide a contemporary update to the existing literature on interventions and summarise much of what is already known and practised in progressive, specialist 'personality disorder' services. Our intention with these principles is that they stipulate an approach to intervention which is not specific to a particular setting or focused on individual pathology. Our hope is that they lend themselves to creative, co-produced interventions and can be used widely and flexibly to inform therapeutic activity across different settings by different workers.

1. The goal of interventions is the development of epistemic trust (or 'how I can learn to trust you and others?')

The ongoing processes of any intervention seek to provide opportunities for people to experience a reduction in heightened epistemic vigilance – a sufficient reduction in order to have opportunities to experience the potential benefits of adaptive attachment and the resolution of intra and interpersonal distress, as well as to reflect and learn from this experience, ultimately facilitating the experience of epistemic trust within the working relationship. These opportunities are for the person to be assisted to access social learning initially in the intervention setting and ultimately in the wider world.

> ## Case study 1: Joe / Core-OM service
>
> Joe received an IPP (Indeterminate Public Protection) sentence for arson and was released many years over tariff. While in prison a pattern emerged: whenever parole was being considered, Joe's behaviour deteriorated and his pending release was stopped. Eventually he was released to an Approved Premise. Joe's Offender Manager, Sara, was keen to establish a working relationship with him to facilitate the sentence plan. However, she noted that there was a distinct sense of 'unease' and 'tension' whenever she met him and she was left feeling after each meeting with a sense of 'anxiety' and 'doom'. Hostel staff also experienced similar feelings in their interactions with Joe. Sara arranged a meeting with the Offender Personality Disorder Pathway Core OM psychologist Maggie, to discuss her concerns. The psychologist formulated in collaboration with Sara the hypothesis that the 'request' by Sara for a working relationship with Joe, which 'required' him to 'think' about himself and others, was at the current time just too intrusive for Joe, and that Sara's sense of unease was related to Joe's heightened epistemic vigilance to the threat he felt that she posed. Sara and Maggie hypothesised that the desire for a typical working relationship was potentially a logical error. Joe's vigilance was formulated to be an adaptive response to his adverse childhood experiences, and indeed had facilitated his literal 'survival'. The formulation identified that to increase Joe's chances of remaining in the community, the 'request' for a 'working relationship' with Sara should be very limited, and for the time being the 'imperatives' of the social environment of the hostel should come to the fore and be the focus of the work. It was assumed that trust would be established not through interpersonal closeness but by Sara's availability and commitment to making things work for Joe. By helping him practically she acted to contain and manage his anxiety and communicate that she could be trusted.

2. Interventions are attuned to individual need and are deliberately focused upon facilitating change in means of survival, connection with others and quality of life (or 'am I going to learn and experience something useful about myself and others by doing this?')

Interventions are any deliberate activities, be they focused upon material, relational or social aspects of a person's life (e.g. housing and resettlement, to care co-ordination, to engagement in daily activity, to formal talking therapy), which are designed to make a useful impact upon and change in service users' circumstances.

This deliberately designed activity consciously accepts that service users are where they are because of disrupted early attachment experiences and trauma, and that people manage these adverse experiences in the contexts of their capacities and the wider cultural, social and physical environments.

Case formulation (Johnstone, 2014) informs the intervention of how to be with the person, of what to predict in terms of working with the person, of how to consciously engage with these dynamics and of where to do the intervention (i.e. the best-fit therapeutic, physical and social environment).

3. Interventions are primarily a relational process (or 'what's going on right here right now between us and what can I/we learn from it?')

Interventions and their contents are primarily vehicles for facilitating an adaptive, learning experience of engaging with and collaborating with another person. Our intentions, as workers, towards people are directly indicated by our ostensive cues (Fonagy *et al*, 2017) – ways of communicating which indicate that we have something in our minds that is worthwhile, interesting, relevant and important for this person. The worthwhileness (the evidence) of engaging in the intervention may be directly and physically tangible (i.e. housing, receiving benefits, making and eating a meal) or less obviously tangible (i.e. an emotional experience, techniques for managing emotion), but ultimately it is the experience of the processes of the relationship that is of primary importance for interventions. It is this relationship, not the content of interventions, which primarily facilitates epistemic trust.

Intervention (beyond immediate crisis intervention) is required to be a place of deliberate therapeutic tension and challenge, which comes about through the active process of mentalisation. The relationship is key to facilitating processes of mentalising (e.g. Bateman & Fonagy, 2004), of the 'sharing' of minds and of the work involved in 'synthesising' the logical position of these minds (Murphy & McVey, 2010). This is needed to indicate to people that it is ultimately tolerable and indeed useful to be 'thought about' and to 'think about' oneself and others. The activity of the intervention, be it predominately physically or verbally orientated, provides the means in the relationship for states of mind to be noticed and considered.

Case study 2: Ruby/care coordination

Ruby was a young adult referred for care coordination from CAMHS. Ruby had a long history of mental health difficulties, including serious self-harm leading to multiple long-term inpatient admissions. Ruby experienced and indicated a distrust of her care co-ordinator, Jack, and often failed to attend appointments. Over time, with careful and deliberate enactment by Jack of his role, guided by explicit reference to therapeutic strategies and phases of intervention, Ruby and Jack were able to develop their therapeutic relationship. In the context of the 'safety' of this relationship, Ruby was able to disclose continuing abuse within her family home. Jack suggested that they meet with a housing and resettlement worker to consider her options. The result of this was Ruby moving into supported accommodation. Jack shared the formulation that he and Ruby had been working on with the accommodation staff team. This facilitated the accommodation workers' ability to communicate with Ruby in an attuned manner, which lowered the potential for making logical errors. For example, Ruby regularly sought contact with staff during the early morning hours. This was initially perceived and understood by the staff as Ruby 'demanding extra and special treatment'. Utilising the formulation facilitated the staff's attitude and understanding of Ruby to move to one of her needing 'proximity to safe and containing attachment' in the context of her experiences of abuse. With this change in Ruby's experience of the staff at night time, Ruby was more able to build relationships with peers and staff, and with Jack was able to reflect upon the experience of these relationships and consequently able to identify their benefits. As Ruby became more settled and was actively 'utilising' the relationships with the accommodation staff, Jack wondered with Ruby about the potential of becoming more active in the wider social environment of the local community. Ruby started volunteering at a local community allotment.

Within the team supervision Jack received, the team noted a number of key events which they hypothesised led to a decrease in Ruby's epistemic vigilance and an increase and expansion in her epistemic trust – Jack's explicit attention to the dynamics and boundaries of the therapeutic relationship, the validation for Ruby of being believed and the containing action of finding new accommodation, the sharing of the formulation with the accommodation staff, and Ruby's engagement in voluntary work. All of these processes led to a sense for Ruby of the potential of other people (the social environment) and their contribution to her sense of well-being and quality of life.

4. Interventions are a collective endeavour (or 'are other people are helping us with this and we are all learning?')

The interpersonal dynamics of the relational work impact upon those delivering interventions. It is essential that these interpersonal dynamics are not just held by the individual worker, but are thought about and considered by a wider team. This wider team provides a team-mind and an external eye on the intervention. This thinking provides new information for the worker to take back into the intervention, but also facilitates the resilience of the individual worker to be able to consistently and usefully engage in the inevitable dynamics of the relationship.

There is a requirement for the learning from the experience of participating in interventions to contribute to ongoing processes of formulation and to inform engagement in other current and future interventions. The service which is providing the intervention is required to have systems in place which facilitate this communication.

Summary

This chapter identified two challenges that services providing interventions face – that our understanding of interventions is limited to those who find meaning in and can access our current interventions, and that we just don't know the needs of the majority of people who are currently excluded or ill-served by what is currently on offer. We have outlined these challenges in the context of prevailing narratives about the need to treat individual pathological processes – narratives which both reinforce and are reinforced by the ongoing development of manualised interventions. We have acknowledged the fact that none of these interventions are seemingly more effective than the other, and the danger – as we see it – of these manualised approaches ultimately being a limiting lens by which to view interventions and their ongoing development.

The alternative frameworks outlined in this chapter indicate, in our view, different ways of intervening. We assert that these frameworks provide the basis upon which to critically consider current approaches and, crucially, to design interventions which can better meet the needs of those who are ill-served by what we offer.

At the heart of what we have outlined here is a values-based approach: we believe that people with a diagnosis of personality disorder should be viewed as citizens with rights and responsibilities, whose presenting difficulties make sense in the context of their experiences of trauma, neglect and loss. The resulting emotional and interpersonal difficulties typically are the very factors which exclude them from accessing potentially helpful, evidence-based interventions. The 'problem of personality disorder', then, must be considered at a social and systemic level rather than a purely intrapsychic level. Pilgrim (2017) suggests that the concept of personality disorder is essentially a set of 'culturally situated judgments' and there are important developments in non-psychiatric perspectives which ask services to radically accept that individuals 'are where they are': that individual change may not be the current goal for interventions, and that more effective ways to relieve distress and reduce risk will be socially, systemically and environmentally focused.

We hope that there is a sense of liberation in what we have outlined. The goal is not attendance in formal therapy; instead, the offer is a relationship which exists within a supportive (team) framework that helps workers retain their minds – to be compassionate, focused and authentic, and to work collaboratively on something that really helps.

References

Bartak A, Andrea H, Spreeuwenberg MD, Ziegler UM, Dekker J, Rossum BV, Hamers EFM, Scholte W, Aerts J, Busschbach JJV, Verheul R, Stijnen T & Emmelkamp PNG (2011) Effectiveness of outpatient, day hospital, and inpatient psychotherapeutic treatment for patients with Cluster B personality disorders. *Psychotherapy and Psychosomatics* **80** 28–38.

Bateman A & Fonagy P (2004) *Psychotherapy for Borderline Personality Disorder: Mentalisation Based Treatment*. Oxford: Oxford University Press.

Bateman A & Fonagy P (2009) Randomized controlled trial of outpatient mentalization-based treatment versus structured clinical management for borderline personality disorder. *American Journal of Psychiatry* **166** 1355–1364.

Bateman AW, Gunderson J & Mulder R (2015) Treatment of personality disorder. *The Lancet* **385** 735–743.

Bateman A, O'Connell J, Lorenzini N, Gardner T & Fonagy P (2016) A randomised controlled trial of mentalization-based treatment versus structured clinical management for patients with comorbid borderline personality disorder and antisocial personality disorder. *BioMedCentral Psychiatry* **16** (304) 1–11.

Beck AT & Freeman A (1990) *Cognitive Therapy of Personality Disorders*. New York: Guilford Press.

Bernstein DP, Nijman HL, Karos K, Keulen-de Vos M, de Vogel V & Lucker TP (2012) Schema therapy for forensic patients with personality disorders: Design and preliminary findings of a multicenter randomized clinical trial in the Netherlands. *International Journal of Forensic Mental Health* **11** (4) 312–324.

Black DW, Simsek-Duran F, Blum N, McCormick B & Allen J (2016) Do people with borderline personality disorder complicated by antisocial personality disorder benefit from the STEPPS treatment program? *Personality and Mental Health* **10** (3) 205–215.

Beck AT & Freeman A (1990) *Cognitive Therapy of Personality Disorders*. New York: Guilford Press.

Blum N, Pfohl B, St. John D, Monahan P & Black DW (2002) STEPPS: A cognitive-behavioral systems-based group treatment for outpatient clients with borderline personality disorder – a preliminary report. *Comprehensive Psychiatry* **43** 301–310.

British Psychological Society (2018) *Power Threat Meaning Framework Overview*. Leicester: BPS.

Budge SL, Moore JT, Del Re AC, Wampold BE, Baardseth TP & Nienhuis JB (2014) The effectiveness of evidence-based treatments for personality disorders when comparing treatment-as-usual and bona fide treatments. *Clinical Psychology Review* **33** 1057–1066.

Cambridge Online Dictionary (2019) Intervention. Retrieved from https://dictionary.cambridge.org/dictionary/english/intervention

Campling P & Haigh R (eds) (1999) *Therapeutic Communities: Past, Present and Future*. London: Jessica Kingsley Publishers.

Cann J, Falshaw L, Nugent F & Friendship C (2003) *Understanding What Works: Accredited Cognitive Skills Programmes for Adult Men and Young Offenders*. Home Office Research Findings Number 226. London: Home Office.

Capone G, Schroder T, Clarke SP & Braham L (2016) Outcomes of therapeutic community treatment for personality disorder. Retrieved from core.ac.uk/download/pdf/74207303.pdf

Chanen AM, Jackson HJ, McCutcheon LK, Jovev M, Dudgeon P, Yuen HP, Germano D, Nistico H, McDougall E, Weinstein C, Clarkson V & McGorry PD (2008) Early intervention for adolescents with borderline personality disorder using cognitive analytic therapy: Randomised controlled trial. *British Journal of Psychiatry* **193** (6) 477–484.

Clarke S, Thomas P & James K (2013) Cognitive analytic therapy for personality disorder: Randomised controlled trial. *British Journal of Psychiatry* **202** 129–134.

Clarkin JF, Yeomans FE & Kernberg OE (1999) *Psychotherapy for Borderline Personality*. New York: John Wiley & Sons.

Clarkin JF, Levy KN, Lenzenweger MF & Kernberg OF (2007) evaluating three treatments for borderline personality disorder: A multiwave study. *American Journal of Psychiatry* **164** 922–928.

Cristea IA, Gentili C, Cotet CD, Palomba D, Barbui C & Cuijpers P (2017) Efficacy of psychotherapies for borderline personality disorder: A systematic review and meta-analysis. *JAMA Psychiatry* **74** (4) 319–328.

Dale O, Sethi F, Stanton C, Evans S, Barnicot K, Sedgwick R, Goldsach S, Doran M, Shoolbred C, Samele C, Urquia N, Haigh R & Moran P (2017) Personality disorder services in England: Findings from a national survey. *BJPsych Bulletin* **41** (5) 247–253.

Davidson K (2007) *Cognitive Therapy for Personality Disorders: A Guide for Clinicians* (2nd Edition). New York: Routledge.

Davidson K, Norrie J, Tyrer P, Gumley A, Tata P, Murray H & Palmer S (2006) The effectiveness of cognitive behaviour therapy for borderline personality disorder: Results from the borderline personality disorder study of cognitive therapy (BOSCOT) trial. *Journal of Personality Disorder* **20** (5) 450–465.

Davidson K, Tyrer P, Tata P, Cooke D, Gumley A, Ford I & Crawford M (2009) Cognitive behaviour therapy for violent men with antisocial personality disorder in the community: An exploratory randomized controlled trial. *Psychological Medicine* **39** (4) 569–577.

Doering S, Horz S, Rentrop M, Fischer-Kern M, Schuster P, Benecke C, Buchheim A, Martius P & Buchheim P (2010) Transference-focused psychotherapy v. treatment by community psychotherapists for borderline personality disorder: Randomised controlled trial. *The British Journal of Psychiatry* **196** 389–395.

Duggan C, Huband N, Smailagic N, Ferriter M & Adams C (2007) The use of psychological treatments for people with personality disorder: A systematic review of randomized controlled trials. *Personality and Mental Health* **1** 95–125.

Emmelkamp PM, Benner A, Kuipers A, Feiertag GA, Koster HC & van Apeldoorn FJ (2006) Comparison of brief dynamic and cognitive-behavioural therapies in avoidant personality disorder. *British Journal of Psychiatry* **189** 60–64.

Fonagy P & Allison E (2012) What is mentalization? The concept and its foundations in developmental research. In: Midgley N and Vrouva I (eds) *Minding the Child – Mentalization Based Interventions with Children, Young People and Their Families*. Hove: Routledge.

Fonagy P & Allison E (2014) The role of epistemic trust in the therapeutic relationship. *Psychotherapy* **51** (3) 372–380.

Fonagy P, Luyten P & Allison E (2015) Epistemic petrification and the restoration of epistemic trust – a new conceptualisation of borderline personality disorder and its psychosocial treatment. *Journal of Personality Disorders* **29** (5) 575–609.

Fonagy P, Luyten P, Allison E & Campbell C (2017a) What we have changed our minds about: Part 1. Borderline personality disorder as a limitation of resilience. *Borderline Personality Disorder and Emotion Dysregulation* **4** (11) DOI 10.1186/s40479-017-0061-9.

Fonagy P, Luyten P, Allison E & Campbell C (2017b) What we have changed our minds about: Part 2. Borderline personality disorder, epistemic trust and the developmental significance of social communication. *Borderline Personality Disorder and Emotional Dysregulation* **4** (9) DOI 10.1186/s40479-017-0062-8.

Friendship C, Blud L, Erikson M, & Travers R (2002) *An Evaluation of Cognitive Behavioural Treatment for Prisoners*. Home Office Research Report Findings 161. London: Home Office

Gibbon S, Duggan C, Stoffers J, Huband N, Völlm BA, Ferriter M & Lieb K (2010) Psychological interventions for antisocial personality disorder. *Cochrane Database of Systematic Reviews*, Issue 6. Art. No.: CD007668. DOI: 10.1002/14651858.CD007668.pub2.

Giesen-Bloo J, van Dyck R, Spinhoven P, van Tilburg W, Dirksen C, van Asselt T, Kremers I, Nadort M & Arntz A (2006) Outpatient psychotherapy for borderline personality disorder: Randomized trial of schema-focused therapy vs transference-focused psychotherapy. Archives of General Psychiatry 63 649–658.

Gilbert P (2010) *Compassion Focussed Therapy – Distinctive Features*. Hove: Routledge.

Grenyer BFS, Lewis KL, Fanaian M & Kotze B (2018) Treatment of personality disorder using a whole of service stepped care approach: A cluster randomized controlled trial. PLoS ONE **13** (11) e0206472. https://doi.org/10.13711/journal.pone.0206472

Haigh R & Lees J (2008) Fusion TCs: Divergent histories, converging challenges. *Therapeutic Communities* **29** 347–374.

Johnstone L (2014) *Formulation in Psychology and Psychotherapy – Making Sense of People's Problems* (2nd edition). Hove: Routledge.

Johnstone L & Boyle M with Cromby J, Harper D, Kinderman P, Longden E, Pilgrim D & Read J (2018) *The Power Threat Meaning Framework: Towards the Identification of Patterns in Emotional Distress, Unusual Experiences and Troubled or Troubling Behaviour*. Leicester: British Psychological Society.

Jorgensen CR, Freund C, Bøye R, Jordet H, Andersen D & Kjølbye ML (2013) Outcome of mentalization-based and supportive psychotherapy in patients with borderline personality disorder: A randomized trial. *Acta Psychiatrica Scandinavica* **127** 305–317.

Koons CR, Robins CJ, Tweed JL, Lynch TR, Gonzalez AM, Morse JQ, Bishop GK, Butterfield MI & Bastian LA (2001) Efficacy of dialectical behavior therapy in women veterans with borderline personality disorder. *Behavior Therapy* **32** 371–390.

Kröger C, Harbeck S, Armbrust M & Kliem S (2013) Effectiveness, response, and dropout of dialectical behavior therapy for borderline personality disorder in an inpatient setting. *Behaviour Research and Therapy* **51** 411–416.

Leichsenring F & Leibing E (2003) The effectiveness of psychodynamic therapy and cognitive behavior therapy in the treatment of personality disorders: A meta-analysis. *American Journal of Psychiatry* **160** 1223–1232.

Leichsenring F, Leibing E, Kruse J, New AS & Leweke F (2011) Borderline personality disorder. *The Lancet* **377** 74–84.

Lewis G & Appleby K (1988) Personality disorder: The patients psychiatrists dislike. *British Journal of Psychiatry* **153** (1) 44–49.

Linehan MM (1993) *Cognitive-Behavioural Treatment of Borderline Personality Disorder.* London: Guilford Press.

Linehan MM, Comtois KA, Murray AM, Brown MZ, Gallop RJ, Heard HL, Korslund KE, Tutek DA, Reynolds SK & Lindenboim N (2006) Two-year randomized controlled trial and follow-up of dialectical behavior therapy vs therapy by experts for suicidal behaviours and borderline personality disorder. *Archives of General Psychiatry* **63** 757–766.

Livesley WJ (2017) *Integrated Modular Treatment for Borderline Personality Disorder – A Practical Guide to Combining Effective Treatment Methods.* Cambridge: Cambridge University Press.

McGauley G, Yakeley J, Williams A & Bateman A (2011) Attachment, mentalization and antisocial personality disorder: The possible contribution of mentalization based treatment. *European Journal of Psychotherapy & Counselling* **13** (4) 371–393.

McMain SF, Links PS, Gnam WH, Guimond T, Cardish RJ, Korman L & Streiner DL (2009) A randomized trial of dialectical behavior therapy versus general psychiatric management for borderline personality disorder. *American Journal of Psychiatry* **166** 1365–1374.

McMurran M, Huband N & Overton E (2010) Non-completion of personality disorder treatments: A systematic review of correlates, consequences, and interventions. *Clinical Psychology Review* **30** 277–287.

Murphy N & McVey D (2010) Fundamental treatment strategies for optimising interventions with people with personality disorder. In: N Murphy and D McVey (eds) *Treating Personality Disorder – Creating Robust Services for People with Complex Mental Health Needs.* London: Routledge.

National Institute for Health and Care Excellence (2009a) *Antisocial Personality Disorder: The Nice Guideline on Treatment, Management and Prevention* (NICE Clinical Practice Guideline No 77). Retrieved from https://www.nice.org.uk/guidance/cg77/evidence/full-guideline-pdf-242104429

National Institute for Health and Care Excellence (2009b) *Borderline Personality Disorder: Treatment and Management* (NICE Clinical Practice Guideline No. 78). Retrieved from https://www.nice.org.uk/guidance/cg78/evidence/full-guideline-pdf-242147197

National Institute for Health and Care Excellence (2009c) *Depression in Adults: Recognition and Management* (NICE Clinical Practice Guideline No. 90). Retrieved from https://www.nice.org.uk/guidance/cg90/evidence/full-guidline-pdf-4840934509

National Institute for Health and Care Excellence (2009d) *Psychosis and Schizophrenia in Adults: Prevention and Management* (NICE Clinical Practice Guideline No. 178). Retrieved from https://www.nice.org.uk/guidance/cg178/evidence/full-guideline-pdf-490503565

NHS England/National Offender Management Service (2015) *Working with Offenders with Personality Disorder – A Practitioner's Guide.* London: NHS England Publications.

Paris J (2013) Stepped care: An alternative to routine extended treatment for patients with borderline personality disorder. *Psychiatric Services* **64** (10) 1035–1037.

Pilgrim D (2017) Incorrigible conduct and incorrigible diagnoses: The case of personality disorder. *Social Theory and Health* **15** (4) 388–406.

Personality Disorder Knowledge and Understanding Framework Partnership (2009) *Developing and Extending Therapeutic Practice – Student Learning Guide.* Nottingham: Open University.

Ramsden J & Lowton M (2014) Probation practice with personality disordered offenders: The importance of avoiding errors of logic. *Probation Journal* https://doi.org/10.1177%2F0264550514523815

Ramsden J, Hirons A, Maltman L & Mullen T (2017) Finding our way: Early learning from the Compass Project, an intensive intervention risk management service for women. *The Journal of Forensic Psychiatry and Psychology* **28** (2) 257–273.

Ramsden, J (2018) 'Are you calling me a liar?' Clinical interviewing more for trust than knowledge with high risk men with antisocial personality disorder. *International Journal of Forensic Mental Health* **17** (4) 351–361. DOI: 10.1080/14999013.2018.1505789

Ryle A (1997) *Cognitive Analytic Therapy for Borderline Personality Disorder: The Model and the Method*. Chichester: John Wiley & Sons.

Simon W (2009) Follow-up psychotherapy outcome of patients with dependent, avoidant and obsessive-compuls*ive personality disorders: A meta-analytic review*. International Journal of Psychiatry in Clinical Practice **13** 153–165.

Stoffers-Winterling JM, Völlm BA, Rücker G, Timmer A, Huband N & Lieb K (2012) Psychological therapies for people with borderline personality disorder. *Cochrane Database of Systematic Reviews*, Issue 8. Art. No.: CD005652. DOI: 10.1002/14651858.CD005652.pub2.

Svartberg M, Stiles TC & Seltzer MH (2004) Randomized, controlled trial of the effectiveness of short-term dynamic psychotherapy and cognitive therapy for cluster C personality disorders. *American Journal of Psychiatry* **161** 810–817.

Warren F, McGauley G, Norton K, Dolan B, Preedy-Fayers K, Pickering A & Geddes JR (2003) *Review of Treatment for Severe Personality Disorder*. Home Office Report 30/03. London: Home Office.

Wierzbicki M & Pekarik G (1993) A meta-analysis of psychotherapy dropout. *Professional Psychology: Research and Practice* **24** 190–195.

Winston A, Laikin M, Pollack J, Samstag LW, McCullough L & Muran JC (1994) Short-term psychotherapy of personality disorders. *American Journal of Psychiatry* **151** 190–194.

Verheul R, Van Den Bosch LMC, Koeter MWJ, De Ridder MAJ, Stijnen T & Van Den Brink W (2003) Dialectical behaviour therapy for women with borderline personality disorder: 12-month, randomised clinical trial in The Netherlands. *British Journal of Psychiatry* **182** 135–140.

Young J (2003) *Schema Therapy: A Practitioner's Guide*. New York: Guilford Press.

Chapter 9:

Service User Involvement and Co-production in Personality Disorder Services: An Invitation to Transcend Re-Traumatising Power Politics

Melanie Anne Ball

Introduction

Across contemporary mental health services, and especially in the context of 'personality disorder' services, it is necessary to push beyond the boundaries of traditional service user involvement and instead adopt the methodology of co-production. This chapter will proffer co-production as a framework for re-assigning power, responsibilities and resources, and consequently as a means of avoiding re-traumatising experiences for those undertaking this work. I will highlight and offer solutions around especially problematic areas, including the identification of examples of 'good enough practice': case studies of innovative service design or delivery to consider replicating in your own settings. The language of 'good enough' has been knowingly selected to reflect the embryonic stage of national development regarding the application of co-production in this area. By the time of your own reading, some of the roles described may have been lost in service transformations or, conversely, identified as national examples of excellence. However, at the time of writing it is too early to tell. It is fair to say, though, that all of the examples given will hold their own idiosyncrasies and challenges, which will not be explored here.

First, though, a note on the terminology of 'personality disorder'. This notoriously controversial diagnosis can be said to cast a vast and dark shadow: reportedly correlating with a shortened life expectancy by 19 years for women and 18 years for men, and affecting 'between 4% and 15%' for North America and Western Europe (Tyrer *et al*, 2015). However, as with most psychiatric disorders, even if the distress is undoubtedly, heartachingly real for the person experiencing it, the absence or presence of personality disorder is impossible to detect absolutely. Where a diagnosis is applied, it is on the basis of a hugely imperfect, highly subjective assessment method, and wholly dependent on the strength of belief in systems such as the Diagnostic Statistical Manual (DSM-5) (American Psychiatric Association, 2013) or International Classification of Diseases and Related Health Problems (ICD-10) (World Health Organisation, 2018). Despite this lack of medical evidence to bolster the construct of personality disorder, a compelling body of evidence is growing to support the notion of personality disorder as a diagnosis with the potential to highly damage and further stigmatise already traumatised people (Sheehan *et al*, 2016; Personality Disorder in the Bin, 2016).

Given these critical voices, the exploration in this chapter is not intended to lend any legitimacy to the terminology services use to describe themselves using the 'personality disorder' term. As such, the guidance I have outlined and considered would apply to working with any group defined by high levels of trauma survival within their collective identity – arguably, that being anyone who has been exposed to the mental health system. This is reflective of my own conceptualisation of the diagnosis' validity in my own life and indicates my own preference regarding redesign of our mental health and social care provision.

Thus, this chapter is indebted to those illuminating critical discourses around the construct of the personality disorder diagnosis. Without it, it would be impossible for myself and many others working from a position of lived experience to move past the injuries sustained by the stigma related to the label in order to think clearly about the politics of co-production and power. It is therefore imperative that both pressure groups opposing the diagnosis and those in a closer relationship with the status quo keep attempting to hear one another with dignity and understanding. However painful, brutal or challenging the alternate perspectives might be, we can't afford to silence valuable voices or shut out people whose experiences challenge our own.

It is also important for me to acknowledge that, throughout this chapter, I will focus primarily on highlighting areas where co-production might present as particularly challenging for those involved as 'registered healthcare professionals' or 'people with professional learning'. I am writing on the assumption that the majority of readers will identify as registered healthcare professionals, and thus I am electing to highlight details that will prove most useful to them. I have chosen to write with this specific focus without the input of a registered healthcare professional co-production partner in order to reverse the common configuration of a person with professional learning writing around the collective experiences of the community with lived experience. As for the challenges uniquely experienced by service users and carers during these processes, I would invite readers to jointly identify how these locally manifest as an ongoing aspect of the co-production process itself.

The case for involvement and co-production

Simply put by The Offender Health Collaboration (2015, p1): 'there is a growing recognition that because of their direct experiences of using services, service users have a unique insight into what works, which can be used to improve services'.
In addition, key legislation surrounding patient and public involvement across services, such as the Health and Social Care Act 2012, as well as guidance from NHS England, the Care Quality Commission (CQC) and other government bodies, demands the involvement of 'people using the service' (regulation 17, Health and Social Care Act, 2012), with the stipulation that providers must 'actively engage, liaise and communicate with Service Users, [...] their Carers and Legal Guardians'. Therefore there is no room for service providers to be passive agents in the process of service user involvement.

It is important that public and patient involvement (PPI), service user involvement and co-production, as well as user-led initiatives and peer support initiatives, are not flippantly conflated into one another. However, they are usually conceptualised to stand in close relationship to one another (e.g. Slay & Stephens, 2013). Arnstein (1969), for example, conceptualises this within her ladder of citizen participation model. A 2009 report jointly produced by the New Economics Foundation and Nesta (Nesta, 2012) further clarifies that co-production 'goes well beyond the idea of "citizen engagement" or "service user involvement" to foster the principle of equal partnership':

> 'Co-production shifts the balance of power, responsibility and resources from professionals to individuals, by involving people in the delivery of their own services. It recognises that "people are not merely repositories of need or recipients of services", but are the very resource that can turn public services around. Coproduction also means unleashing a wave of innovation about how

*services are designed and delivered [...] It offers to transform the dynamic
between the public and public service workers, putting an end to "them" and
"us". Instead, people pool different types of knowledge and skills, based on lived
experience and professional learning.' (p11)*

The process-oriented benefits of co-production are often an integral aspect of
anecdotal evaluation or reflections on outcomes. For example, the transformational
and re-energising experience of working alongside someone in their recovery from
a condition once believed to be 'untreatable' (as is often the case in co-production
related to personality disorder) should not be underestimated. Indeed, interactions
which reinforce the overarching reason for holding hope can be argued as a
protective measure against staff burnout. Similarly, the level of authenticity
required from all in order to undertake a co-production process is often an effective
way of meeting divisive notions of 'us' and 'them'; the emphasis on working
across boundaries allows those engaged as registered healthcare professionals to
relinquish their supposed expertise potentially in a radically freeing way. The relief
of being able to acknowledge not having the answers, and the notion that some
answers may, in fact, sit with the affected community, can lead to innovative and
positive discourse which removes the barriers to working effectively together.

Equally, the direct benefits to those with lived experience being involved should
not be minimised. Notably, co-production supports people with lived experience to
tell their story with purpose in a way that minimises opportunities for tokenistic
engagement or exploitation. In addition, co-production and the way in which it
emphasises people as assets, and places responsibility on locating assets rather
than deficits within all, supports those with lived experience to continue on a
journey of integration of the whole self. Thus, the unhelpful binary division common
for those of us with a lived experience of receiving and recovering from a personality
disorder diagnosis – of a high-functioning able side versus the deficient and sick
identity – is challenged via the process. Over time, in its place, a conceptualisation
of value and meaning can be located in 'the lost years', which in turn, leads many
to an eventual sense of overall purpose. I would assert that, for this community, the
benefit of integrating the side of oneself which has been most loathed and berated
for its inability or dysfunction with the strengthening self-image of someone
who has something to offer the world can be transformational, and is therefore
especially important to consider when selecting an involvement methodology.

Though the business case specific to systems related to personality disorder
is still in its infancy, there is substantial evidence to support co-production in
terms of more generic mental health. Nesta's People Powered Health programme,
which included 'people helping people (peer support); [...] and user co-design
and co-delivery' suggested 'savings of at least £4.4 billion a year [for the NHS

in England]' (Nesta, 2013). Similarly, an ImROC (Implementing Recovery through Organisational Change) briefing paper on the business case for recovery specifically states that 'a review of evidence on co-production in mental health identified a number of studies [...] associated with reduced healthcare costs' (Slade *et al*, 2017, p24).

The selection of involvement methodology should be decided upon in relation to the context of the involvement activity. Though eventually cost-effective, co-production is often considered to be resource-intensive and often includes the necessity to train all contributing to the process to a level of equal literacy regarding the approach. In certain health settings, such as palliative care, it might be highly challenging to adhere closely to strict co-production principles and more appropriate to undertake other forms of involvement or engagement. Where this is the case, it is important to be transparent regarding the departure from the preferred model of co-production, and regularly revisit dialogue raising awareness of how this maintains some of the less helpful power relations.

In my own observations, the selection of methodology is often not context-driven and is instead dictated less thoughtfully by local culture. Patient leadership theorist David Gilbert considers the insight and wisdom of those with lived experience to be 'jewels from the caves of suffering' (Gilbert, 2019, p4). He goes on to highlight problematic relationships that are established by the methodology adopted to access these 'jewels', commenting: 'traditional patient and public engagement relies on (child–parent) feedback or (adolescent–parent) "representative" approaches that fail to value this expertise and buffers patients' influence' (p4).

Shifting the balance of explicit power

Gilbert articulates a correlation between involvement methodology and the impact on relationships between people with lived experience and those involved as registered professionals. This illuminates the first reason why co-production is a preferable method for undertaking involvement-related activities with populations for whom significant relationships may have been traumatising: the potential it has to mitigate adverse effects on relationships. Co-production principles have the potential to redress power imbalances, and instead of reinforcing historically disempowered roles, the co-production partners with lived experience are elevated to empowered roles of equality. Given the prevalence of adverse childhood experiences for those who have received a personality disorder diagnosis, it is clear to see how a coerced infantilisation via a disempowered role in more tokenistic involvement activities might lead to potentially re-traumatising experiences. For example, processes that come to feel exploitative or entrapping can re-enact and reignite the traumas of an abusive caregiver causing harm. The foundational principles of co-production have the potential to protect everyone against these experiences. Often, those with lived experience of how re-traumatising these experiences can be are best placed to advise on and facilitate processes which avoid them; the role of the lived experience practitioner as a professional facilitator of co-production processes will be discussed later in this chapter.

Notably, the principles of co-production dovetail with the underlying philosophies of effective clinical interventions for those of us who have received a diagnosis of personality disorder. Unlike pharmaceutical interventions, psychotherapy cannot be forced: it is inherently co-productive as a process and requires some level of mutuality, reciprocity and collaboration between the person with the lived experience and the individual with a clinical training, all of which are features of co-production as it is defined by Nesta (2012). Therefore, the less empowering and more traditional involvement models are not viable options for this group of services or the people who populate them. Admittedly, it should be queried whether the mental health industry at large wishes to continue replicating coercion, infantilisation and restriction in any of its involvement activities. Particularly as critiques regarding the validity of all diagnostic labels increase, if involvement methodologies were commonly selected on the basis of accessibility and suitability for the context and groups with which they were being applied, one might see a surge in the use of co-production and a mammoth reduction in less empowering involvement processes. There is a bizarre hypocrisy to the expectation that people should tolerate a less empowering engagement style as they move into their recovery than that which they experienced during a co-productively undertaken treatment process.

'Good enough' practice example:

West London Health Trust (WLHT) Managed Clinical Network (MCN), Network Coordinator

The Managed Clinical Network at West London Health Trust holds the primary task of delivering training and consultation to improve the quality of care for those with difficulties associated with the diagnosis of personality disorder. The MCN has developed a co-produced, whole systems approach and works across West London Health Trust and beyond, delivering training to staff, service users and carers to NHS, third and independent sector organisations. The team comprises a team manager, and two Network Coordinators.

The team's approach to work is totally co-produced, including the two Network Coordinator roles within the team established on a 'mirror image' model, with one

continued ➜

post-holder primarily informed by training in a traditional health discipline, and the 'mirror image' post-holder primarily informed by their own lived experience and extensive experience of professionally utilising this in systems related to personality disorder. WLHT MCN's commitment to hold both experiential and training-based knowledge in equally high regard is evident in the identical banding and naming of the two Network Coordinator posts. As a consequence, the following is achieved:

- Organisational commitment to co-production and the value of expertise brought by LXP is modelled.
- Power is symbolically more balanced.
- Responsibility is shared.
- Value of expertise indicated through banding of post and balanced 'sharing' of resource.

Shifting the assumed balance of resources

Co-production next consolidates its suitability for personality disorder contexts in the way it shifts the balance in resources. We have seen a 'good enough practice' example of how this might relate to tangible resources such as payment and we will come to see how this relates to resources such as employment structures and staff support. However, I would also like to present the potency of psychological resources: structures which support us to think about ourselves and be able to reflect on our experiences in order to develop self-awareness. It is particularly important that in 'shifting the balance' of these resources we identify all of the emotional 'baggage' brought to the process, including that of the registered professionals.

This chapter has consciously avoided explicitly addressing some of the commonly perceived 'challenges' (usually asserted by professional service providers) which tend to be referred to as a rationale for avoiding co-produced ways of working. This avoidance reflects a central argument of this chapter – that the majority of these barriers relate to worker and organisational anxiety. For example, earlier in the chapter, it was suggested that co-production helps professionals to abandon their expertise. It was suggested that this might be 'radically freeing'. It is, however, acknowledged that this may also be anxiety-provoking, given that so much personal identity is frequently invested in professional expertise and knowledge.

The notion of organisational anxiety and the emergence of 'social defences' (Menzies-Lyth, 1960) is pertinent here. It is a central assumption of this book that organisations experience anxiety in relation to the task of caring for and/ or managing other human beings, especially where those human beings are

experiencing distress. Arguably, barriers to humane ways of working with others
(let alone involvement activity) serve to protect the workforce from this anxiety
at the expense of the service user.

One way in which organisations tend to protect themselves from anxiety about
'not knowing' in the arena of co-production is to uphold an assumption that those
with a primary background of professional learning are more 'psychologically
healthy' or 'self-aware' than their counterparts with lived experience. Next, I will
give examples of how this assumption can be problematic. We will explore how
a flattened hierarchy of power and equity in accessing structures that support
reflection can be protective. Alison Cameron (2015) is often cited as referring to
co-production as feeling 'messy and risky'. This author states: 'If we can take the
risk of emerging from our boxes of "patient" or "professional" and venture into the
territory where boundaries are blurred, and both "sides" are prepared to walk in the
shoes of the other, then we have the potential to create something radically new.'

In this blog, Cameron isn't referring to specific co-production around personality
disorder systems, and yet many readers whose experiences of co-production have
been solely within personality disorder-specific contexts will recognise these
feelings. Often the 'mess' that Cameron refers to within any co-productive process
is mistaken to be an aspect of the specific environment in which the co-production is
taking place, or, worse, a symptomatic by-product of the group of people with lived
experience who are undertaking the co-production as partners.

When the imperfect, human and 'messy' co-production process is pathologised,
it may begin to stir echoes of the roles that all co-production partners have
brought with them to the table. Indeed, the interpersonal challenges associated
with gathering any group of imperfect humans to work collectively may come to
the surface – and at times, some of these interactions may even feel impacted
upon by someone's personality imperfections. But these challenges must not be
conceptualised as someone's 'schemas' beginning to dictate their interactions or
some kind of inner 'beast' escaping from its usual dialectical behaviour therapy
(DBT)-fashioned imprisonment. When these interpretations enter the process,
positions that began in a state of equilibrium are interrupted. By this point, the
registered healthcare professional has reverted to observing their co-production
partner, poised to detect any hint of pathology, whilst the understandably
outraged, misinterpreted person with lived experience is left to protest their sanity.
Furthermore, traumatic memories of prior stigmatising interactions with healthcare
professionals – of being over-pathologised, unheard, disbelieved, demonised or
dismissed – can be stirred up while the apparent response from their co-production
partner is to locate all of the 'mess' within the person with a diagnosis. Thus, an
uncomfortably familiar (and potentially re-traumatising) trope is played out.

Another way in which organisational anxiety at the sharing of power is avoided is, perhaps, through adopting a position of smug vindication at the expression of any distress by the person with a diagnosis. Often this vindication is accompanied by an ego-centric sigh of 'well, what did we expect? Of course it's going to be like this – they're [unwell/service users/patients/mad people/personality disordered]!' The most disturbing version of this statement is accompanied by a pseudo-compassionate, highly paternalistic reflection on the co-production process, as if its eventual failure was inevitable: 'of course they sabotaged it – just like whenever they try to do anything involving relationships'. Often in environments with particularly combative cultures, statements such as these support the notion that working with people with a personality disorder is so especially challenging that it is impossible for anyone aside from the registered health professional to do 'properly'. The supposed 'sabotage' of the co-production process on behalf of the person with a diagnosis is in fact, unconsciously or not, a far more complicated sabotaging power play on behalf of their (anxious) co-production partner.

This is not to say that colleagues should stand by cooly should their co-worker begin to experience work as overwhelming, triggering or disempowering. It is incumbent on any healthy organisation to ensure that all workers are looked out for and looked after. In the interests of managing organisational anxiety, it is suggested that explicit discussions about power form part of the co-production process. These discussions, though at times uncomfortable to navigate, can ensure transparency around problematic organisational responses and reduce the perceived personal nature of the interactions and the likelihood of any party internalising the fallout of the process 'messiness'. There can be a radically re-orienting shift once power imbalance and influence is acknowledged within the process via contextualising the dynamics within a theoretical framework, and especially one that considers the systems and roles as opposed to the individuals and personalities within the process. This chapter invites the registered health professional to reflect on their professional identity and how anxiety associated with its maintenance (or loss) may interfere with ambitions around co-production. In a blog written for the BMJ, for example, Anna Mead Robson acknowledges data presented at the International Congress of the Royal College of Psychiatrists in 2010 which suggested that broad perceptions of psychiatry were that it was one of the least competitive medical specialties, and that 'one-quarter of the psychiatrists said they avoid disclosing their profession in social situations. One-third said their family was disappointed in their career choice' (Mead Robson, 2010). With such challenging and stigmatised professional identities adopted as a starting point, perhaps it is no surprise that some individuals within these professional groups feel a need to inflate their own professional self-image and reinforce the perceived importance of their work – in the process unintentionally dehumanising their client groups – as a protective strategy for psychic survival that creates further challenges for undertaking effective co-production.

Organisationally sanctioned social defences may mean that it is not necessarily realistic to expect registered healthcare professionals to have workplace cultures which support the required level of reflection to notice and consider their emotional responses to the co-production process. It is likely that many practitioners may have never had the opportunity to develop this level of reflectivity and self-awareness. Somewhat ironically, of the two groups of co-producers, it may well be the service users or lived experience practitioners who are more capable of this level of reflection, as frequent graduates of long-term psychotherapy programmes, where tools to support self-reflection and self-awareness are developed. Similarly, it is often assumed that the experience of returning to work somewhere of therapeutic significance will be most challenging for the lived experience practitioner.

On my own journey, however, I experienced the opposite: it was those who had previously known me as a patient who found my return most disturbing. In particular, the psychotherapy staff seemed to find my existence more challenging than my nursing colleagues. Those who were accustomed to working collaboratively alongside people, with 'what's strong, rather than what's wrong', appeared to find my integration into the team notably easier.

In attempting to understand the disturbance provoked by my presence, I considered what significance the theoretical approach of the service might hold – in this instance, a psychoanalytically informed context. Though I have described therapy as inherently collaborative, there does appear to be a spectrum of power relations between the schools of psychotherapeutic approaches. Theoretical approaches with a heavier emphasis on the role of the unconscious (thus a powerful force which is usually familiar to the therapist and unfamiliar to the client) commonly disempower the client and renders them less knowledgeable than the therapist. Once therapy has ended, these imbalanced power dynamics cease to exist. Freud described the notion of the uncanny as a specific type of fear conjured by 'what was once well known and had long been familiar' (Freud, 1919). He continues that the effect 'often arises when the boundary between fantasy and reality is blurred'. Perhaps in having to re-meet a client, who was 'once well known and had long been familiar' but now seems different, the therapist's fantasy of eternal omnipotence and omniscience in relation to the inner world of the client is powerfully extinguished?

Whether we suppose that the uncanny might be at work or not, it is perhaps more useful to consider an organisational dynamics perspective (and, in the spirit of co-production, to emphasise the potential asset as opposed to deficit). This perspective is particularly useful due to its ability to reframe these experiences as less personally provoked and more systemically driven. Frequently, when an ex-service user joins a team which had previously treated them, a 'therapeutic hangover' (Ball, 2017) can be defaulted to as a result of everyone involved awkwardly attempting to negotiate these 're-meeting' interactions without any guidance or framework. Therefore, the provision of supervision for all parties is imperative to make sense of the new interpersonal power dynamics congesting the space between these new colleagues. Otherwise, the person with lived experience, confronted with the emotionally overwhelming behaviour acted out by their new colleagues, is potentially sabotaged in any chance of being able to sustain their employment or engagement in the co-production process. At worst, such strong feelings of confusion, betrayal and hurt might be invoked that the emotional wounds attained can trigger a preventable relapse.

'Good enough' practice example

A number of NHS trusts across the country include lived experience practitioners within their multidisciplinary teams (referred to with varying job titles). One of these was Leeds and York Partnership NHS Foundation Trust, which co-developed and co-delivered a citywide DBT Skills programme with a lived experience practitioner (LXP), entitled as a service user consultant. The role of the LXP within this team was to co-deliver the DBT skills group, including leading mindfulness sessions, and to 'illuminate/reframe teaching through personal experiences' (Ellis *et al*, BIGSPD Conference 2018).

The LXP also contributed to the team by attending weekly consult meetings, including input to referrals, and supporting team thinking by viewing the work through a different lens. The team noted that this included a function of regulating 'thinking around issues, dilemmas and perspectives' (ibid). Notably, when an evaluation of the LXP's contribution to the service was undertaken, 100% of both staff and service users described it as either 'very helpful' or 'somewhat helpful' to have the lived experience practitioner contributing to the group facilitation and/or staff consult (ibid).

In another service, Central and North West London (CNWL) NHS Foundation Trust's Westminster Personality Disorder Pathway Services have also developed an Advanced Lived Experience Practitioner role. The 'Wesminster Personality Disorder Pathway Advanced LXP', employed at the same banding as a traditionally trained colleague in a 'mirror image' role, works with a small caseload of people in both individual and group contexts. Although both roles are designed to be nearly identical, unlike their traditionally trained counterpart, the Advanced LXP holds the 'added value' of being able to use their insights and reflections from their own lived experience to foster hope and build rapport with the individuals they work with.

Both roles also hold the task of training and consulting to the Community Mental Health Team in which they are based, local inpatient mental health services and GPs, supporting other staff groups to develop confidence, skills and knowledge related to treating people with a diagnosis of personality disorder.

Shifting the balance of implicit power of responsibility

Finally, we will examine how the application of co-production to personality disorder-specific contexts can create a shift in the implicit power dynamics related to responsibility. One of co-production's most attractive attributes is that in the invitation to work across boundaries, the unhelpful positioning of the registered healthcare professional as holding ultimate responsibility for identifying solutions can be abandoned. This can be liberating and re-humanising: allowing them to not know the answers, make mistakes and ask for help. Sometimes it even gifts the opportunity for their own lived experiences to be declared. Equally, the person with lived experience has to move out of the historically disempowered and passive role and embrace the opportunity to become a more active agent.

Cameron (2015) writes: 'This is not about professionals having to relinquish power in an already chaotic and uncertain climate, but about strengthening the power base so there is more of it to go around'.

In order to strengthen this power base, a skillmix review and subsequent integration of new lived experience practitioner roles within the multidisciplinary team (MDT) can be a good place to start. However, only the creation of roles with seniority and responsibility demonstrates a true organisational commitment to re-balancing the power imbalances. In order for such roles to be developed, pioneers often have to raise awareness of the potential of excellence from people with lived experience, and even in the most compassionate and well-intentioned teams, it is often necessary to educate and challenge low expectations set by entrenched stigmas. The organisation Implementing Recovery through Organisational Change (ImROC) highlights the importance of 'team preparation' in relation to the peer support workforce in mental health systems.

There are also often misconceptions surrounding the complexity and emotional demands presented by lived experience practitioners' work, and so highly challenging tasks can be assigned to people who aren't adequately prepared or supported to undertake it. Ideally, lived experience practitioners should be well established in their own self-management and personal recovery, in order to expertly advise, facilitate and support those in earlier stages of self-management to safely engage in co-production activities. This is especially true in contexts associated with high levels of risk – an aspect of sharing responsibility is co-productively creating an assessment of what feels safe and realistic, and ensuring that supportive resources are available to have ongoing dialogue around this for when the details or thresholds inevitably change.

If a lived experience practitioner, as an expert advisor on involvement and co-production, can curate a spectrum of co-production (and, where necessary, involvement) activities for the local service user and carer population, the organisation is more likely to quickly understand the value of lived experience practice and less likely to anxiously undermine the role by contextualising the continued contact with mental health services as a sign of pathology or dependence, or a lack of ability or 'readiness' to pursue other career options. Related to this, reference to those with professional learning as 'the staff' or 'the professionals' suggests that the lived experience practitioner fits neither of these descriptors – that however excellent the quality of their work and attitude to their career, their contribution can never match that of their colleagues. The inherent suggestion here is the notion that lived experience contributions are less valuable and should serve only temporarily as a route 'back' from illness – a stepping stone into the working world.

If co-production requests that we see people for their assets, as opposed to perceived deficits, it follows that we recognise the skills, qualities and prior learning that people bring with them to lived experience-specific roles, including identification of those which are especially useful and relevant for the task at hand. Lived experience practitioners need to be highly skilled professionals in a number of areas in order to challenge, role-model and function overall in the often hostile environments that they work in. The lived experience practitioner should hold professional expertise in skilfully sharing aspects of themselves and their own stories, as well as the broader contexts of stories, including socio-political themes relating to commonalities in experience. Lived experience practitioners also skilfully share stories they have been witness to and work as community connectors. This connecting role provides platforms and opportunities for more diverse stories to be heard and have influence, including the stories of those who do not wish or hold capacity to undertake a co-production process. By the point of progression into senior lived experience practitioner roles, they should be able to contribute knowledge as an expert regarding the concept of personal recovery, having a broad knowledge of varied experiences and narratives, underwritten by a sophisticated understanding of the politics and ethics surrounding their field of work. For involvement processes to benefit from a vast array of contributing perspectives, it is crucial that the lived experience practitioner is aware of their role as a community connector and adequately prepared to engage with the communities relevant to their role. If the lived experience practitioner is able to engage with broader groups, then an array of involvement activities can be undertaken, which provides a variety of opportunities for a diverse and larger population to contribute to. At times, this might include more 'traditional' and less collaborative forms of involvement, but when these activities are always undertaken as co-productively as possible and are organised as a spectrum of work by a lived experience practitioner, there is less chance of a dangerously tokenistic process. When the role of a lived experience practitioner is conceptualised as such, we reduce the notion of 'expiration dates' on relevant lived experience. With more traditional involvement processes, there is often a question of how long someone can feed back their experience until they are eventually commenting on a system that no longer resembles that in which they received care. Spectrums of involvement opportunities should also support the development of those service users involved to develop skills to prepare for volunteering, employment or training, including as lived experience practitioners.

This development through involvement and co-production activities into lived experience practice is likely to, and should run concurrent with, the person's movement into a personal recovery. This is important as professionally utilised lived experience within mental health systems needs to be that of a lived experience of personal recovery, as opposed to solely being a lived experience of service access or distress. If lived experience practitioners only have experience of what doesn't support their mental health and well-being, and have never experienced tools which supported them to move into a recovery (whether those tools were provided by services or not), their ability to work effectively and sustainably within the system is likely to be limited.

When the terms 'service user' and 'lived experience practitioner' are assumed to be interchangeable, it is suggested that the influence of the 'master identity' of the lived experience practitioner as a patient has an irreversible impact, further consolidating the unhelpful binary of 'us' and 'them' between registered healthcare professionals and those otherwise engaged in involvement activities. For those of us undertaking this work from a perspective of lived experience, the suggestion is that anything we have learned prior to or within our employment is irrelevant compared to the influence of our former disturbance. Similarly, the concept that training as a nurse or psychologist might so permanently affect one's perspective that it cannot be influenced by any additional training, never mind any transformative life experiences (including experiences of distress and even receiving a diagnosis themselves), further calcifies this 'us' and 'them' binary and, simultaneously, divisions between the two groups.

Furthermore, if the lived experience practitioner is assumed as a 'professionalised patient voice', it is often next posed by a registered healthcare professional that 'we all have lived experience of being patients; I'm a patient of my GP/own therapist'. Though there is some truth to this, there are profound differences in undertaking a highly invasive process of self-examination motivated by career progression, such as engaging in psychotherapy while training as a psychotherapist, as opposed to the motivating hope that one might respond to life-saving treatment. As a survivor, comparisons such as these can feel akin to a comparison between undergoing cosmetic breast enhancement motivated by dreams of a Hollywood career and undergoing a double mastectomy in order to survive aggressive breast cancer.

Microaggressions such as these are unfortunately common for lived experience practitioners, and in attempting to understand them it is helpful to return to the theme of organisational anxiety. At the time of writing, most mental health services are underfunded, short-staffed and poorly resourced, backdropped by consistent media hysteria about the 'failing' NHS. As many registered professionals battle impending burnout, the lived experience practitioner gets to '[do] all the things that used to be the nicest bits of [their] job. Now all [they] have left is the paperwork' (Ball *et al*, 2018). Furthermore, the lived experience practitioner reports deep satisfaction and reward in their work, while their colleague struggles to survive. Perhaps it is unsurprisingly intolerable for the registered healthcare professional to experience a profound loss so linked to their own core identity – that being the loss of the fantasy of what life as a healthcare professional would be – while perceiving themselves to be in such close proximity to the beneficiary of their loss. Finally, inherent to the lived experience practitioner undertaking work traditionally done by registered healthcare professionals is the suggestion that someone without that professional's level of education and/or experience could undertake aspects of their role competently. Indeed, it might be even more disturbing to suggest that a 'mad person' might be capable of undertaking one's duties with the same quality and diligence.

In order to combat the idea that lived experience-specific roles do not require skills or knowledge, they should be designed with specific job descriptions, person specifications and Agenda for Change-banded salaries, like all other posts. Roles should also be appropriately advertised via NHS Jobs, as when roles are stepped into on the basis of nepotism, there can be re-traumatising parallels to being selected from a peer group and prepared (or groomed) for a 'special' role. Without appropriate contracts of employment or any protecting rights, exploitation can become more likely. As has been well established within trauma-informed theory, for those of us for whom boundaries have not historically always been safe, consistent or healthy, there may be additional necessity to establish more considered boundaries in order to stay mentally well. If personality disorder services then go on to actively sabotage and undermine any safe boundaries around ex-service user engagement, the apparent hypocrisy can be devastating. Thus, the formalities and protections afforded by contracted employment serve to ensure the service benefits from deliverable objectives within the job description and annually at appraisal; these lend a level of assurance for the organisation anxious about co-production. Placing LXP roles on exactly the same footing as registered health professionals means that all the same checks and balances can be employed if necessary and, conversely, the lived experience practitioner is afforded some level of security and equity with their colleagues in terms of rights and rewards.

Formal employment processes such as these would also be likely to protect against the common financially discriminatory practices that many lived experience practitioners face. A survey undertaken in 2018 suggested that of more than 100 people with lived experience of personality disorder working in mental health systems, more than 70% had attained university qualifications to undergraduate or masters degree level, and yet more than 70% of these people were earning less than £25,000 per year (Ball *et al*, 2018). As well as frequently undervaluing lived experience practitioners by offering low-banded contracted roles, rarely full-time permanent positions, many trusts insist on short-term project work, and so lived experience practitioners have to work as self-employed contractors with far fewer employment rights.

Ensuring robust processes around staff (or involvement personnel) support can also be an important aspect of managing risk. Ensuring DBS checks, documentation around well-being planning and access to staff support such as the Employee Assistance Programme and Occupational Health can be protective measures in relation to risk. Undertaking proactive processes such as collaborative safety planning also reduces the likelihood of any disproportionate or disempowering decision making, and, conversely, raises the likelihood of positive risk-taking. Though this chapter has not specifically focused on contexts where risks are likely to be especially high, such as forensic settings, measures such as these should be considered as imperative to undertaking co-production and involvement projects and processes within these systems.

Another important resource for supporting lived experience practitioner staff or those undertaking involvement activities is supervision. As well as generic clinical supervision for those working clinically, the provision of discipline-specific supervision between lived experience practitioners is crucial to ensure longevity to withstand difficult experiences such as those described thus far in this chapter.

'Good enough' practice example

Emergence Plus CIC

Prior to its closure in August 2016, Emergence Plus CIC was the leading national user-led organisation focusing on personality disorder. Emergence Plus was a key partner in the design, development and delivery of the Knowledge and Understanding Framework for Personality Disorder training. Additionally, it held responsibility for the contractual delivery and staffing of a number of lived experience practitioner roles embedded in NHS personality disorder services in

continued ➜

London and other regions (referred to at the time as 'service user consultancy' roles). Embedded into the costing for all contractual provision were supervisory structures for all their staff. Emergence Plus, brokering the staffing and negotiated terms of employment, protected and advocated for the rights of the lived experience practitioners as well as quality assurance and sustainability in the practice development.

Largely established by ex-residents of the Henderson Hospital Democratic Therapeutic Community, and thus informed by the organisation's ethos, Emergence Plus nationally role-modelled co-production at all levels in its work. Though a user-led organisation, Emergence Plus sought to influence systems by working from within them. As a result, it insisted upon working from a co-produced model in the delivery and development of the majority of its work. Despite its size ruling out the provision of any official HR department, Emergence Plus developed highly supportive processes and procedures as an employer of lived experience practitioners. Each of us who worked for Emergence Plus had a professional development plan and a designated supervisor who we would meet regularly for supervision, and all staff were made aware of the level of responsibility that they had to assume regarding their own health and well-being. Well thought out, considered governance and robust processes such as these allowed Emergence Plus to nationally role-model. As a result the organisation had an outstanding reputation of reliability and excellence, which surpassed the aforementioned 'low bar' of expectation regarding lived experience practice and repositioned it in a space that felt both attainable to those with lived experience and deeply inspiring and valued by those without.

Local support for the hosting, creation and implementation of peer supervision structures such as those once utilised by Emergence Plus CIC can be a first step in ensuring safe and 'good enough' practice. However, further provision internally within services is required in order for lived experience practitioners to feel well supported and valued, and therefore for the work undertaken to fulfil its greatest potential.

ImROC, national experts on peer working in statutory settings, state that it is essential for peer workers to receive training and supervision so that they can do their best work in generic mental health settings, and advocate for proactive well-being planning. Lived experience practitioners within personality disorder-specific contexts may encounter unique challenges that require consideration, such as the specific theoretical approach of some of the services. My own recommendation from reflecting on my own experiences as a lived experience practitioner in a personality disorder service read as follows:

- Reflection upon how the theoretical and philosophical framework of the service fits, or might be antagonistic to, the role and place of peer workers in the clinical team.

- Training for the whole staff team prior to the peer's induction regarding the benefits of peer-based roles, including open discussion about their views and support for the addition of peer workers in the organisation.

- The recruitment occurring in pairs, in order for the chances of isolation for the peer worker to be reduced.

- An initial training in peer support/peer-based working to be provided for the peer worker as a part of their induction process.

- Provision of clinical and management supervision for the peer worker which is embedded in to the organisation.

- 'Sponsorship' from another organisation serving the same client group, ideally sharing a theoretical approach, who have successfully incorporated peer workers into the team, especially for the peer worker and their supervisor or line manager.

(Ball, 2017)

Clearly, co-production and involvement projects require sufficient resource investment in order to provide such support. Processes related to co-production and lived experience practice that are rushed, undertaken as a 'side of the desk' duty or not appropriately resourced will struggle to provide the level of support that is ethically and responsibly required. They require staffing from individuals who are passionate and informed about the nature of the work as a collaborative process.

Where permanent posts cannot be created for lived experience practitioners, a budget should be provided to ensure parity between day rates of freelance lived experience practitioners and those whom they are tasked to co-produce with. There should not be an expectation of one half of the co-production group contributing to service improvement or co-delivery on the basis purely of 'wanting to give something back', which is burdened with the suggestion that something was initially taken unjustly. An offender 'gives something back' to the community following a criminal act; a lived experience practitioner, with skills and knowledge related to healthcare and a first-person knowledge of recovery, has simply accessed an extensive, immersive and unusual form of experiential training in preparation for their role.

Conclusion

This chapter has sought to unpack some common experiences in relation to co-production in NHS personality disorder services. Informed by my own perspective as a lived experience practitioner who has undertaken this work, I have sought to organise my own ideas, experiences and theories around three co-production pillars: redressing explicit power imbalance, resource imbalance and responsibility imbalance. I have attempted to blend my own observations and experiences with those of my peers and allies, while offering some hopeful solutions that you might replicate to safeguard all involved. The limitations to my own understanding, of course, factor into my writing and I have referred consistently to the systems I am more familiar with: the context of dedicated English and Welsh NHS personality disorder services. I have not explored the innovations within forensic services in the same geographical region, nor innovative practice being undertaken in Scotland, Northern Ireland or the Republic of Ireland or nations further afield, of which I am sure there is much. For readers working within more diverse settings than those that I have primarily held in mind, I acknowledge that the concepts, challenges or examples of how best to undertake this work may not always be perfectly 'drag and drop' in their application to your contemporary setting. That being said, I hope that for any practitioner, whether trained via lived experience or via professional learning, this chapter might suggest thoughts and ideas that can be applied. More importantly, I hope you might finish reading with a refreshed resolve regarding the importance of thoroughly reviewing the skill mix of your team in order to include lived experience practitioners, thus raising the likelihood of optimum service delivery for those in need. Finally, I hope that the publication of more case studies of good practice in this field grows, inspiring confidence in the process and generating momentum surrounding the all-important interruption of the status quo of historical power dynamics within mental health services.

References

American Psychiatric Association (2013) *Diagnostic and Statistical Manual of Mental Disorders* (5th edition) Arlington, VA: APA.

Arnstein S (1969) Arnstein's ladder. Retrieved from http://www.citizenshandbook.org/arnsteinsladder.html

Ball M (2017) Walking the tightrope: incorporating the voice of lived experience into a personality disorder service. *The Psychotherapist* **66** Summer. Retrieved from https://issuu.com/ukcp-publications/docs/the_psychotherapist_summer_2017_iss

Ball M, Stirling F & Whyte T (2018) *Breaking The Glass Ceiling of Service User Involvement*. British and Irish Group for the Study of Personality Disorder Conference 2018, Cardiff. YouTube video of slides accessible at https://bigspd.org.uk/conference-2018/

Cameron A (2015, May) Classics: Co-production – Radical roots, radical results. *The Edge* **8**. London: NHS Improving Quality.

Ellis S, Demaine S & Zamir A (2018) *Innovation and Involvement in Times of Austerity: The development of a Citywide DBT Skills Group Programme Incorporating Service User Involvement in Its Delivery.* BIGSPD Conference 2018, Cardiff.

Freud S (1919) *The Uncanny*. London: Penguin Books.

Gilbert D (2019) Rethinking engagement. *British Journal of Psychiatry Bulletin* **43** 4–7 doi:10.1192/bjb.2018.55

Mead Robson A (2010, 28 June) Psychiatry – a specialty for failures? [blog post] Retrieved from https://blogs.bmj.com/bmj/2010/06/28/anna-mead-robson-psychiatry-%E2%80%93-a-specialty-for-failures/

Menzies-Lyth I (1960) Social systems as a defense against anxiety: An empirical study of the nursing service of a general hospital. *Human Relations* **13** 95–121.

Nesta (2012) People-powered health co-production catalogue. Retrieved from: https://media.nesta.org.uk/documents/co-production_catalogue.pdf

Nesta (2013) The business case for people powered health. Retrieved from https://media.nesta.org.uk/documents/the_business_case_for_people_powered_health.pdf

Sheehan L, Nieweglowski K & Corrigan P (2016) The stigma of personality disorders. *Current Psychiatry Reports* **18** (11) https://doi.org/10.1007/s11920-015-0654-1

Slade M, McDaid D, Shepherd G, Williams S & Repper J (2017) *Recovery: The Business Case*. Nottingham: ImROC.

Slay J & Stephens L (2013) Coproduction in mental health: A literature review (commissioned by MIND). Retrieved from https://neweconomics.org/uploads/files/ca0975b7cd88125c3e_ywm6bp3l1.pdf

Offender Health Collaboration (2015) Liaison and diversion manager and practitioner resources: Service user involvement. Retrieved from https://www.england.nhs.uk/commissioning/wp-content/uploads/sites/12/2015/10/ohc-paper-06.pdf

Personality Disorder in the Bin (2016) [blog posts]. Retrieved from https://personalitydisorderinthebin.wordpress.com

Tyrer P, Reed GM & Crawford MJ (2015) Classification, assessment, prevalence, and effect of personality disorder. *The Lancet* **385** (9969) 717–726.

World Health Organisation (2018) International classification of diseases and related health problems (11th edition) Retrieved from https://icd.who.int/browse11/l-m/en

Chapter 10:

Partnership Working

David Harvey and Bernie Tuohy

> ### Governance principles
> Services working in partnership should ensure they work to uphold:
> - Shared partnership structures
> - A relationship focus
> - Clarity about the primary task and roles
> - Shared values and culture
> - Collective and containing leadership

Introduction

For services supporting people who may attract a diagnosis of personality disorder, partnership working is worthy of consideration due to a range of potential benefits for service users. However, effective partnership working is not yet fully understood, and as a consequence this way of working can be perilous and the pitfalls underestimated. In this chapter it is suggested that many threats to partnership working come from not acknowledging, or attending to, powerful responses in the workforce and wider systems that ultimately undermine the endeavour.

It is argued that services working in partnership to support those whose problems are consistent with the diagnosis should focus on the conditions around the partnership itself in order to notice, understand and manage any problematic service responses that may increase repeated exclusion and 'failure'. Five conditions are outlined that may assist partnerships to avoid such hazards and meet service user needs more effectively. These conditions are: *shared structures; relationship focus; a focus on the primary task and clarity about roles; shared values and culture; and collective and containing leadership*.

What is partnership working?

In the 1990s New Labour promoted partnerships spanning health and social care to provide 'joined up, seamless solutions' for complex and overarching social issues, thus tackling the wider determinants of poor outcomes, such as social exclusion, crime and substance misuse (Dickinson, 2007; Rittel & Webber, 1973; Glasby & Lester, 2004; Boydell & Rugkasa, 2007). Partnerships may exist on an operational level (between front-line workers with a local remit to deliver projects to address specific problems), at a strategic level (between senior managers and elected members as a multi-issue collaboration with an agenda-setting capacity) or at a commissioning level (Glasby & Lester, 2004; Lasker & Weiss, 2003; Boydell & Rukkasa, 2007). However, partnership as a concept has been poorly defined in the health and social care literature, with no universally accepted definition (Carnwell & Carson, 2009; Wildridge *et al*, 2004; Institute for Public Policy Research, 2001). Some have defined partnerships along a continuum defined by activity and proximity, for example from *isolation* (involving no joint activity); through *encounters* (ad hoc contacts) and *collaboration* (joint working as the central activity); to *integration* (services having no separate identities in terms of activity) (Hudson *et al*, 1997). Others have defined partnerships along a continuum defined by 'depth' of relationship, for example, from consulting with each other through joint management to a formal merger (Peck & Crawford, 2004).

Partnerships occur between organisations, agencies, individuals or disciplines; have common aims and visions; involve joint rights, responsibilities and resources; may create new structures and processes; aim to provide better access to better services for service users; aspire to equality and trust; and strive to achieve more than an individual agency can (Wildridge *et al*, 2004). Among these comprehensive and complex definitions and descriptions of partnership, the simplicity of the definition offered by Huxham & Vangen (2005, p4) is appealing – 'any situation in which people are working across organisational boundaries towards some positive end' – as it captures the many guises of partnership work that can be beneficial to service users who may attract a diagnosis of personality disorder.

Why consider partnership working?

When supporting service users with 'personality disorder', there are two main factors that, when combined, mean partnership working is worthy of consideration. These factors are: multiple health and social needs; and the potential for service fragmentation when providing for multiple, complex and differing needs.

Multiple health and social needs

People who face problems consistent with a diagnosis of personality disorder can have a constellation of interrelated needs across various domains, including mental health, substance misuse, physical health, education, social care and criminal justice (Mind, 2018). There are significant rates of mental health problems within this population (Zanarini *et al*, 2004), with high rates of depression, eating disorders, anxiety, suicidal behaviours and substance misuse identified (Samuels, 2011; Zimmerman *et al*, 2005; Department of Health, 2009). Research has also highlighted associations with physical health problems, including obesity, chronic pain and chronic health conditions, such as liver transplant and having HIV-seropositive status (Dixon-Gordon *et al*, 2015).

People within this group also face many profoundly difficult social problems, meaning that, unsurprisingly, a strong association has been found between 'personality disorder' and an increased likelihood of lower levels of income (Sareen *et al*, 2011). Estimates suggest that approximately two-thirds of street homeless people meet the diagnosable criteria for a personality disorder but struggle to access services, meaning any support will largely come from homelessness services alone (Middleton, 2008; Shelter, 2008). Parents who are – or who could be – diagnosed with personality disorder are often parenting while managing emotional and interpersonal difficulties, stress and low self-confidence, often without the support needed to optimise parent–child interactions and child development (Petfield *et al*, 2015; Moss *et al*, 2002).

Multiple service providers and the potential for fragmentation

No one agency will be able to provide the appropriate level of support and intervention required to meet the unique constellation of multiple, inter-related needs of an individual whose difficulties may attract a diagnosis of personality disorder (NIMHE, 2003). This is because people's needs are not organised in line with service provision across welfare services (Glasby *et al*, 2010).

People are therefore obliged to engage with multiple providers negotiating complex service divisions (Glasby *et al*, 2010; Douglas, 2009; Tait & Shah, 2007). As a result the experience of service users is dependent upon the effectiveness of system behaviour and service co-ordination to access appropriate support (Mind, 2018).

Mainstream services frequently struggle to co-operate to provide appropriate support and intervention for people whose difficulties are consistent with the diagnosis of personality disorder, and, as a consequence, individuals are frequently excluded (NIMHE, 2003). Mental health services and practitioners are often reluctant to work with this client group (Dale *et al*, 2017), citing lack of skills, believing service user needs are too complex or the risks too high, or suggesting the likelihood of improvement from intervention is too low (Crisp *et al*, 2016). This exclusion can leave a person's needs unmet and distress unacknowledged or uncontained, increasing the chances of repeated assessment, exclusions, 'failures' and rejection, often via unsuitable, short-lived interventions via A&E departments or acute inpatient services (Shaikh *et al*, 2017; NIMHE, 2003). In the criminal justice system, a lack of appropriate service provision and co-ordination has meant people with this presentation and these needs are sent from court to police custody or prisons, which are ill equipped to meet their needs (Revolving Doors Agency, 2019), and from where they are released with little or no appropriate support (Edgar & Rickford, 2009). Where service users do gain access to an appropriate service, a lack of partnership working can often lead to difficulties at points of transition. Frequently, these difficulties stem from a lack of understanding and/ or appreciation about the importance of relationships that the individual has had with staff and the service, and the subsequent distress experienced when this is 'threatened' by endings. Attachment relationships which have brought a sense of personal meaning and emotional containment are often lost at transition or not shared across different contexts and, instead, people are subjected to repeated assessments. Not only can this reinforce a fragmented, 'unknown' sense of one's self and one's life story, but it also means that rich, co-produced and/or personally relevant learning (which would support care planning, risk management and pathway planning) is not shared and 'held' within the system.

Exclusion and inappropriate support is, therefore, exacerbated for this already deeply disadvantaged service user group by service fragmentation and the difficulties services have in working together. Distress may be compounded for a group of people with multiple needs who understandably struggle to assimilate and 'fit into' a rigid system. By creating links between the criminal justice system, mental health services, substance misuse services, housing and welfare advice and parenting support services, partnership working offers the possibility of relating to a 'whole person' (Banks, 2002; Revolving Doors Agency, 2019; Women in Prison/ Barrow Cadbury Trust, 2017). This increases the chances of multiple, integrated, comprehensive and co-ordinated responses, which are recognised as key for people who may attract a personality disorder diagnosis (NIMHE, 2003; DoH, 2009; NICE, 2015; Mind, 2018).

Is partnership working effective?

High-quality evidence of partnership effectiveness is scarce and the literature focuses on theoretical or descriptive aspects of partnerships as opposed to effectiveness (Perkins *et al*, 2010). Consequently much partnership work is 'faith-based' or ideologically determined (El Ansari & Weiss, 2006). Commissioners or providers may assume partnership working is beneficial, preferable, intuitive and 'common sense' (Fischbaker-Smith, 2015; Dickinson & Glasby, 2010). However, this underestimates the complexities involved and can lead to under-resourcing and underestimation of the time and effort required (Wildridge *et al*, 2004). There are no quick fixes or easy answers that emerge from partnership working (Glasby & Lester, 2004). It can be time-consuming, render services less responsive to need and opportunities and impact on staff time because of increased bureaucracy (Boydell & Rugkasa, 2007; Peck, 2002). The abundance of potential pitfalls can result in spending more time on the mechanisms of partnership than on achieving the outcomes (Wildridge *et al*, 2004), leading some to conclude it is best avoided unless the benefits of collaboration clearly outweigh the benefits of working alone (Huxham & Vangen, 2005).

Given so little is known about effective outcomes for partnership working, evaluation is important, but complex. Partnerships often offer multi-faceted interventions and need time to establish long-term outcomes (Dowling *et al*, 2004). Perhaps this explains the reported tendency for partnerships to focus on *process evaluation* over *outcome evaluation* (Boyduch & Rugkasa, 2007). The focus of outcome evaluation is the impact of partnership activity in relation to its main aim (Carnwell & Carson 2009), such as on service users' lives and well-being. The focus of process evaluation is *how* the partnership work is carried out, such as the development, management, learning and activity of a partnership. While important, process evaluation does not assist providers and commissioners to make informed decisions based on clear impact at the front line (Yeomans, 2007; Boydell & Rugkasa, 2007). Carrying out and disseminating outcome *and* process evaluation will help stakeholders to plan services thoughtfully. Networks or communities of partnerships that are willing to share their learning for the wider benefit of service users and all stakeholders would help augment the limited evidence base.

The emotional world of partnership working

Groups and organisations are susceptible to anxieties and emotional pressures (Halton, 1994). These, along with any resultant problematic responses such as conflict, splits, indignation, apathy, distancing, idealisation or acquiescence, threaten a partnership's ability to function optimally and so meet the needs of service users. Problematic responses can be inadvertent attempts by individuals or teams to manage anxieties originating from a range of sources – the high risks and complex presentations of the client group; each partner unknowingly working towards a different aim; authority of either partner being unclear or challenged; commissioning arrangements based on 'contract and competition'; or policy-driven changes external to the partnership (Boydell & Rugkasa, 2007; Obholzer & Zagier Roberts, 1994; Hudson, 2004; Burns *et al*, 2018). For services working with those who have the most distressing histories and who live with overwhelming levels of emotion, the anxieties are amplified (Clulow, 1994) and responses of the organisation to manage those anxieties arguably more problematic (Obholzer & Zagier Roberts, 1994). However, in spite of the multiple, perilous anxiety-inducing challenges of partnership work, its objective, rational and structural aspects have received more attention in the literature than its irrational, unconscious and subjective aspects (Horwarth & Morrison, 2007).

It is a central theme of this book that organisations unconsciously seek to manage anxiety within the workforce through processes, procedures, policies and practices, which, on the surface, appear rational and reasonable, but which ill serve the needs of the service user group (Barrett, 2011; Gabriel & Carr, 2002). Menzies-Lyth (1960) called these organisationally sanctioned practises 'social defences'. If left unexamined, social defences can threaten the effectiveness of partnership work (Obholzer & Zagier Roberts, 1994).

> Jane was in custody due to an offence of arson following a crisis in her mental health. She was now nearing release. Her probation officer referred Jane to a local housing project. The referral was declined automatically without an assessment because 'arson offences' was an exclusion criteria for the housing project. Her probation officer felt pressured to find Jane housing and, frustrated by what he perceived to be a lack of flexibility, spoke to the housing project manager, explaining that Jane's risks were considered to be manageable and offering extra support from probation. The housing manager, however, was adamant that the risks were not manageable, she could not set a precedent and she had to adhere to the project policy. She declined to attend a professionals meeting.

In the above case we can see how anxieties relating to risk on both sides of a potential partnership increased tensions and made collaboration less likely. It is possible that the blanket 'exclusion criteria', a seemingly reasonable organisational measure, potentially constituted a social defence – a way of protecting the housing project from having to confront the anxieties and complexities of housing someone who may pose a risk of arson. One option may have been to consider what would need to be in place to allow for the policy to be relaxed. Partnership work involving an arson specialist from the fire brigade and mental health services, along with a housing worker and MAPPA, may have assisted. This may have resulted in a package of support to assist Jane's pathway, including a property with its own entry access, agreed safety equipment (smoke alarms, fire proof bedding/furniture), specialist mental health support for Jane and specialist risk consultation from probation.

An awareness of authority in partnerships

In single-agency (or single-practitioner) work, specific expertise is used to try to meet service user need. This expertise affords authority, defined as 'the right to make an ultimate decision … to make decisions which are binding on others' (Obholzer & Zagier Roberts, 1994, p39). This authority permits the prioritisation of specific values, the channelling of resources and the taking of certain courses of action. In partnership, each party contributes different areas of expertise to serve the needs of service users in an integrated, multi-faceted manner and this merging of expertise has the potential to bring with it often unspoken complexities regarding authority. In partnership there is a requirement that resources are shared and decision-making negotiated. The notion of absolute, fixed and constant clarity regarding authority may be challenged, introducing a new set of anxieties in relation to the work.

A proposed pilot involved a low secure 'personality disorder' inpatient unit and a third sector housing provider working in partnership to review the readiness of patients to move into community settings. This was offered as an alternative to the more traditional method which involved the hospital making decisions about readiness for transition and then referring to the housing provider. Under the new arrangement, it was anticipated that the housing provider's specialist skills and knowledge about 'personality disorder' and housing options could facilitate a more seamless and responsive approach, reducing delayed discharges, increasing the likelihood of identifying compatible placements and thus positive settlement within the community. However, concerns were raised by the clinical management team in the hospital, which stated that they had the statutory responsibility for the decision to discharge and that the pilot complicated lines of responsibility for the risk management. The pilot proposal was swiftly rejected.

In the above example, we might hypothesise that the potential partnership innovation (which may well have assisted some service users to move on sooner from hospital) was threatening to authority conferred through established practices.

While the hospital would retain the statutory responsibility and authority in this sense, the pilot would still open up their decision-making to scrutiny and curious enquiry through negotiation and consideration of alternative perspectives, thus making authority more ambiguous. While governance arrangements and role responsibility would no doubt need careful articulation, it could be that these 'reasonable' reasons to not consider the pilot were, in fact, methods of avoiding a situation within which expertise and decision-making would be questioned by a partner. Preventing the pilot project allowed those concerned to avoid the emotional impact of a blurring of absolute authority on the hospital management and staff.

We don't mean to imply that decision-makers and those with authority in organisations always cling mindlessly to authority, but rather that, where there is an invitation to examine decisions, especially where risk is concerned, there can be understandable anxieties. If it is accepted that anxiety associated with negotiated decision-making is a necessary by-product of shared authority within partnerships (at least when they are in their infancy), then stakeholders need to ensure that there are structures and processes which enable good oversight of the partnership and healthy conditions for it to mature. We would argue that it is detrimental to a healthy collaboration not to at least acknowledge that there will be instances where decision making authority is confused or contested (Obholzer & Zagier Roberts, 1994; Wildridge *et al*, 2004). If left unacknowledged, there is the potential for conflict and subjugation (perceived or otherwise) provoking anxiety for individuals (Obholzer & Zagier Roberts, 1994), especially if shifts in associated resources are involved (Fischbaker-Smith, 2015). To manage these anxiety-provoking situations, partnerships may start to function as 'tokenistic talking shops' or 'good behaviour partnerships' to collusively avoid conversations and agreements about these difficult issues (Boydell & Rugkasa, 2007). Alternatively, partnerships may come to use 'cultural differences' to mask or conceal issues and discussions about authority, decision-making parameters, control, devolution and accountability (Fischbaker-Smith, 2015). It is advisable therefore to uphold a mindful awareness of the emotional world of a partnership.

How do you get good outcomes in partnership working?

The paucity of literature and research in this area means that no one definitively knows the answer to this question. In the absence of a robust evidence base, Boydell & Rugkasa (2007) suggest that services/stakeholders should aim to learn about, and try to create, the *conditions* that *may* mean partnerships can have a positive impact. In the specific context of supporting service users whose difficulties are consistent with a personality disorder diagnosis, any conditions and learning need to take into account the powerful emotions and problematic organisational responses that may be triggered by the work.

What follows is a range of descriptions of specific conditions that may increase the chances of noticing, understanding and managing the many perils of partnership work when supporting services users who may attract a personality disorder diagnosis. We have labelled these five conditions *shared structures, relationship focus, focus on the primary task and clarity about roles, shared values and culture* and *collective and containing leadership*. They are intended to be applicable for partnership working with an individual service user, at an operational level, a strategic level or a commissioning level. Each one is presented separately for the sake of parsimony, but in reality they are inter-linked and overlap, whereby the strengthening of one may well strengthen others.

Shared structures

The need for clear structures within the clinical care, systemic and administrative management of people with 'personality disorder' is widely accepted (Murphy & McVey, 2010; Campbell & Craissati, 2018; Livesley, 2003). In partnership work these need to be *shared structures*. Shared structures are the agreed processes about how the work will be carried out and/or the planned meetings and forums in which partners come together for communication, pooling of expertise, information sharing, understanding, negotiation and escalation of issues. The nature and extent of these structures will vary depending on context and the level of the partnership. The shared nature of the structures may be enacted via co-authoring of all documents or policies, co-chairing or rotating chairing responsibilities, alternating the location of meetings across each partner's premises, clear links from shared processes or meeting structures into the relevant polices and forums of each partner organisation or clear partnership representation at as many levels as appropriate, including senior management boards.

A local authority and mental health trust had embedded mental health workers in children's services to enhance mental health support for young mothers whose children were on the edge of being taken into care. Over time it emerged that the mental health workers were focused on the needs of the mothers and this conflicted with the priorities of the social workers, whose focus was on the safety of the children. The local authority managers expressed concerns that their staff were being unduly influenced by the mental health workers, impairing the safeguarding of the children,

continued ➔

while there were other instances of the social workers withdrawing from the mental health workers, believing they did not understand their area of work. The mental health workers started to notice that they were not being notified of joint home visits and started to feel powerless and hopeless. These issues were raised in individual line management in both agencies and were escalated through the respective governance arrangements. There were no joint forums or meetings where these concerns and tensions could be thought about and worked through, and this increased the likelihood of a split and othering between the workers and their organisations. As a consequence the mental health workers were withdrawn from the team.

In the example above we can see how there was a lost opportunity to sustain the functioning of this partnership through shared structures – joint forums, meetings, processes and escalation procedures. A series of monthly meetings at all levels (for front-line staff, for operational managers and for senior management) may have allowed for the challenges, which were perhaps predictable and inevitable, to be discussed, understood, escalated where necessary and managed by all levels. Representation from both agencies at all levels with a clear expectation of attendance may have assisted further. The emotional world of this partnership can be understood somewhat through the nature of its emotive and challenging task – to manage what will often be conflicting needs of mothers and their children. Shared structures may have been unconsciously avoided to circumvent confronting these tensions, but may also have reduced the capacity of the partnership to manage the competing aims of each agency in ways that, first and foremost, kept children safe and mothers supported.

The purpose of shared structures is not solely administrative. They also act as an important emotional container within the work. Deviation from the 'usual' structures and processes also provides important information for the partnership. These deviations are a barometer to notice both conscious and unconscious pushes and pulls in the work, which need attending to. When partnerships notice that structures and processes are not being adhered to as agreed, they can then make conscious, deliberate decisions to understand and rectify the drift or to be flexible and clarify the rationale for intentionally deviating from them.

Of course, a counterproductive organisational response to shared structures may be a rigid adherence to them which could, for example, manage organisational concerns about losing control, but not assist the partnership in achieving its aims. An ability to find a balance between both adherence to structure and a need for flexibility is a fundamental aspect of partnership working, enabling creativity and innovation in complex contexts.

Relationship focus

Partnerships are built on relationships (Wildridge *et al*, 2004). Nurturing these can facilitate learning about partners; offer alternative perspectives; provide a more holistic understanding of the issues; enable the sharing of expertise; develop trust, mutual respect, loyalty and commitment; and reduce stereotyping of one another (Boydell & Rugkasa, 2007; Glasby & Lester, 2004). In systems that support people who may attract a diagnosis of personality disorder it is not uncommon for there to be relationship difficulties between different parts of a system (Burns *et al*, 2018). These strains may be clearly visible (such as conflict and disagreements about access to services, 'treatment' or pathways) or there may be more subtle signs of difficulties between partners, such as withdrawal, acquiescence, apathy or superficial engagement (e.g. non-attendance at meetings; lack of meaningful, tangible input; or non-responsiveness to requests or ideas). All of these difficulties pose a threat to the partnership and to meeting the needs of service users effectively. It is judicious to consider whether these kinds of problems are 'symptomatic' of the challenges of partnership working.

When difficulties emerge in a partnership relationship it is imperative that all partners come together to think about and understand the problem. In doing so, a partnership increases its capacity to 'think about itself' and so confront and contain its own powerful feelings with a view to continuous learning and development. Managing differences, barriers, tensions and drifts between partners can legitimately occupy considerable time, especially in systems working with complex needs and high risks (Burns *et al*, 2018). Attempts to actively manage problems between partners via open and reflective discussion increases the possibility of resolution and strengthening the relationship (Boydell & Rugkasa, 2007). By noticing difficulties and resolving them in realistic ways, there is an increased likelihood that effort can be re-focused on meeting the needs of service users.

A 'mentalising' partnership (one which is able to think about itself in relation to all its parts and the wider system) is a significant achievement given the inherent levels of anxiety within systems which work with significant emotional disturbance and risk. One might expect conversations which increase the capacity of the partnership to 'mentalise', to be avoided or for relationship difficulties in the partnership to be dismissed, ignored, minimised or explained away. It is therefore not sufficient to rely on good intentions or some attentive individuals to ensure difficulties are noticed and discussed. Mechanisms that prompt partners to monitor, understand, manage and learn from problems in their relationship need to be embedded within the shared structures. This ensures that staff at all levels are responsible for a relationally-focused culture. Mechanisms to prompt these conversations may include a regular agenda item of 'partnership health check-in' meetings; clear processes for registering frustrations or difficulties in the partnership; having shared forums for review, feedback discussion and learning which is then disseminated; or performance or commissioning meetings to include concrete, specific examples of on-going or 'resolved' partnership difficulties. These structural mechanisms acknowledge that a core aspect of the work is to accept and legitimise the likelihood of relationship difficulties between partners and manage this proactively through noticing, understanding and resolving challenges together.

A focus on the primary task and clarity about roles

A focus on the primary task and clarity regarding aims and roles both contribute to the containment of a workforce, fulfilment of goals and optimum functioning of teams and organisations. As such, they should be articulated as clearly as possible in partnership working (Stokoe, 2011; Obholzer & Zagier Roberts, 1994; Glasby & Lester, 2004; Carnwell and Carson, 2009; Glasby et al, 2010). Zagier Roberts (1994, p38) articulates these questions as being focused on what the desired 'output' is of the organisations and 'how the system (group, department or organisation) proposes to bring this about'.

Identifying and agreeing shared aims in partnership working with individuals presenting with multiple and complex needs is a challenge, as each service or stakeholder will by virtue of their role and expertise bring a different emphasis and approach to the issues being addressed. Indeed, the rationale for partnership working is that no one organisation is able to meet the diverse needs of individuals in receipt of care, and thus differences in emphasis and priorities are to be expected and encouraged. How these differences between partners are understood, prioritised and co-ordinated in order to provide a considered and coherent response to individuals is, however, ripe for confusion and ambiguity. For example, bringing together different models of understanding, such as medical, psychological, social and criminogenic needs, may lead to a lack of clarity about the primary task for any partnership (Limb, 2018). The criminal justice system may consider its main aim to be public protection or social order, while healthcare agencies may see the main aim of the work to assess and offer 'treatment' for 'symptom reduction'. At the same time, social services may see their aim as enhancing social welfare, while the third sector may aim to flexibly assist recovery in a way the public sector cannot. Moreover, each partner may have clear ideas and cultural practices regarding how these aims are achieved that will differ from one another. Additionally, the emotional experience of the work of either partner, or the partnership itself, and any resultant responses may pull activity 'off course', moving it away from an agreed partnership goal. These responses may be manoeuvres that protect the workforce itself from powerful anxieties or emotions (referred to as anti-task behaviour by Zagier Roberts, 1994).

Difficulties in being able to provide clarity about roles can also arise from the requirement within some partnerships for roles to be more flexible. Arguably, partnership working necessitates the need for an 'evolved workforce' – a workforce which shares and utilises skills which, traditionally, may be seen as belonging to the other partnership organisations, meaning that there may be little in terms of a 'pre-existing template' of a role. To illustrate, in the previous example it was, perhaps, necessary for a successful partnership endeavour for the mental health and social workers to evolve and 'borrow' some of the skills of the other to help them in their partnership task. Without structures for understanding how to do this so that each role retains clarity whilst contributing to the overarching primary task, partnerships potentially face a level of confusion, anxiety, and reduced job satisfaction and morale (Glasby & Lester, 2004). For roles in partnership a balance needs to be struck between flexibility and innovation on the one hand, and clarity, role definition and professional accountability on the other.

Darren had diabetes and a diagnosis of personality disorder. His self-care and management of his physical health was poor. Mainstream services struggled to engage with him and he would regularly miss outpatient appointments at the diabetes clinic. He had on occasion become verbally hostile at the diabetes clinic and was at risk of being excluded. His diabetes nurse and mental health care co-ordinator developed a joint care plan with Darren. His care co-ordinator recommended some joint home visits with the diabetes nurse, who would also offer emotional support via planned telephone contact between appointments to develop a trusting relationship. The manager of the diabetes clinic was irritated that his staff were being asked to address the mental health needs of service users and to do outreach work, both of which were outside of their usual practice. He contacted the CMHT manager to express his frustration about them acting outside of their remit and 'telling the diabetes clinicians what to do'. The CMHT manager acknowledged the lack of discussion at a management level about the appropriateness of the plan, given the requested 'extension' of the nurse's role, and suggested a joint meeting to think about next steps and how the services could work together to support Darren to manage his diabetes.

Darren's emotional and relationship difficulties jeopardised his access to physical health services. Partnership working clearly had the potential to meet his multiple needs in a joined-up way, but was almost thwarted by difficulties between services. The care plan required flexibility around the role of the diabetes nurse to prevent Darren being excluded from services. Unacknowledged issues of authority seemed to threaten the partnership working as the manager was undermined by his resources being used in such a way and had little opportunity to understand or negotiate this. The effort made to reach out to the other service, and the idea of spending time to work together on this, were instances of a relationship focus on the partnership itself, avoiding further tensions, and being able to support Darren as effectively as possible.

Shared values and culture

Values serve as standards to evaluate actions, policies, people and events; they inform desirable goals that motivate action and impact on every decision almost always unconsciously (Schwartz, 2006). Values inform culture. A higher level of agreement between partners regarding joint values may assist successful working (Fischbacher-Smith, 2015).

Nowadays many organisations develop explicit values, which are unlikely to be controversial or highly incompatible between partners. For example, the NHS values are cited as *working together for patients, respect and dignity, commitment to quality of care, compassion, improving lives and everyone counts* (Department of Health and Social Care, 2015). These explicit values can be distinguished from assumed, implicit values – for example, Yeomans (2007) suggests that NHS values and culture may actually focus on a readiness to medicalise or detain those in distress, whereas the third sector may hold alternative perspectives. Tait and Shah (2007) suggest that it is the underlying and assumed values of each partner that are capable of destabilising partnerships, even when structures, policies and procedures have been agreed. These implicit values, which are often outside conscious awareness, significantly influence decisions and behaviours and, if left unacknowledged or not understood, contribute to relationship difficulties in partnerships such as conflicts or splits, impairing the integrated support offered to a service user.

Establishing explicit, shared values and discussing how those values might be enacted may assist in bringing more implicit assumptions of both partners to the surface, thus increasing the capacity of each partner to 'notice itself' and understand previously unseen and problematic aspects of its own practice. Acknowledging cultural differences between partners may reduce the potential for unexpected confusion, conflict or competing priorities. Jointly developed values may also act as a commonality to guide and anchor activity but without eradicating the necessary differences in perspectives and expertise which each partner brings. A key task is noticing which values are shared and agreeing how those values would be enacted in the partnership in concrete ways. This may include embedding shared values in structures and clear processes so they guide behaviour and practice, as opposed to being tokenistic or rhetorical. Agreeing strategic aims and objectives in partnership may, for example, act definitively to define shared value-driven expectations for the service. Partners may also use values to inform operating procedures or terms of references for meetings. Partners and commissioners may agree for clear examples to be evidenced in performance reports of how shared values are enacted by the partnership.

Collective and containing leadership

Partnership working requires 'systems leaders' (Limb, 2015) or 'boundary spanners' (Williams, 2002), who work across and within organisational boundaries. This often involves leading without the clear authority afforded by a hierarchy in a single-agency context (Goodwin, 2000; VanVactor, 2012).'Command-and-control' leadership has limited applicability in partnership work as it can create a culture of scapegoating and 'fear of failure' because of a displacement of responsibility onto individuals, thus hampering an appetite for genuine innovation and learning. Alternatively, it is suggested that collective leadership is best suited to partnership working, where everyone takes responsibility for a venture in its entirety, not just for one's own work or organisation. There is a focus on continual learning through dialogue, debate and discussion to understand difficulties and ways forward, all of which needs constant focus and nurturing. Continual learning from innovation in partnership is a legitimate outcome in itself (Glasby *et al*, 2010), provided it is used to improve and refine practices to meet the needs of service users as effectively as possible.

Boundaries between services can provide clarity and containment for the workforce, so innovation and learning in partnership may lead to some uncertainty and so anxiety (Burns *et al*, 2018). As practitioners and services intentionally move into 'unknown territory' to learn more about effectively supporting service users in partnership to overcome long-standing difficulties of exclusion and 'failure', leaders will need to give joint consideration to how they can safely manage risks associated with the work, meaning risks to service users, staff and the public and risks to quality, staffing, statutory duties, reputation and business objectives or finances (NHS National Patient Safety Agency, 2008). In attending to these risks, leaders are implicitly attentive to some of the more unacknowledged, unconscious anxieties associated with the negotiation and sharing of decision-making.

Moreover, in partnerships supporting service users who present with complex needs, there is still much to be learned about 'what works'. Partnerships working together to innovate and learn may need to be able to tolerate unknowns as opposed to absolute truths (Burns *et al*, 2018). A key task, therefore, for leaders in partnerships is to effectively manage anxieties in the workforce and wider system and to balance the dialectics inherent in the work – ambiguity vs clarity; structure vs. flexibility; risk vs progress; relationship vs task focus. Tending to the conditions around the partnership – as outlined throughout this chapter – may augment the workforce's capacity to notice, understand and safely manage anxieties and extreme, problematic responses. This can help ensure safe innovation and manageable levels of uncertainty. Unsurprisingly, leaders' own responses to the challenges and complexities will inform the overall culture of a partnership (Fischbacher-Smith, 2015), meaning that, by role modelling collaboration and containment, leaders have the capacity to influence front-line work between staff and service users.

As a response to anxieties in the system, leaders in partnership may experience a pressure to behave in ways that do not enact the values of collective, containing leadership. Signs of this may include debate and dialogue consistently being shut down, processes and procedures frequently being discarded or not being open to questioning or curious enquiry, partnership decisions not being made together, routinely only focusing on the needs of one partner/agency or innovative solutions being discounted without clear, scrutinised rationales. Leaders should entertain the possibility that these kinds of responses (in themselves or in others), rather than problems *per se*, could be inadvertent ways for parts of the system to manage the anxieties associated with risks and ambiguities (and may be accompanied by outwardly reasonable justifications grounded in 'organisational practices'). Leading in a collaborative and containing way, which is sustainable, is emotionally and practically demanding. Leaders will likely benefit from structural, organisational and relational support, which includes an acknowledgement of the perils, challenges and benefits of partnership work, especially from those that lead the leaders.

Concluding comments

Partnership work is challenging, yet can be profoundly satisfying. Meeting the needs of people who rely on services requires us as professionals and services to think not just about the emotional world of service users, but about our own emotional world and how we, and the services and organisations we make up, work together and cope with the stresses and strains of the work we do, sometimes inadvertently exacerbating difficulties or repeating harmful patterns for those who use services. The conditions outlined in this chapter are by no means definitive and are merely offered to provoke thought and dialogue between all stakeholders. It is hoped that they can provide a focal point to continue learning and innovating to meet service user need effectively, safely and compassionately – in partnership.

References

Ball R, Forbes T, Parris M & Forsyth L (2010) *The Evaluation of Partnership Working in the Delivery of Health and Social Care*. Sterling: Sage Publications.

Banks P (2002) *Partnerships under Pressure: A Commentary on Progress in Partnership –Working between the NHS and Local Government*. London: King's Fund.

Barrett J (2011) Sustainable organizations in health and social care: Developing a 'team mind'. In: D Reiss and A Rubitel (eds) *Containment in the Community*. London: Routledge.

Boydell LR & Rugkasa J (2007) Benefits of working in partnership: A model. *Critical Public Health* **17** (3) 217–228.

Burns M, Campbell C & Craissati J (2018) The offender personality disorder pathway: Modelling collaborative commissioning in the NHS and Criminal Justice system. In: C Campbell and J Craissati (eds) *Personality Disorder Offenders: A Pathway Approach*. Oxford: Oxford University Press.

Campbell C & Craissati J (2018) *Managing Personality Disordered Offenders: A Pathway Approach*. Oxford: Oxford University Press.

Carnwell R & Carson A (2009) The concepts of partnership and collaboration. In: R Carnwell and J Buchanan *Effective Practice in Health, Social Care and Criminal Justice: Working Together* (2nd edition). London: Open University Press.

Clulow C (1994) Balancing care and control: The supervisory relationship as a focus for promoting organizational health. In: A Obholzer & V Zagier Roberts (eds) *The Unconscious at Work: Individual and Organizational Stress in the Human Services*. London: Routledge.

Crisp N, Smith G & Nicholson K (2016) *Old Problems, New Solutions – Improving Acute Psychiatric Care for Adults in England*. London: The Commission on Acute Adult Psychiatric Care.

Dale O, Sethi F, Stanton C, Evans S, Barnicot K, Sedgwick R, Goldsack S, Doran M, Shoolbred L, Samele C, Urquia N, Haigh R & Moran P (2017) Personality disorder services in England: Findings from a national survey. *BJPsych Bull* **41** (5) 247–253.

Department of Health (2009) Recognising complexity: Commissioning guidance for personality disorder services. Retrieved from https://lx.iriss.org.uk/sites/default/files/resources/dh_101789.pdf

Department of Health and Social Care (2015) The NHS Constitution for England. Retrieved from https://www.gov.uk/government/publications/the-nhs-constitution-for-england/the-nhs-constitution-for-england#nhs-values

Dickinson H (2007) Evaluating the outcomes of health and social care partnerships: The POET approach. *Research Policy and Planning* **25** 79–92.

Dickinson H & Glasby J (2010) Why partnership working doesn't work. *Public Management Review* **12** (6) 811–828.

Dixon-Gordon K, Whalen D, Layden B & Chapman A (2015) A systematic review of personality disorders and health outcomes. *Canadian Psychology* **56** (2) 168–190.

Douglas A (2009) *Partnership Working*. London: Routledge.

Dowling B, Powell M & Glendinning C (2004) Conceptualising successful partnerships. *Health and Social Care in the Community* **12** (4) 309–317.

Edgar K & Rickford D (2009) *Too Little Too Late: An Independent Review of Unmet Mental Health Need in Prison*. London: The Prison Reform Trust.

El Ansari W & Weiss E (2006) Quality of research on community partnerships: Developing the evidence base. *Health Education Research* **21** (2) 175–180.

Fischbacher-Smith M (2015) Mind the gaps: Managing difference in partnership working. *Public Money and Management* **35** (3) 195–202.

Gabriel Y & Carr A (2002) Organizations, management and psychoanalysis: An overview. *Journal of Managerial Psychology* **17** (5) 348–365.

Glasby J, Dickinson H & Miller R (2010) Partnership working in England – where we are now and where we've come. *International Journal of Integrated Care* **11** DOI: 10.5334/ijic.545

Glasby J & Lester H (2004) Cases for change in mental health: Partnership working in mental health services. *Journal of Interprofessional Care* **18** (1) 7–16.

Goodwin N (2000) Leadership and the UK health service. *Health Policy* **51** (1) 49–60.

Her Majesty's Inspectorate of Constabulary and Fire & Rescue Services (HMICFRS) (2018) *Policing and Mental Health: Picking Up the Pieces*. London: HMICFRS.

Horwarth J & Morrison T (2007) Collaboration, integration and change in children's services: Critical issues and key ingredients. *Child Abuse and Neglect* **31** (1) 55–69.

Hudson B (2004) Analysing network partnerships: Benson revisited. *Public Management Review* **6** (1) 75–94.

Hudson B, Hardy B, Henwood M & Wistow G (1997) Strategic alliances: Working across professional boundaries: Primary health care and social care. *Public Money and Management* **17** (4) 25–30.

Huxham C & Vangen S (2005) Managing to Collaborate: The Theory and Practice of Collaborative Advantage. Abingdon: Routledge.

Institute for Public Policy Research (2001) *Building Better Partnerships: The Final Report of the Commission on Public Private Partnerships*. London: IPPR.

Lasker R & Weiss E (2003) Broadening participation in community problem solving: A multidisciplinary model to support collaborative practice and research. *Journal of Urban Health* **80** (1) 14–47, 48–60.

Limb M (2015) NHS should develop 'system leaders' who work across organisations. *British Medical Journal* 350:h2855.

Livesley J (2003) *Practical Management of Personality Disorder*. New York: Guilford Press.

Menzies I (1960) The functioning of social systems as a defence against anxiety: Report on a study of the nursing service of a general hospital. *Human Relations* **13** (2) 95–121.

Middleton R (2008) *Brokering Reality: A Review of Service Provision in Leeds for Homeless People with Personality Disorder/Complex Needs*. Leeds: Community Links.

MIND (2018) 'Shining lights in dark corners of people's lives': A Consensus Statement for people with complex mental health difficulties who are diagnosed with a personality disorder. Retrieved from https://www.mind.org.uk/media/21163353/consensus-statement-final.pdf

Moss H, Lynch K, Hardie T & Baron D (2002) Family functioning and peer affiliation in children of fathers with antisocial personality disorder and substance dependence: Associations with problem behaviors. *The American Journal of Psychiatry* **159** (4) 607–614.

Murphy N & McVey D (2010) *Treating Personality Disorder: Creating Robust Services for People with Complex Mental Health Needs*. Chichester: Routledge.

National Institute for Health and Clinical Excellence (2015) *Personality Disorders: Borderline and Antisocial* (NICE Quality Standard QS88). Retrieved from https://www.nice.org.uk/guidance/qs88

National Institute for Mental Health in England (2003) No Longer a Diagnosis of Exclusion. Retrieved from http://personalitydisorder.org.uk/wp-content/uploads/2015/04/PD-No-longer-a-diagnosis-of-exclusion.pdf

Obholzer A & Zagier Roberts V (1994) *The Unconscious at Work: Individual and Organizational Stress in the Human Services*. London: Routledge.

Peck E (2002) Integrating health and social care. *Managing Community Care* **10** (3) 16–19.

Peck E & Crawford A (2004) *'Culture' in Partnerships: What Do We Mean by It and What Can We Do About It?* Leeds: Integrated Care Network.

Perkins N, Smith K, Huner D, Bambra B & Joyce K (2010) 'What counts is what works'? New Labour and partnership in public health. *Policy & Politics* **1** 101–117.

Petfield L, Startup H, Droscher H & Cartwright-Hatton S (2015) Parenting in mothers with borderline personality disorder and impact on child outcomes. *Evidence Based Mental Health* **8** (3) 67–75.

Revolving Doors Agency (2019) *In Ten Years' Time: Improving Outcomes for People with Mental Ill-Health, Learning Disability, Developmental Disorders or Neuro-Diverse Conditions in the Criminal Justice System*. London: Bradley Report Group.

Rittel HWJ & Webber MM (1973) Dilemmas in a general theory of planning. *Policy Sciences* **4** 155–169.

Roberts Z (1994) The organisation of work: Contributions from open systems theory. In: A Obholzer and V Zagier Roberts (eds) *The Unconscious at Work: Individual and Organizational Stress in the Human Services*. Routledge: London.

Samuels J (2011) Personality disorders: Epidemiology and public health issues. *Int Rev Psychiatry* **23** (3) 223–233.

Sareen J, Afifi T, McMillan K & Asmundson G (2011) Relationship between household income and mental disorders: Findings from a population-based longitudinal study. *Arch Gen Psychiatry* **68** (4) 419–427.

Schwartz S (2006) A theory of cultural value orientations: Explication and applications. *Comparative Sociology* **5** (2–3) 137–182.

Shaikh U, Qamar I, Jafry F, Hassan M, Shagufta S, Odhejo YI & Ahmed S (2017) Patients with borderline personality disorder in emergency departments. *Frontiers in Psychiatry* **8** 136.

Shelter (2008) A long way from home: mental distress and long-term homelessness - a good practice briefing. Retrieved from https://england.shelter.org.uk/professional_resources/policy_and_research/policy_library/policy_library_folder/a_long_way_from_home_mental_distress_and_long-term_homelessness__a_good_practice_briefing

Tait L & Shah S (2007) Partnership working: A policy with promise for mental healthcare. *Advances in Psychiatric Treatment*, 13, 261–271.

Tyrer P (2014) Personality disorders in the workplace. *Occupational Medicine* **64** (8) 566–568.

VanVactor JD (2012) Collaborative leadership model in the management of health care. *Journal of Business Research* **65** (4) 555–561.

Wildridge V, Childs S, Cawthra L & Madge B (2004) How to create successful partnerships – a review of the literature. *Health Information and Libraries Journal* **21** Suppl 1. 3–19.

Williams P (2002) The competent boundary spanner. *Public Administration* **80** (1) 103–124.

Women in Prison/Barrow Cadbury Trust (2017) Corston 10: The Corston Report 10 years on. Retrieved from https://www.womeninprison.org.uk/perch/resources/corston-report-10-years-on.pdf

Yeomans D (2007) Take your partners please: Invited commentary on … Partnership working. *Advances in Psychiatric Treatment* **13** 272–275.

Zanarini M, Frankenburg F, Hennen J, Reich D & Silk K (2004) Axis I comorbidity in patients with borderline personality disorder: 6-year follow-up and prediction of time to remission. *Am J Psychiatry* **161** (11) 2108–2114.

Zimmerman M, Rothschild L & Chelminski I (2005) The prevalence of DSM-IV personality disorders in psychiatric outpatients. *Am J Psychiatry* **162** (10) 1911–1918.

Chapter 11:

Outcomes

Mary McMurran

> ### Governance principles
>
> Services should:
>
> - Collaborate with other researchers including service users to inform research priorities
> - Be vigilant to adverse outcomes
> - Seek to use common outcome measures across sites to allow for data sharing and comparison
> - Seek objectivity as much as possible
> - Seek to develop case formulations collaboratively with service users

Introduction

The purpose of this chapter is to address an apparently straightforward question: how do we assess the outcomes of clinical and psychosocial work with people diagnosed with 'personality disorder'? It is necessary at this very early stage to clarify that it is not the remit of this chapter to critique the construct of personality disorder. The standpoint here is to accept that many interventions and services are aimed at alleviating the problems experienced by people diagnosed with personality disorder, and it is these interventions and services that need to be evaluated. Addressing the question of outcomes will not result in a comprehensive list of assessment instruments: this chapter is not a shopping catalogue. One reason for this is that outcomes are of interest to a range of people, including commissioners of services, service providers, clinicians and therapists, researchers, research funders and, last but not least, the person in treatment. These categories of stakeholder have different requirements of outcomes, including measurement of effectiveness, cost effectiveness and cost efficiency. There are very many assessments that cover these areas. Rather than list them, the plan is to cover some issues in outcome assessment, with specific attention to the perspective of service users, who are the people being assessed. All stakeholders, service users included, need valid and reliable outcome measures: measures that really get to the crux of the matter and which give consistent results under similar conditions. This applies whether assessing outcomes is a clinical pursuit with individual clients or a research endeavour comparing groups of people.

The content of the chapter will cover diagnostic assessments and problem-focused outcome measures. All of these methods of assessment have their place in measuring aspects of people's problems and assessing how effective and cost-effective interventions to ameliorate these problems can be in resource limited services. In each section, the fundamental questions that will be addressed are to what extent the service user is meaningfully involved in the assessment, and what value service user involvement brings to the assessment. These questions will be posed in relation to research, diagnosis, symptom checklists, patient-focused outcomes and costs. Following this, influences that compromise the validity and reliability of measures will be described. Awareness of these pitfalls should enable assessors to minimise problems. The chapter will conclude with suggestions for best practice in assessment.

Research

Research is one of the cornerstones of evidence-based practice, with outcomes from treatment effectiveness studies informing the commissioning of services and the practice of clinicians working with people diagnosed with personality disorders. This section addresses setting the agenda for research into developing effective interventions with people diagnosed with personality disorders. Researchers, particularly those that are aiming to access funding for their research from national and international funding bodies, are bound by the priorities of funding bodies and by good scientific practice. Researchers must adhere closely to these requirements to stand any chance of acquiring funding in a domain where funding is scarce and there is fierce competition. Funding bodies have been criticised for under investing in mental health research, with only 5.5% of the UK's health research budget devoted to mental health (Mental Health Foundation, 2016). This is despite the high prevalence of mental health problems, including personality disorder: almost 14% of the UK adult population screen positive for personality disorder (Moran *et al*, 2016).

Researchers who are fortunate to acquire funding are likely to have met requirements for good research, which includes selecting valid, reliable and worthwhile measures. These would likely assess outcomes, processes and service use. Outcomes are what researchers intend that treatments will achieve; processes are the means whereby those outcomes are achieved; service use is an indicator of both individual well-being and cost to society and may include not only costs to health services but also costs of social care, criminal justice and employment benefits. Outcomes supply information on the effectiveness of treatment; outcomes, along with the amount and type of treatment received and the use of services, are measures that are used to calculate the cost-effectiveness of interventions.

Research into problems associated with personality disorder and the implementation of empirically supported treatments is not quite the objective science and decision-making that one might expect. Two questions will be considered here: first, what topics are chosen for research? Second, are treatment trials as good as they are supposed to be?

Prioritisation of the problems that are worthy of research funding, developing interventions to address those problems and designing methods of evaluating their effectiveness and cost-effectiveness used to be done without much in the way of consultation with those affected by these matters. This has changed. The James Lind Alliance (JLA) (www.jla.nihr.ac.uk) aims to change the way research funding is granted by raising awareness of research questions that are of direct relevance to service users, carers and clinicians. Named after an Edinburgh physician who, in 1747, confirmed the superiority of citrus fruits in the diet of sailors over other remedies for preventing and treating scurvy, the JLA brings patients, carers and clinicians together in priority setting partnerships (PSPs) to identify the top ten priorities for research in any field of health research. Unfortunately, to date no PSP has yet been constituted to consider priorities for personality disorder research.

The National Institute for Health Research (NIHR), a major UK funding body for health research, has driven patient and public involvement (PPI) in research (see www.invo.org.uk). The idea behind PPI is that research should not be an activity done by professionals *on* or *for* patients or clients, but rather *with* or *by* patients or clients and the general public. PPI can influence research priorities, research design and research methods. This includes the choice of domains to be assessed and the type of outcome measures used in research. Co-production, which is perhaps the pinnacle of PPI, is where researchers, practitioners and the public (which includes patients, potential patients, carers and people from patient representative organisations) collaborate equally on all aspects of a project from the very early design stages right to the end (Involve, 2018). At a broader level, service users can be involved in the commissioning of research, thus improving its relevance, and as research ambassadors to facilitate the implementation of research findings (National Institute for Health Research, 2018). This is mentioned here as an important reminder to researchers and intervention developers of the need to work with service users in the research process.

The 'gold standard' research design for evaluating the effects of treatment is the randomised controlled trial, although there is a critique to be made about the validity of importing medical model-based research methods to evaluate complex personal and interpersonal problems. Adequately sized trials are difficult to conduct; therefore, preliminary work is done to pave the way. This would include a proof of concept study of the intervention to check its acceptability to those who deliver and receive it and to ascertain its practicability. Then a feasibility trial would be conducted to check if people can be recruited to the study, randomised to different groups and retained to complete follow-up assessments. In mental health research in general, and in personality disorder research in particular, good results from the early stages of treatment evaluations have not always been replicated in full-scale trials (Crawford et al, 2016). Examples from trials in personality disorder treatment that have not supported active treatment include psychoeducation and problem solving (PEPS) versus usual treatment (McMurran et al, 2017), lamotrigine as a treatment for people diagnosed with borderline personality disorder versus a placebo (Crawford et al, 2018), and cognitive analytic therapy for adolescents diagnosed with borderline personality disorder versus good clinical care (Chanen et al, 2008). The reasons for this may be bias in feasibility studies, which may be run by product champions or may have too few participants to detect an effect reliably, or methodological flaws in full-scale trials, such as the fidelity of the intervention being compromised in the roll-out across therapists and sites or recruitment bias driven by clinical concerns. Furthermore, the accepted criterion for any treatment to be considered empirically supported is that at least two independent, well-conducted randomised controlled trials or single case experiments with a sample size of three or more should support the treatment; where only one RCT or single case experiment supports the treatment, then it is considered only promising. By these standards, most treatments for people diagnosed with personality disorder are promising at best (McMurran & Crawford, 2016).

Consequently, evidence-based clinical guidelines and treatment recommendations for people diagnosed with personality disorder are rare, and those that have been produced have focused primarily on the treatment of people diagnosed with borderline personality disorder (American Psychiatric Association, 2001; Australian Government National Health and Medical Research Council, 2013; National Institute for Health and Clinical Excellence, 2009a). These guidelines place considerable emphasis on general management and the context in which psychological treatments are offered and delivered and include actively involving people in treatment decisions, the need for contingency and crisis plans and the importance of explaining boundaries prior to the start of treatment. The positive impact of good clinical management may also help explain why clinical trials of psychological treatments show little or no additional benefit when compared with structured clinical care that is delivered in a consistent and supportive manner.

Levels of outcome assessment

Assessments can address different levels or domains of a problem and its treatment, depending on the purpose of the assessment. Diagnosis may be required to describe the population that accesses a service or for a person to access that service in the first place. The nature of the problem can be assessed by psychometrically developed measures, self-reported experiences, diary keeping and, more recently, methods using mobile technology (Areàn *et al*, 2016).

Personality disorder diagnosis

Assessing personality disorder either as a clinical need or an outcome measure is fraught with problems, including the excessive co-occurrence of different personality disorders, the heterogeneity of people diagnosed with any disorder owing to the way only some (e.g. any three of eight) of the criteria need to be met, and the stability over time of personality disorder diagnoses (Skodol, 2012). The co-occurrence of personality disorders, commonly referred to as comorbidity, leads to problems in choosing which disorder to focus on as an outcome measure. A personality disorder diagnosis requires a positive identification of only a subset of several listed criteria, meaning that the person's unique problems are not emphasised. In illustration, arithmetically there are 247 ways of meeting the criteria for borderline personality disorder, and 848 ways of meeting the anti-social personality disorder criteria (Arntz, 1999; Widiger & Trull, 1994). Hence, people with the same diagnosis may have very different problem profiles. Thus, a personality disorder diagnosis is not individually informative as an outcome measure. Indeed, personality disorder diagnoses give little information about the problems currently experienced by the individual, these being the problems for which the person has sought help and where improvement is desired, and, of course, these complex problems cannot be reduced to the binary outcome of personality disorder present or absent. Furthermore, the conceptualisation of personality disorder is that it is a condition that is stable across time, which offers little scope for change. Even where remission from a diagnosis is evident, this is not equivalent to remission of problems (Maden & Fowler, 2015).

Unsurprisingly, many service users perceive the label as having little functional value, negatively affecting their identity, reducing hope for recovery and interfering with service provision (Perkins *et al*, 2018). Consequently, one might expect some resistance to personality disorder assessment, which may affect validity, particularly where self-report measures are used. Structured interview assessments, such as the International Personality Disorder Examination (IPDE; Loranger *et al*, 1999) and the Structured Clinical Interview for Axis II disorders (SCID-II; First *et al*, 1997), give more valid diagnoses, but these are mostly lengthy and time-consuming. Even with thorough structured assessments, there remain the problems of diagnostic co-occurrence, heterogeneity of problem profiles and lack of uniqueness to the individual.

These problems with personality disorder diagnoses have recently led to major changes in classification systems. Both the fifth edition of the American Psychiatric Association's (APA's) Diagnostic and Statistical Manual (DSM-5; APA, 2013a) and the eleventh edition of the World Health Organization's International Classification of Diseases (ICD-11; World Health Organization, 2018) have viewed personality disorders less as discrete clinical entities and more as constellations of maladaptive personality traits that impair everyday functioning, particularly in the realm of interpersonal behaviour.

In the DSM-5, the 'emerging' hybrid model requires assessment of the level of impairment in functioning and associated personality traits, matching these with six personality disorder types. First of all, functioning is assessed in two domains with two elements in each: (1) Self, which includes (a) identity and (b) self-direction, and (2) Interpersonal, which includes (a) empathy and (b) intimacy. These elements are assessed using the Level of Personality Functioning Scale (American Psychiatric Association, 2013a, p775).

If functional impairment is present, then the next step in the alternative model is the assessment of personality traits. The Personality Inventory for DSM-5 (PID-5; American Psychiatric Association, 2013b) assesses traits in five broad domains, consisting of 25 specific trait facets. These domains are: (1) Negative affectivity (vs. Emotional stability); (2) Detachment (vs. Extraversion); (3) Antagonism (vs. Agreeableness); (4) Disinhibition (vs. Conscientiousness); and (5) Psychoticism (vs. Lucidity). The pattern of functional impairment and traits may match one of six personality disorder types: antisocial, avoidant, borderline, narcissistic, obsessive-compulsive and schizotypal.

ICD-11 also sees personality disorder as essentially reflecting disturbed interpersonal behaviour, but proposes a more radical departure by jettisoning personality disorder categories altogether in favour of a completely dimensional system of classification where assessment of the severity of personality disorder is paramount. Severity ranges from mild (not associated with substantial harm to self or others) to severe (associated with a past history and future expectation of severe harm to self or others that has caused long-term damage or has endangered life) (Tyrer *et al*, 2015). Clearly, assignment to one of the severity groups depends heavily upon the diagnostician's interpretation of a person's emotions and behaviour. However, severity can also be examined psychometrically. Olajide *et al* (2018) have developed the Standardized Assessment of Severity of Personality

Disorder (SASPD), a nine-item checklist, which asks respondents to rate their experiences as not problematic through to severely problematic with respect to relationships, emotion regulation, impulsivity and independence. Preliminary research indicates that the SASPD is reliable and that valid cutoffs can be identified for mild and moderate personality disorders. The value of this instrument for use as an outcome measure remains to be examined. ICD-11 also proposes assessment of dysfunctional personality traits in five trait domains: negative affect, dissocial, disinhibition, obsessional-compulsive and detachment. These new approaches potentially change the landscape of assessment of personality disorder, with severity being the focus.

New methods of personality disorder assessment developed for diagnostic purposes, particularly severity assessments, may lend themselves to measuring change over time, and hence may have usefulness as treatment outcome measures. Nonetheless, diagnosis remains a label visited upon the service user by a clinician, albeit based largely on information provided by the person in assessment, and frequently augmented by information from health records and clinical observation. Other types of measure focus more closely on the concerns of the individual.

Symptom checklists

Symptom severity checklists can be used to measure treatment progress and outcomes. These can be general, such as the global measure of disability, the World Health Organization Disability Assessment Schedule Version 2.0 (WHODAS 2.0; World Health Organization, 2010), which is a self-assessment of functioning in six areas: cognition (understanding and communicating); mobility; self-care; getting along with people; life activities (domestic, work/school, leisure); and participation in communities and society. The WHODAS 2.0 is available online and is reproduced in DSM-5, along with scoring instructions. Similarly, the Clinical Outcomes in Routine Evaluation – Outcome Measure (CORE-OM) is a pan-diagnostic measure of health and well-being (Evans et al, 2000; see CORE webpage www.coreims.co.uk).

There are also some symptom checklists specific to personality disorder, the best developed arguably being those assessing borderline symptoms, such as the clinician-rated Zanarini Rating Scale for Borderline Personality Disorder (ZAN-BPD; Zanarini, 2003) and the self-report Borderline Symptom List (BSL; Bohus et al, 2007). These measures focus on pertinent areas of functioning, such as relationships, affect regulation, self-harm and feelings of emptiness.

To be useful, these measures should be valid, reliable and sensitive to change (Zanarini et al, 2010). Meeting these criteria allows for data to be shared and compared across client groups and intervention types in both research and clinical practice. However, the interpretation of change in checklist scores is not a simple matter. It is important to know if positive change in a checklist score is associated with meaningful real-life change. Does change on a checklist score indicate genuine improvement? That is, is the person happier, calmer and getting into fewer predicaments? What degree of change in a checklist score is associated with symptom improvement? Is change on some checklist items more strongly associated with better functioning than scores on other items? That is, are some domains of functioning more important than others?

Symptom checklists go a considerable way towards accessing and assessing the degree of the actual problems faced by the person in treatment. Not only can total scores be calculated but also individual items can highlight areas of concern that need to be targeted for intervention and assessed for change. Nonetheless, the areas of enquiry into functioning and problems are determined by researchers and clinicians, not the individual him or herself. This leads us to consider the obvious strategy of asking clients directly about their problems and their responses to treatment.

Patient-focused outcomes

Gilbody *et al* (2003), in a review of outcomes in mental health research, noted that, in healthcare generally, there had been increasing interest over the past few decades in 'patient based outcomes, which measure the impact of illness or healthcare interventions on the individual and how they live their day-to-day life' (p8). The traditional measures of death, disease and expenditure began to be augmented by measures of the patient's perspective: how the individual subjectively experiences illness, the associated level of distress and the consequent psychological and social functioning are all captured in the concept of 'quality of life' (QoL). Of course, in mental health services, the assessments of 'disorders' are *de facto* measures of subjective phenomena, often combined with measures of functioning.

In 2016, NHS England published a document on developing quality and outcomes measures for use in mental health services. They placed emphasis on collaboration and co-production with experts by experience, clinicians and voluntary sector organisations to help ensure that services and interventions would be accessible and appropriate for people of all backgrounds, ages and experience, leading to system wide buy-in, which may support the achievement of outcomes. Their guidance was that the effectiveness of interventions should be measured through patient-reported outcomes measures (PROMs), alongside clinician-reported outcomes measures (CROMs). PROMs measure what service users consider to be important. Taking measures before and after treatment is of clinical value, and aggregated data can inform patient choice, service development and commissioning. PROMs measure general quality of life and there are condition-specific PROMS

(Devlin & Appleby, 2010). Some attention has been given to PROMS for mental health (Schmidt *et al*, 2000), with a recent focus on recovery in the development of the Recovering Quality of Life (ReQoL) assessment (Keetharuth *et al*, 2018), but there is no nationally accepted PROM for personality disorder.

A focus on the problems most relevant to the client is clearly important. Hasler *et al* (2004) found that clients who had completed treatment for psychiatric disorders experienced outcomes beyond reducing the symptoms of a disorder, including finding meaning in life and improving self-worth, and that there were differences between diagnostic groups in valued outcomes. Using only problem severity checklists might, therefore, miss some therapeutic gains. The message here is simply that people want various outcomes from treatment and clinicians cannot guess what any client might prioritise. Participants could be asked to identify their most important treatment goals and rate their progress towards these goals before, during and after treatment. The CORE Goal Attainment Form guides this procedure (see www.coreims.co.uk). Additionally, the most important areas for change can be assessed and agreed through collaborative case formulation.

Formulation is the preparation of an evidence-based explanation of a person's difficulties – their form, their origins and their development and maintenance over time (Hart *et al*, 2011; Sturmey & McMurran, 2019). The formulation is intended to generate an individually relevant treatment plan that will ameliorate the difficulties presented. The process involves specifying the problems to be addressed; identifying the predisposing, precipitating and perpetuating factors; and hypothesising what interventions might work to effect positive change. Outcome measures will relate to these specific aims. This formulation would be constructed in co-production with the individual concerned. In a meta-analysis of psychotherapy research studies, Tryon and Winograd (2011) found a substantial positive relationship between goal consensus and collaboration and therapy outcomes. This highlights the importance of identifying treatment goals collaboratively in the early stages of therapy.

Costs

One outcome that is of interest to commissioners, service providers and researchers is the costs incurred by people before and after treatment. People diagnosed with personality disorder are high users of medical, psychiatric and emergency healthcare services (Byrne *et al*, 2014). The wish is for treatments to be effective, and one measure of effectiveness might simply be a reduction in costs. Caution is required in judging effectiveness on costs alone; after all, death can be a relatively cheap outcome. Cost-effectiveness is the more balanced calculation. Costs that are included in calculations vary among studies to include health, social and criminal justice costs. These are measured by instruments such as the Client Service

Receipt Inventory (Beecham & Knapp, 2001). Effects for economists are generally identified as quality adjusted life years (QALYs), which are estimates of the years of life remaining following a particular intervention and weighting each year with a quality of life score measured in terms of the person's ability to carry out the activities of daily life, and freedom from pain and mental disturbance measured using instruments such as the EQ-5D (EuroQoL Group, 1990).

Discord between outcome measures

Definitions of personality disorder are multi-faceted and, as outlined above, outcomes can focus on diagnosis, symptom severity, client self-report of emotional and behavioural functioning and specific problem resolution, costs, and cost-effectiveness. What if these various measures are discordant? There may be a lack of synchrony between what people in treatment report and objective measures: people may feel better without any tangible improvements, or may feel worse but appear to have improved in the eyes of others. This latter point should give clinicians pause for thought before they discharge people who are less overtly troublesome but are unhappy.

Where multiple measures are taken, there is a chance of a random positive finding, and the more measures used the greater the chance of this. In some cases, this may lead to uninformed (or even unscrupulous) cherry picking. Stating a primary outcome minimises this problem. Where results are inconsistent, clarification needs to be achieved through collecting qualitative information from service users and considering theoretical explanations for asynchrony. An additional problem with multiple measures is the plain one of overburdening the respondent, sometimes to the point of them losing the will to complete any measure. Practical clinicians and researchers will aim to avoid this problem.

Influences on outcome measurement

Modes and methods of data collection affect outcomes. The information collected depends on what you ask, how you ask, when you ask and who is asking. Answers are affected by matters such as whether or not the questions being asked are meaningful to the respondent, how the respondent is feeling at the time of the assessment, the mode of assessment and the relationship between the assessor and the respondent. Obvious impediments to valid assessment are whether the client can read or hear and understand the questions, bearing in mind that some people with poor literacy may conceal their difficulties to avoid embarrassment. Clearly, respondents can choose to be truthful or deceptive, depending on what is to be gained or lost in the assessment situation, but there are also situational demands that affect people's responses. These influences will be addressed in this section.

Memory and meaning

Symptom checklists and interview schedules ask for information about the past, and often force answers into categories such as 'frequently – often - sometimes – never' or 'no symptoms – mild symptoms – moderate symptoms – serious symptoms – severe symptoms'. Recall of experiences, particularly highly emotional experiences, is subject to bias, for instance the tendency to be disproportionately influenced by the most recent or most intense experience when asked to average across all experiences and the tendency to base estimates of frequency and severity of variable experiences according to personal theories (Solhan *et al*, 2009). Furthermore, even though the categories of scales are defined for respondents, there may be lack of agreement on what constitutes frequency or severity. This can lead to errors that can affect treatment decisions and outcome measurement. The effects can be minimised by asking people to focus on specific experiences and record these as they happen or shortly afterwards (e.g. daily rating scales and diaries).

Rigorous ongoing assessment lends itself to single case design methodology for evaluating treatment outcome (Barlow *et al*, 2009). Single case designs, which are not to be confused with narrative case studies, use the participant as his or her own experimental control. Change is assessed by repeated measures of the treatment target from baseline, through treatment, to follow-up. This design is person-specific and allows for individual differences in responsiveness to treatment.

Confirmation bias

A major issue to be taken into account when measuring outcomes is cognitive bias. Lilienfeld and Lynn (2014) outline the major important biases operating in assessing treatment effectiveness. The first is confirmation bias, which is looking for the outcome you expect. Researchers are keen for their interventions to prove effective, and precautions need to be taken to avoid bias. This is addressed by employing researchers who are blind to the treatments that research participants have undertaken (or not undertaken) when outcomes are assessed. Similarly, in clinical practice, therapists aim to help their clients and they wish for positive outcomes; therefore, that is what they are inclined to see. As Lilienfeld and Lynn (2015) point out, this is nothing to do with therapist competence; rather, we are all susceptible to cognitive biases and it is simply that these normal processes apply to therapists in the therapy environment. It is good practice in some clinical fields that the person evaluating the outcomes of interventions should not be the clinicians who delivered the interventions. Clinicians in any service might therefore offer to evaluate each other's work via a peer exchange resource. Lilienfeld and Lynn also advocate 'debiasing strategies' such as deliberately considering the alternative or opposite to your expected outcome.

You won't find what you don't look for

The corollary of the confirmation bias is failing to see what else is happening besides that which you expect to find; that is, you don't see what you are not looking for. In both research and clinical practice, this can mean not seeing improvement in unexpected areas or being unaware of trajectories of regression and improvement. People are complex, with their functioning in numerous domains interconnected in contingent, synergistic and interactive ways. Changing one aspect of the system will have knock-on effects on other aspects. Trying to measure complex systems where altering one thing changes others is challenging and risks overlooking positive outcomes where there is actual change, and, of course, negative change where none was expected.

Some therapies can make some people worse. Lilienfeld (2007) evidences examples of harmful therapies, which include critical incident stress debriefing, scared-straight programmes for young offenders and grief counselling for normal bereavement. Given this knowledge, it would seem obvious that researchers and clinicians should attend to possible negative outcomes from therapy (McIntosh *et al*, 2019). Adverse events and adverse effects are often not referred to in treatment or even research literatures. For clarity, the term adverse events is generally used to describe observable events, such as self-harm, overdose or suicide attempt, whereas adverse effects are more subjective, such as an increase in depression, relationship dissatisfaction or loneliness.

Duggan *et al* (2014) examined protocols and final reports of 82 trials funded by the NIHR between 1995 and 2013. Of the 44 psychological intervention trials, 19 (43%) mentioned adverse events in protocols or final reports, compared with of 11 of 14 (79%) drug trials. The definition of adverse events in these trials followed research guidelines and focused on death, hospitalisation or disability; they were not tailored to the population in treatment. Duggan *et al* provide the example of people in treatment for borderline personality disorder, where some hospital attendance for self-harm is not unusual but hospital treatment might count as an adverse event. Furthermore, self-harm might be unrelated to treatment but related to other events in a person's life, such as relationship, work or financial problems.

In both treatment evaluations and clinical practice, theory drives the interventions, the treatment targets and the outcomes to be measured. Why, then, should theory not similarly drive considerations of harmful effects? In a trial of psychoeducation and problem solving (PEPS) for adults with personality disorder (McMurran *et al*, 2017), recruitment was halted when the Data Monitoring and Ethics Committee observed that more adverse events had occurred in the PEPS arm than in the usual treatment arm. While the difference was not statistically significant, the numbers were worrying: 117 adverse events among 60 participants in the treatment arm and 76 adverse events among 39 participants in the usual treatment arm. These events included deaths (four in the PEPS arm – two from natural causes and two from suicide, one of which occurred before the start of treatment; none in the usual treatment arm). Most adverse events were of severe substance use and self-harm. There may have been a bias in adverse event recording since there were more follow-up days in the treatment arm. However, there was great difficulty in establishing whether or not adverse outcomes were actually related to the treatment. The team proposed that, in future, protocols for treatment and evaluation should state *in advance* what adverse effects might theoretically be attributable to the intervention and if these are likely to be short-term effects due to temporary destabilisation or serious adverse effects that suggest that treatment should stop. This clearly has implications for assessment of outcomes. How should adverse effects be assessed? When should these effects be assessed to establish whether they are transitory or long lasting? And how can the relationship between adverse effects and treatment be established? This last point clearly requires the input of the person experiencing adverse effects, but this is by no means straightforward, since effects – negative or positive – may be attributed erroneously to treatment.

Response biases

Just as there may be a therapist bias to notice positive outcomes, service user information can also be subject to bias. People in therapy may evidence a social desirability response bias, that is, perceived undesirable thoughts, feelings or behaviours are under-reported and those perceived as desirable are over-reported (Edwards, 1957). This may also be expressed as a tendency to report positive therapy outcomes to please the therapist. This tendency can be measured using a social desirability scale, such as the Marlowe–Crowne inventory (Crowne & Marlowe, 1960). High levels of social desirability responding would cast doubt on the validity of self-report outcome measures. Service users may also be susceptible to an effort justification bias, which is a psychological process whereby outcomes are skewed towards the positive in justification of the effort expended (Cooper & Axsom, 1982). Report biases can be minimised by building a strong therapeutic relationship that promotes openness, but bear in mind that biases are subconscious; they are not deliberate attempts to mislead.

Ways forward

Having addressed issues in outcome assessment, it remains to indicate how organisations and services could use this information to improve their methods. There is no single, simple recipe for good practice; rather, those involved in evaluation need to use the information to make the best choices in their circumstances. What follows, therefore, is not prescriptive.

Formal agreements

Opportunities for research priority setting (e.g. JLA), agreeing common outcome measures to allow for comparisons across research studies and service evaluations, and defining relevant patient-related outcome measures (PROMS) have not been sufficiently developed in personality disorder work. Key to developing protocols for research and evaluation is co-operation between researchers, clinical staff and service users. User-led or user-controlled organisations have a major role to play but these require support, both financial and organisational. One example of a service user-controlled personality disorder organisation was the excellent Emergence in England and Wales, which has regrettably folded as a result of financial unsustainability. Commissioners, practitioners and service users need to place collaboration on their agenda and take up opportunities for influencing research and practice. One relevant recent development that may form the vehicle for such collaborations is the formation of 'communities of practice' (Wenger, 1998). A community of practice is a group of practitioners, which may include experts by experience, identified by a shared domain of interest, who are engaged in activities and discussions to share and develop best practice.

Adverse outcomes

Researchers and clinicians should be vigilant for adverse effects and adverse events. Exactly what they should be vigilant for should be based on theoretically driven hypotheses, as is the method for determining which positive outcomes are expected. That is, practitioners should consider the potential effects of their interventions in both positive and negative lights, using their academic and clinical knowledge to predict what might go wrong as well as what might go well. This ranges from acceptable side effects, whether temporary or permanent, to more serious negative effects that are likely in the course of treatment. For example, a temporary increase in distress in the process of trauma-related therapy may be considered acceptable in light of longer-term benefits. By contrast, an approach aiming to empower a person in an abusive relationship may exacerbate risk. To a large degree, the treatment recipient is the one to decide what is acceptable. However, service users can only make the decision to take the risk of any adverse outcomes that may accompany positive change if they are fully informed. Not only do they need to be informed of the potential risks of undertaking treatment, but safeguarding procedures need to be put in place to protect against harm. These include designing crisis management plans, a well-established practice whereby clinicians and service users jointly identify signs of deterioration and make plans for how to cope or get help. However, it must be noted that there is an absence of research on the effectiveness of crisis plans for people diagnosed with personality disorder (Borschmann *et al*, 2012). This absence of evidence could usefully be corrected.

Linden (2013) offers a useful checklist for investigating and recording negative effects for use in research and clinical work. He lists classes of negative events, including lack of treatment effect; patient non-compliance; emergence of new symptoms; deterioration of symptoms; strains in the patient–therapist relationship; strains in the patient's work, family or life circumstances; illness; or negative well-being. Clinicians should be vigilant for these matters. When unwanted outcomes are observed, service users should be asked about the circumstances to elucidate the relationship to treatment. Upon investigation, these may or may not be related to the therapy.

While not all negative outcomes will be measured psychometrically, where they are then, as with all measures, those selected should be reliable and valid. Often, these will be the same measures that aim to assess positive change (e.g. anxiety or depression may decrease or increase) and assessment at baseline allows for observation of change in either direction.

Outcome measures

Common outcome measures should be promoted to allow for data sharing and comparison across research studies and service evaluations. These will be drawn from different levels of assessment, as identified earlier in the chapter, depending on the purpose of the evaluation: service-level or individual-level evaluation. At the individual level, additional measures can address unique needs. It should be remembered that most psychometric outcome measures are proxy measures of real-life change, so the choice should be of those that have been validated against meaningful clinical outcomes. Questionnaires and checklists can be impersonal and are therefore usefully augmented by PROMS and patient diaries.

Selection of outcome measures should be a collaborative approach at all levels. In research, there is a strong drive to include service users on research teams at the point of designing studies, when outcome measures are selected. This collaborative approach has the potential to enhance their relevance while abiding by scientific principles. In practice, collaboration with clients regarding the choice and range of outcome measures is likely to improve response rates and validity of responding.

Multiple measures will usually be required to address different domains, including symptoms, social functioning, and service use. Attention could also usefully be paid to physical health outcomes (Dixon-Gordon *et al*, 2015). There may well be disparities of results across measures. While the use of multiple measures can be useful to search for concordance, there is the risk of random results, that is, a chance finding. To avoid this, it is important to select a primary outcome measure, this being the single most important outcome expected as a result treatment. This should be stated in advance and be based on logic (i.e. a theory-driven hypothesis). In doing so, false positives (and negatives) are avoided.

Biases

Lilienfeld *et al* (2014) provide helpful safeguards against a number of biases in evaluating therapies. The case for using well-validated and reliable measures has already been made. These should be applied both before treatment and after treatment to assess outcomes. Furthermore, assessing people repeatedly and over the long term enables a check on fluctuations of response. Of course, repetition can create its own problems by overloading respondents, so repeated measures need to be selected and used judiciously, with shorter measures amenable to more frequent use.

Treatment outcome evaluation should ideally be conducted by someone blind to the expected outcomes. In clinical settings, blind assessment is usually not possible, but what should be possible is case evaluation by personnel uninvolved in therapy. Clearly, the individual's therapist should not be the one to evaluate the therapy that he or she has been delivering.

In addition to outcomes, it is also important to measure mediators of change. These tell us if the intervention is working (or not) in the way intended. Ideally, an objective measure should be used. For example, if the goal is to help people reduce depression, and the means by which the intervention aims to achieve this is through increasing physical activity, then activity trackers or mobile apps can be used to monitor activity. This guards against reliance on self-report outcomes that may be biased by social desirability or outcome justification biases. Of course, objective measures that rely on gadgets may prove out of reach of cash-strapped services, and evaluators may have to rely on corroborative evidence from significant others.

Case formulation

The importance of co-production of intervention planning, implementation, and evaluation was mentioned earlier. Where outcomes are concerned, it is essential to reach an agreement with the individual about what is to be measured, how and when. Such an agreement maximises the chances that assessments will be meaningful, valid and regularly completed. The lynchpin of this co-production is the case formulation, developed jointly with the individual concerned and resulting in agreed treatment targets, treatment methods and process and outcome evaluations.

Conclusion

To return to the question posed at the outset: how do we assess the outcomes of clinical and psychosocial work with people diagnosed with personality disorder? Readers may be disappointed but probably not surprised to learn that there is no simple and definitive answer. There is work to be done to clarify best and most important outcomes for research and practice, care to be taken in design and application of measures, and collaboration with service users to be purposefully and meaningfully undertaken to advance knowledge and practice.

References

American Psychiatric Association (2010) Practice guideline for the treatment of patients with borderline personality disorder. Retrieved from http://psychiatryonline.org/pb/assets/raw/sitewide/practice_guidelines/guidelines/bpd.pdf

American Psychiatric Association (2013a) *Diagnostic and Statistical Manual of Mental Disorders* (5th edition). Washington, DC: APA.

American Psychiatric Association (2013b) *The Personality Inventory for DSM-5 (PID-5)*. Retrieved from http://www.psychiatry.org/APA_DSM5_The-Personality-Inventory-For-DSM-5-Brief-Form-Adult.pdf

Areàn PA, Ly KH & Andersson G (2016) Mobile technology for mental health assessment. *Dialogues in Clinical Neuroscience* **18** 163–169.

Arntz A (1999) Do personality disorders exist? On the validity of the concept and its cognitive-behavioral formulation and treatment. *Behaviour Research and Therapy* **37** S97–S134.

Australian Government National Health and Medical Research Council (2013) Clinical practice guideline for the management of borderline personality disorder. Retrieved from https://www.nhmrc.gov.au/about-us/publications/clinical-practice-guideline-borderline-personality-disorder

Barlow DH, Nock MK & Hersen M (2009) *Single Case Experimental Designs: Strategies for Studying Behaviour Change* (3rd edition). Boston: Pearson.

Beecham J & Knapp M (2001) Costing psychiatric interventions. In: G. Thornicroft (ed) *Measuring Mental Health Needs*. London: Gaskell.

Bohus M, Limberger MF, Frank U, Chapman AL, Kühler T & Stieglitz RD (2007) Psychometric properties of the Borderline Symptom List (BSL). *Psychopathology* **40** 126–132. DOI: 10.1159/000098493

Borschmann R, Henderson C, Hogg J, Phillips R & Moran P (2012) Crisis interventions for people with borderline personality disorder. *Cochrane Database of Systematic Reviews*, Issue 6, Art. No.: CD009353. DOI: 10.1002/14651858.CD009353.pub2

Byrne M, Henagulph S, McIvor RJ, Ramsey J & Carson J (2014) The impact of a diagnosis of personality disorder in service usage in an adult community mental health team. *Social Psychiatry and Psychiatric Epidemiology* **49** 307–316. DOI: 10.1007/s00127-013-0746-3

Chambless DL & Hollon SD (1998) Defining empirically supported theories. *Journal of Consulting and Clinical Psychology* **66** 7–18. DOI:10.1037/0022-006X.66.1.7

Chanen AM, Jackson HJ, McCutcheon LK, Jovev M, Dudgeon P, *et al* (2008) Early intervention for adolescents with borderline personality disorder using cognitive analytic therapy: Randomised controlled trial. *British Journal of Psychiatry* **193** 477–484. DOI: 10.1192/bjp.bp.107.048934

Cooper J & Axsom D (1982) Effort justification in psychotherapy. In: GW Weary & H Mirels (eds) *Integrations of Clinical and Social Psychology*. New York: Oxford University Press.

Crawford MJ, Barnicot K, Patterson S & Gold C (2016) Negative results in phase III trials: Cause for concern or just good science? *British Journal of Psychiatry* **209** 6–8. DOI: 10.1192/bjp.bp.115.179747

Crawford MJ, Sanatinia R, Barrett B, Cunningham G, Dale O, Ganguli P *et al* (2018) The clinical effectiveness and cost-effectiveness of lamotrigine in borderline personality disorder: A randomized placebo-controlled trial. *American Journal of Psychiatry* **175** 756–764. DOI: 10.3310/signal-000617

Crowne DP & Marlowe D (1960) A new scale of social desirability independent of psychopathology. *Journal of Consulting Psychology* **24** 349–354. DOI:10.1037/h0047358

Devlin NJ & Appleby J (2010) Getting the most out of PROMS: Putting health outcomes at the heart of NHS decision making. Retrieved from https://www.kingsfund.org.uk/sites/default/files/Getting-the-most-out-of-PROMs-Nancy-Devlin-John-Appleby-Kings-Fund-March-2010.pdf

Dixon-Gordon KL, Whalen DJ, Layden BK & Chapman AL (2015) A systematic review of personality disorders and health outcomes. *Canadian Psychology* **56** 168–190. DOI: 10.1037/cap0000024

Duggan C, Parry G, McMurran M, Davidson K & Dennis J (2014) The recording of adverse events from psychological treatments in clinical trials: Evidence from a review of NIHR-funded trials. *Trials* **15** (1) 335. DOI: 10.1186/1745-6215-15-335

Edwards AL (1957) *The Social Desirability Variable in Personality Assessment and Research*. New York: The Dryden Press.

EuroQol Group (1990) EuroQol: A new facility for the measurement of health-related quality of life. *Health Policy* **16** 199–208. DOI: 10.1016/0168-8510(90)90421-9

Evans C, Mellor-Clark J, Margison F, Barkham M, Audin K, Connell J & McGrath G (2000) CORE: Clinical outcomes in routine evaluation. *Journal of Mental Health* **9** 247–255. DOI: 10.1080/jmh.9.3.247.255

First MB, Gibbon M, Spitzer RL, Williams JBW & Benjamin LS (1997) *Structured Clinical Interview for DSM-IV Axis II Personality Disorders*. Arlington, VA: American Psychiatric Publishing, Inc.

Gilbody S, House AO & Sheldon TA (2003) Outcome measures in psychiatry: A critical review of outcomes measurement in psychiatric research and practice. Report 24, Centre for Reviews and Dissemination, University of York. Retrieved from https://www.york.ac.uk/media/crd/crdreport24.pdf

Hart S, Sturmey P, Logan C & McMurran M (2011) Forensic case formulation. *International Journal of Forensic Mental Health* **10** 118–126. doi: 10.1080/14999013.2011.577137

Hasler G, Moergeli H & Schneider U (2004) Outcome of psychiatric treatment: What is relevant for our patients? *Comprehensive Psychiatry* **45** 199–205. doi:10.1016/j.comppsych.2004.02.001

Involve (2018) Guidance on co-producing a research project. Retrieved from http://www.invo.org.uk/wp-content/uploads/2018/03/Copro_Guidance_Mar18.pdf

Keetharuth A, Brazier J, Connell J, Bjorner J, Carlton J, Taylor Buck E, Ricketts T, McKendrick K, Browne J, Croudace T & Barkham M (2018) Recovering Quality of Life (ReQoL): A new generic self-reported outcome measure for use with people experiencing mental health difficulties. *The British Journal of Psychiatry* **212** (1) 42–49. DOI: 10.1192/bjp.2017.10.

Lilienfeld SO (2007) Psychological treatments that cause harm. *Perspectives on Psychological Science* **2** 53–70. DOI: 10.1111/j.1745-6916.2007.00029.x

Lilienfeld SO & Lynn SJ (2015) Errors/biases in clinical decision making. In: RL Cautin and SO Lilienfeld (eds) *The Encyclopaedia of Clinical Psychology*. New York: Wiley.

Lilienfeld SO, Ritschel LA, Lynn SJ, Cautin R & Latzman RD (2014) Why ineffective psychotherapies seem to work: A taxonomy of causes and spurious therapeutic effectiveness. *Perspectives on Psychological Science* **9** 355–387. DOI: 10.1177/1745691614535216

Linden M (2013) How to define, find and classify side effects in psychotherapy: From unwanted events to adverse treatment reactions. *Clinical Psychology and Psychotherapy* **20** 286–296. DOI: 10.1002/cpp.1765

Loranger AW (1999) *International Personality Disorder Examination* (IPDE). Odessa, FL: Psychological Assessment Resources.

Maden A & Fowler JC (2015) Consistency and coherence in treatment outcome measures for borderline personality disorder. *Borderline Personality Disorder and Emotion Dysregulation* **2** (1). DOI: 10.1186/s40479-014-0022-5

McIntosh LG, McMurran M, Taylor PJ & Thomson LDG (2019) Gaps in measures of adverse outcomes relating to psychological interventions. *Criminal Behaviour and Mental Health*, in press.

McMurran M & Crawford MJ (2016) Personality disorders. In: CM Nezu & AM Nezu (eds) *The Oxford Handbook of Cognitive and Behavioral Therapies*. New York: Oxford University Press.

McMurran M, Day F, Reilly J, Delport J, McCrone P, Whitham D, *et al* (2017) Psychoeducation and problem solving (PEPS) therapy for adults with personality disorder: A pragmatic randomized controlled trial. *Journal of Personality Disorders* **31** (6) 810–826. DOI: 10.1521/pedi_2017_31_286

Mental Health Foundation (2016) *Fundamental Facts about Mental Health 2016*. Mental Health Foundation: London.

Moran P, Rooney K, Tyrer P & Coid J (2016) Personality disorder. In: S McManus, P Bebbington, R Jenkins & T Brugha (eds) *Mental Health and Wellbeing in England: Adult Psychiatric Morbidity Survey 2014*. Leeds: NHS Digital.

National Institute for Health and Clinical Excellence (2009). *Borderline Personality Disorder: Treatment and Management*. London: NICE. Retrieved from https://www.nice.org.uk/guidance/CG78

National Institute for Health Research (2018). The public as our partners: NIHR Central Commissioning Facility 2017/2018 highlights report. Retrieved from https://www.nihr.ac.uk/about-us/how-we-are-managed/coordinating-centres/nihr-central-commissioning-facility/Documents/CCF_PPIEreport17_18SHORT.pdf

NHS England & NHS Improvement (2016). Delivering the five year forward view for mental health: Developing quality and outcomes measures. Retrieved from https://www.england.nhs.uk/mentalhealth/wp-content/uploads/sites/29/2016/02/mh-quality-outcome.pdf

Olajide K, Munjiza J, Moran P, O'Connell L, Newton-Howes G, Bassett P, Akintomide G, Ng N, Tyrer P, Mulder R & Crawford MJ (2018) Development and psychometric properties of the Standardized Assessment of Severity of Personality Disorder (SASPD). *Journal of Personality Disorders* **32** 44–56. DOI: 10.1521/pedi_2017_31_285

Perkins A, Ridler J, Browes D, Peryer G, Notley C & Hackmann C (2018) Experiencing mental health diagnosis: A systematic review of service user, clinician, and carer perspectives across clinical settings. *The Lancet* **5** (9) 747–764. DOI: 10.1016/S2215-0366(18)30095-6

Schmidt LJ, Garratt AM & Fitzpatrick, R (2000) Instruments for mental health: A review. Retrieved from http://phi.uhce.ox.ac.uk/pdf/phig_mental_health_report.pdf

Skodol AE (2012) Diagnosis and DSM-5: Work in progress. In: TE Widiger (ed) *The Oxford Handbook of Personality Disorders*. New York: Oxford University Press.

Solhan MB, Trull TJ, Jahng S & Wood PK (2009) Clinical assessment of affective instability: Comparing EMA indices, questionnaire reports, and retrospective recall. *Psychological Assessment* **21** 425–436. DOI: 10.1037/a0016869

Sturmey P & McMurran M (2019) Case formulation for personality disorders: Tailoring psychotherapy to the individual client. In: U. Kramer (ed) *Case Formulation for Personality Disorders*. Amsterdam: Elsevier.

Tryon GS & Winograd G (2011) Goal consensus and collaboration. *Psychotherapy* **48** 50–57. DOI: 10.1037/a0022061

Tyrer P, Reed G & Crawford MJ (2015) Classification, assessment, prevalence, and effect of personality disorder. *The Lancet* **385** 717–726. DOI:10.1016/S0140- 6736(14)61995-4

Wenger E (1998) *Communities of Practice: Learning, Meaning, and Identity.* Cambridge: Cambridge University Press.

Widiger TA & Trull TJ (1994) Personality disorders and violence. In: J Monahan and HJ Steadman (eds) *Violence and Mental Disorder: Developments in Risk Assessment.* Chicago: University of Chicago Press.

World Health Organization (2010) Measuring health and disability: Manual for the WHO Disability Assessment Schedule, WHODAS 2. Retrieved from: http://apps.who.int/iris/bitstream/handle/10665/43974/9789241547598_eng.pdf;jsessionid=6C8D88CE87C11F9F24A0A772719AD641?sequence=1

World Health Organization (2018) *11th Revision of the International Classification of Diseases* (ICD-10). Geneva: WHO.

Zanarini MC (2003) Zanarini Rating Scale for Borderline Personality Disorder (ZAN-BPD): A continuous measure of DSM-IV borderline psychopathology. *Journal of Personality Disorders* **17** 233–242. DOI: 10.1521/pedi.17.3.233.22147

Zanarini MC, Stanley B, Black DW, Markowitz JC, Goodman M, Pilkonis P, Lynch TR, Levy K, Fonagy P, Bohus M, Farrell J & Sanislow CA (2010) Methodological considerations for treatment trials for persons with borderline personality disorder. *Annals of Clinical Psychiatry* **22** 75–83.

Chapter 12:

Contained and Containing Teams

Jo Ramsden

> Governance principles:
> - ■ Teams need to articulate how they work to notice and contain the inevitable anxiety experienced by workers
> - ■ Teams need to articulate how they are working to define and serve their primary task.
> - ■ Teams need to articulate how they are working to create and maintain high performing transdisciplinary teams

Introduction

This chapter will set out a particular approach to team-working. The approach here is one which seeks to maximise the therapeutic potential of the team by ensuring structures are in place which better enable authentic, compassionate therapeutic relationships with individuals who may be described as having a 'personality disorder'. Of particular importance are structures which enable teams to work effectively with the strong emotions that inevitably result as part of the work.

One of the areas of interest for this book is the fundamental importance of the emotional impact of the work, which we view as having the potential to undermine effective and therapeutic service delivery (see Barrett, this edition). It is a key assertion of this book that services working with people who might be described as having a 'personality disorder' confront powerful emotional processes (e.g. Obholzer & Zagier Roberts, 1994) which frequently subvert and distort some of the relational work which we know is helpful to people in distress.

While much of the existing literature for working with 'personality disorder' recognises the potential for problematic interpersonal dynamics, the emotional impact of the work is often positioned as secondary to what is often implicitly situated as being the 'real work'. Staff are reminded to pay attention to 'burnout' (e.g. NHS England & NOMS, 2015) and the importance of supervision is well endorsed. However, how this emotional impact may itself fundamentally prevent or obstruct authentic, therapeutic relationships is less well discussed. This is despite a general acknowledgement that the work is itself relational.

To illustrate this point, a treatment focus tends to prevail within the literature, meaning that much which is written about work with this client group has its roots in a biomedical or pathology-focused approach. Such an approach tends to position the clinician as a dispassionate expert, immune to (or well equipped to manage) the emotional impact of the work. For example, Young *et al* (2003) discuss the importance of the therapy relationship and illustrate the role that the therapist's own emotional processes can play in problematic interactions. The ability of the therapist to be aware of and notice their own emotional responses is considered essential for good therapeutic work by these authors and they illustrate a number of ways in which the work might trigger the therapist's own problematic schema response. Nonetheless, the therapist's ability to recognise and address their own reactions is described as a relatively straightforward process which seemingly underplays the significance of what Obholzer and Zagier Roberts (1994) describe as a 'major source of stress' associated with working with people who are suffering. For these authors, therapeutic processes which require individuals to notice and address this stress as part of their everyday work also ignores the fact that it is so frequently 'kept out of awareness not only by personal defences but also by collective ones' (p49).

In other examples, the clinician's emotional responses to the work are considered to be essentially benevolent. For example, Evershed (2011) discusses the importance of boundaries in therapeutic work with patients with 'personality disorder' in secure settings and argues that boundary violations tend to occur due to 'a benign intent on the part of the clinician to meet the needs of the patient' (p134). In other words, the clinician is considered to consciously and dispassionately act in a way which breaches the established 'rules' of therapy so as to better enable a therapeutic process. In this instance, no consideration is given to factors within the clinician that might be distorting the boundaries of therapy, such as their own fear, anxiety or desperation. The potential for the worker to feel something less compassionate towards the client (Hinshelwood, 2002) is not considered.

In underplaying the impact of the work on the workforce and overstating the capacity of workers to manage it, much of the literature fails to acknowledge the importance of an organisational capacity to contain emotion (Miller, 1993) and the reality that practices inevitably and unconsciously emerge which serve to manage workers' anxiety, often at the expense of service users. These social defences (Menzies-Lyth, 1960) are often felt to be professionally responsible and appropriate to the workplace culture and, as such, they tend to be left unexamined and unquestioned.

The governance principles upheld by this chapter serve, therefore, to ensure that teams are working to develop structures which allow them to better notice and understand social defences and, in doing so, to act as processors and containers for the inevitable emotional impact of the work (Barrett, this edition). The principles (as with all the principles in the book) are intended to prescribe a way of working which is less about doing and more about noticing and questioning why things are done in the way that they are done. On the face of it, these principles may look to the reader as if they would lead to endless questioning and reflection (rather than action). It is important, therefore, to also ensure that there are structures which facilitate 'doing' by allowing teams to be assured that their practice is sound. The aim of this chapter is, therefore, to articulate principles which allow for the conditions to be in place for the development of curious, compassionate and effective teams.

While this chapter will uphold the importance of team working, it will also discuss some of the limitations of a traditional multi-disciplinary team (MDT) approach (especially in relation to complex emotional difficulties). In particular, it will be argued that unthinking MDT working may constitute a social defence: having different disciplines around the table can feel to the team to be inherently more responsive and as if better decisions are made when in fact these teams are often unhelpfully incoherent in their work. Un-integrated team working allows for the team to avoid some of the more problematic tensions that are likely to be present, even though these tensions may well be informative and important for working authentically and courageously with the client group. As such, this chapter will outline a more complex approach to MDT working where efforts are made to ensure that different roles and approaches are integrated and harmonised in order to achieve a more robust and effective team which is focused on mutually dependent goals (Murphy & McVey, 2010). The governance principle which is upheld is one where teams should be able to evidence the efforts they are making to ensure a highly integrated team. Suggestions will be made for how this might be achieved.

Relational approaches to the work

For someone new to working with 'personality disorder', the important work (from reading the literature) would appear to be the application of a particular therapeutic modality to reduce the symptoms associated with 'personality disorder'. There is plenty of literature available to help the new practitioner by evidencing the relative effectiveness of various approaches, such as schema-focused (e.g. Masley *et al*, 2012), mentalisation-based therapy (e.g. Bateman & Fonagy, 2009), dialectical behaviour therapy (e.g. Bohus *et al*, 2004) or cognitive analytic therapy (e.g. Kellett, 2011). However, despite the prevalence of literature to evidence the positive impact of these different approaches, the iatrogenic effect of psychotherapy has also been highlighted (e.g. Fonagy & Bateman, 2006) and no one therapeutic modality has emerged as more effective than any other (Bateman *et al*, 2015). As a consequence, all this research activity has ultimately failed to underpin a consistent approach to service commissioning and design (Evans *et al*, 2017). Evans *et al* (2017) use their description of the evolution of personality disorder services to argue that there is 'a disparity between what we know and what is being delivered'. These authors suggest that the treatment focus within the literature has been 'conflated' with the need for safe and robust pathways. They point to the need for better research into current clinical practice ('what we know') to inform minimum standards for service delivery.

Arguably, 'what we know' is that working to care for and/or manage people who present in a way which is consistent with a 'personality disorder' diagnosis is a far more complex process than all the treatment manuals and randomised controlled trials into effective 'treatment' approaches would suggest. 'What we know' would appear to underpin some of the contemporary approaches to specialist work with 'personality disorder'. These approaches seek to build on the initiatives that drew attention to the failure of mental health services to provide an adequate response (e.g. National Institute for Mental Health in England, 2003; Department of Health, 2009) while also de-emphasising the expert classification process that, traditionally, has underpinned service provision and driven so much research in the biomedical, pathology-focused tradition. These new approaches tend to critique the diagnostic process, and emphasise service user involvement and the importance of the relational conditions which are required for any effective service response to 'personality disorder'. For example, recent guidance for community teams on working with 'personality disorder' highlights the therapeutic importance of every interaction (Department of Health, 2014). This guidance exhorts professionals to respond in a curious and compassionate way, stressing that the way in which any relationship is conducted (whether or not it is a formal therapy relationship) will ensure that it is potentially helpful. The widely adopted Enabling Environments (EE) framework (e.g. Royal College of Psychiatrists, 2019) requires services to evidence how they uphold standards that enable a sense of belonging and safety. The EE framework states that the nature and quality of relationships are of primary importance. The national offender personality disorder (OPD) pathway strategy (Joseph & Benefield, 2012) ensures that services are delivered in partnership and identifies those eligible for those services not through diagnosis but through screening for the difficulties typically associated with the classification. It is a contractual requirement of those delivering services on the OPD pathway to evidence how they are involving service users and how they work to ensure that relationships are high-quality and support therapeutic change.

Challenges to providing relationally focused work

Despite this contemporary focus on relational awareness, it is also widely acknowledged in the literature that the term 'personality disorder' describes ways of relating that tend to obstruct or distort the development of healthy relational bonds and attachments. In other words, the very nature of 'personality disorder' means that the relational work required is effortful and complex. Young *et al* (2003) describe how behaviours which are consistent with a 'personality disorder' diagnosis typically obscure affective states making it difficult for workers to understand the emotional world of those using their services. Bateman and Fonagy (2004) describe how problems with mentalising or understanding mental processes (skills which facilitate effective interpersonal relationships) are characteristic of 'borderline personality disorder'. Recent guidance highlights how intuitive risk management strategies for an offending population (where there is a high prevalence of the problems associated with 'personality disorder') is frequently flawed (Blumenthal *et al*, 2018). These authors stress the importance of what are often counterintuitive risk management strategies which require a sophisticated understanding of the emotional world of the individual. Other authors have pointed to some of the problematic errors of logic (Murphy & McVey, 2010; Ramsden & Lowton, 2014) that workers often make when relying on their own attachment experiences to inform what are assumed to be helpful ways of relating.

To put all this in a less intellectualised or theoretical way: teams working with individuals who are deeply distressed work every day with the traumatic consequences of that distress. Workers regularly encounter and manage incidents of often serious self-harm, for example, or violent behaviour which is profoundly frightening and upsetting. The histories of the individuals cared for are, typically, appalling and the work often requires the management of interpersonal encounters characterised by abuse, hostility, indifference, etc.

Her own abusive upbringing meant that Natalie was frequently afraid of staff on her ward. Those she was most afraid of could not pass her without her yelling at them that she hoped their children got cancer, and that they were stupid and rubbish at their job. On one occasion, while out for a walk in the hospital grounds, Natalie started to find the conversation she was having with the nurse who was accompanying her difficult and triggering of her fear. In a distressed rage she kicked a passing cat so hard that it was stunned and helpless. As the cat lay at her feet Natalie continued to kick it, much to the extreme anguish of the nurse.

Even though a wealth of psychological theory and guidance is available to help workers understand the relational challenges in the work, the ability of many services to provide the effective therapeutic relational environment required is questionable. Service users frequently complain that their treatment at the hands of services is often inadequate, sometimes abusive and cruel. On social media, there is a proliferation of service user groups (and sympathisers) decrying the treatment that they have received and demanding a more compassionate approach:

> *'Imagine a publicly funded service where staff repeatedly with no sense of shame or morality call rape victims "vindictive and manipulative" and follow that with "and make fake accusations". And tell survivors of abuse they have "an exaggerated [sense] of being wronged'*
>
> (LittleMy1234, 2019) Twitter post. Retrieved from https://twitter.com/littlemy1234/status/1085318671436779521)

> *'We have to work against the overt and covert use of "PD" or "PD traits" to give an excuse to neglect, abuse or gaslight patients that professionals find difficult'*
>
> Shrink_at_Large, 2019, Twitter post. Retrieved from https://twitter.com/shrink_at_large/status/1087843731544391680)

Their experiences would appear to be validated by the literature, which highlights the negative attitudes and damaging counter-transferential experiences that staff have when working with people who present in a way consistent with a 'personality disorder' diagnosis (e.g. Freestone *et al*, 2015). For example, difficulties with 'patient behaviour' and GP–patient relationships were two of the major themes uncovered by Wlodarczyk *et al* (2018) in their exploration of GPs' experiences of providing care to people with 'borderline personality disorder' in primary care in Australia. Similarly, Hong (2016), in describing the experiences of people with 'borderline personality disorder' accessing emergency hospital treatment, highlights increased negative attitudes that staff have towards this patient group and the volatile interactions which frequently characterise these encounters. Murphy and McVey (2010) list a number of difficulties that staff face when working with this service user group and suggest that these emotional reactions can affect clinical judgement and 'restrict the capacity of staff to be effective' (p21). Community guidance for working with personality disorder notes 'cutting off from service users and treating them in a distant, superior or critical way' as one of the 'common defences against the distress stirred up by getting involved in the work' (Department of Health, 2014, p69).

Stacy was frequently admitted to an acute ward throughout her early adulthood for periods of distress when she was self-harming and suicidal. She became aware of the exasperation of staff and got used to a level of dismissiveness from them which was deeply upsetting. On one occasion, when she was lying on her bed in profound distress, she became aware of the conversation around her; the nursing team were discussing stripping her and putting her, naked, into seclusion. The tone of the conversation was that the nursing team could no longer put up with her behaviour and she needed to be 'taught a lesson'. The nurses' conversation triggered memories and emotions associated with early childhood sexual abuse for Stacy and served to compound her suffering.

The need for a mind on the team

The psychodynamic literature seeks to explain why teams are often so ineffective at providing the relational conditions that service users want and need. In her seminal paper, Menzies (1960) explains how social defences proliferate in teams which are unconsciously seeking to manage the inevitable anxiety that is an inherent part of the work of caring for other human beings. These social defences (which manage anxiety in the workforce often at the expense of the service user) frequently fail to be noticed by teams and can go on to form the foundation for ineffective or even damaging workplace cultures. Menzies (1960) describes how social defences remain unexamined by being organisationally sanctioned: they are experienced by workers as normal, professional, inevitable and responsible and go on to constitute a set of cultural norms which are mindlessly upheld. Main (1990) describes how workplace cultures get taught and transmitted from worker to worker, becoming ever more rigid and increasingly hard to notice. Foster (2001) suggests that a 'mindless' approach to the work, where the emotional experience of it is split off, is often necessary to manage the stress of working in helping professions where there is a 'duty to care'.

These authors illustrate how, despite a theoretical understanding of the demands of the work, service providers are likely to be unconsciously pulled into a way of practising which is, at best, ill attuned to the needs of the service user. Practices which are experienced by service users as thoughtless or even cruel may, despite our best efforts, unconsciously emerge. Hinshelwood (2002) describes the 'almost always unrecognised' (S20) impact of the work on service providers, who, he believes, frequently go on to perpetrate a form of unconscious abuse against those in care. Hinshelwood argues that this unconscious abuse is the consequence of an inability of workers to think about and understand what is happening to them when they care for others who have experienced abuse early in life. The blog extract below illustrates how even well-intentioned, compassionate workers may fall into practice which is likely to be experienced by service users as unhelpful.

> 'she screams and laughs at me because I try to help using therapy words which have no meaning for her … I don't know what to do and I don't know how to help. I get paid to help people and I don't know how to help her. She is so frightened and she has nothing and I can't make it better. I'm lost and confused and probably ashamed. I struggle onwards within my frame of professionalism – expecting these words to click as much with her experience as they did with me when I studied them and wrote them in essays and used them to explain myself to other professionals. Her ridicule and desperation push me further away into my shame. It would be easy to blame her for this moment and I could walk away, intact. It almost comes to me – "this is your problem, not mine", "if you don't want to be helped…"'

(Pegortwo, 2017)

Evidently, given the different positions that service providers and users occupy in terms of power, the social defences that teams may utilise have the capacity to be seriously damaging to users of the service. Indeed, the author has suggested the possibility that 'personality disorder' is co-constructed when powerful organisational dynamics serve mindlessly to blame, punish etc. traumatised individuals (Ramsden, 2018). Having a mind on the team, refers, therefore, not just to the social defences that can emerge but also to the power relations that enable the most damaging practices (Johnstone *et al*, 2018).

The work of services supporting, caring for and managing people who present in a way which is consistent with a 'personality disorder' diagnosis is often intensely emotionally demanding. Finding a way through the disorientation and distress that is an inherent part of the work is, therefore, the important work. This emotional labour, where it is ignored, underemphasised and/or misunderstood, will underpin damaging and ineffective practice that works to defend us, as workers, from the difficulties. Where we work effectively with the emotion, there is a mind within the team on what is happening to us and what, therefore, we can assume is also happening to our service user.

How MDT working can be a social defence

MDT working can feel like an inherently sensible approach to the work: multiple perspectives are available for checking practice and holding each other to account; care and treatment are inherently more holistic. However, it is common for MDT members to be working on discrete and often contradictory goals based on ill-coordinated professional assessments. As a consequence, MDT working can be unhelpfully incoherent. Confusion can reign at times over which direction to take and which professional experience most legitimately informs therapeutic goals and/or assessments.

Sarah and her psychologist had worked hard at understanding some of the barriers to her progress. Of significance were the lies that Sarah had told throughout her personal and working life to mask and manage what were profound experiences of shame associated with her lack of education and social status. Together they explored how, ultimately, these lies compounded her shame and did little to allow her to grow into being the person she wanted to be. In her sessions with the occupational therapist, Sarah asked if she could go out to the local art gallery and museum. On these trips Sarah would talk animatedly about the art/exhibitions and it appeared to the occupational therapist that the trips were good for Sarah's mood and self-esteem. In contrast, in her psychology sessions, Sarah talked about feeling out of place, humiliated and ashamed on these visits. She felt conspicuously different to the other people she encountered and described how she had to 'put on a mask'. The psychologist, pleased with Sarah's apparent capacity to reflect on her internal state, asked the occupational therapist to refrain from responding to her requests to visit places that had 'high intellectual status'. The occupational therapist, feeling that Sarah benefited greatly from the trips, was reluctant to do so.

One common theme in the literature which seeks to describe the relational challenges that teams face is 'splitting'. Teams working with individuals who present with behaviour consistent with the diagnosis are frequently described as being vulnerable to this phenomenon. 'Splitting' refers to often highly adversarial and deeply problematic differences of opinion within teams, and frequently its occurrence is ascribed to the service user group, who are described as individuals who 'split teams' or 'exploit' existing cracks and weaknesses in teams. Thankfully, this view of indecision and/or conflict within teams as being the result of core pathology within individual service users now seems out of date, with authors typically referring to the role played not by the service user, but by the team's own transference issues (Tyrer & Bateman, 2004; Wilmot & Evershed, 2018).

For the purposes of this chapter it is also possible to view ill-coordinated MDT working as a social defence which works to guard workers against the anxieties that may lead to damaging splits. Working to integrate assessments, harmonise treatment goals and seek clarity about an individual through multiple perspectives requires effortful attention to reconciling differences within the team. It brings with it the inevitable anxiety that an individual professional assessment may be irrelevant, misplaced or overstated, or that workers may need to confront biases, bigotries or blind spots. It is, arguably, easier to work in silos and to allow individual professionals to do their own work. In the example above, one can imagine how the work may continue separately, with both professionals pursuing what each feels to be a helpful approach with Sarah. We can imagine how the MDT may sanction this with the overarching perspective that 'everything which appears to be helping is a good thing'. In this way, clarity about the meaning underlying the different messages is not sought and what those inconsistencies may mean about Sarah's relationships with her workers fails to be understood.

Governance principles

The following are principles which are upheld by this chapter as being important for governance committees in ensuring that their teams are working to maintain a culture of containment and learning (Miller, 1993). These principles are intended to be upheld together as they work together to provide the necessary conditions. For example, teams may be able to evidence reflective space and structures which allow for the containment of anxiety, but without other forms of evidence (e.g. about how they are seeking to fulfil the primary task), this reflection may become purposeless and ill defined. In other words, one of these principles may start to constitute a social defence without the checks and balances provided by all three principles working together.

The importance of co-production and involvement of service users cannot be overstated. Each of these principles will be more effectively upheld where there is a culture of negotiating and sharing power with people who have experience of using services. In essence, the voices of these service user experts will always help teams to notice their practice, stay focussed on what's important and better articulate the overarching goals which help teams to remain coherent and integrated.

Teams need to articulate how they work to notice and contain the inevitable anxiety experienced by workers

Teams should be able to articulate a number of measures that they have in place for enabling every team member to notice and question practice which would appear to be emerging as a result of anxiety in the workforce. Regular supervision is likely to be a common measure, as is some form of individual appraisal, development and monitoring process. Of importance for teams is also likely to be a framework which allows everyone to understand and share a language around this endeavour. Sharing papers (such as the psychodynamic literature cited here) which seek to explain organisational responses to the work and the social defences which can emerge is likely to be helpful. Service user experience can also add to awareness within the team of the impact of their practice. For example, there is now a recognition of the importance of service user experience in training staff to manage incidents which may lead to the use of restraint (e.g. MIND, 2015).

It can also be helpful to ensure that case discussion allows the team to notice and question practice. One example from our team is a structure for clinical case discussion (based on the Balint group structure) which requires the team to draw on the resources within the room to help understand the case (Balint, 1957): all team members are placed on a rota to present clinical or organisational dilemmas. Time slots for presenting, for questions and for discussion (by a team of consultants) are tightly monitored by the chair. A team of observers are explicitly required to observe the processes in front of them and report them so they can be used by the presenter and consultants to deepen their understanding of the issue. Where possible, roles should be taken by people who have experience of having used services so that the conclusions and recommendations of the meeting can be co-produced. Through this structure all members of the team (however senior and experienced) have their responses to the work noticed and queried by colleagues. Inevitably, this brings with it the requirement that leaders within the team have particular qualities. Of importance is the ability for those in senior positions to truly uphold a perspective that they are just as likely as everyone else to respond anxiously to the work (and to practice in a way which is not task-focused through being anxiety-based). Boldly recruiting leaders who have the humility and the emotional resilience to allow their practice to be questioned is another way in which teams may evidence their efforts to support the development of a contained and containing team.

To add to this, leaders within contained and containing teams should also work to resist and manage anxiety which can be transmitted through them from higher up in the organisation. One relevant example is when harmful incidents occur which require the team to examine their practice. Inevitably, incidents of this kind (especially where there is a danger of reputational damage) can lead organisations to respond anxiously, punitively and without humility or a genuine focus on learning. Although it would be disingenuous to overlook the very legitimate anxiety that stems from a process that could lead to disciplinary action, the reality in most cases is that failures tend to be systemic (rather than personal). Leaders of effective teams should be genuinely committed to learning about problems with processes and systems before allocating blame to individuals. In viewing themselves as part of the system that contributed to any failure in practice, leaders inevitably work to both protect workers from organisational anxiety and to enable the team to learn.

Teams need to work to define and articulate how they work to ensure practice which serves the primary task

Zagier Roberts (1994) defines an organisation's primary task as the task it must perform in order to survive. This author goes on to explain how definition of the primary task in organisations which 'exist to change or help people' (p30) is particularly difficult and how confusion about what the task is (or should be) is a major source of individual and organisational stress.

Teams need, therefore, to continually seek to identify what is required of them by the external environment – to identify the task they need to achieve to be able to survive in the world. In reality this is likely to mean being accountable to commissioners, partner organisations, regulators and service users (Liberman *et al*, 2001). Through seeking to understand these demands and by explicitly placing the team within the context of these demands, leaders within the group are likely to ensure a sophisticated work group focused on real-world survival. Where this primary task-focused activity does not take place, the emotional demands of the work may well distort the process, leading groups into believing that their survival depends on meeting the needs of the internal environment. Zagier Roberts (1994) describes how 'anti-task' activity is driven by anxieties about psychological survival.

Where teams are working to define and to serve their primary task there is likely to be engagement with stakeholders, including service users, and an explicit narrative within the team about the drivers and the evidence base for the work they are doing, as well as the demands and changes to the landscape within which the team is operating. Understanding day to day what is required of the team by the world outside of them is paramount, as is working to identify when practice is working to serve those demands.

Teams seeking to practice in this way should be able to evidence an active programme of stakeholder engagement, of learning from stakeholders and of adaptation in response to that learning. Where there is service development, teams should be able to trace the origin of those developments back to external demands on the work or to learning from some other endeavour (such as service evaluation) which seeks, ultimately, to serve what is understood to be the primary task.

It is notable that, in many clinical settings, what are understood to be the clinical tasks are somewhat divorced from what are understood to be the operational tasks (managing finances, reporting activity, etc.) In many instances, the clinical work is often believed to be 'under attack' from the operational pressures on the service. Operational managers can feel lonely and isolated within a team that sees the priorities that they hold as irrelevant, punitive or short-sighted. As a consequence, clinical staff and operational managers can become alienated. In writing about the contributions of Wilfred Bion to organisational consultancy, Jon Stokes (1994) distinguishes between a work group mentality (which is focused on the primary task) and a basic assumption mentality (where the group are avoidant of the primary task and the real-life work that needs to take place). Arguably, a gulf between clinical and operational demands constitutes an avoidance of the real-life tasks which need to be undertaken by the team. As a consequence, a team focused on the primary task should be able to evidence strong links between clinical and operational leaders within the team.

Co-producing the work with service users (and involving them as much as possible in other ways) is likely to help teams to stay well connected with tasks that are essentially about helping human beings. Service users should routinely be included as stakeholders for consultation but the more they involve the people who use it, the more teams will be confident that their service is relevant and important.

Teams need to articulate how they are working to create and maintain high-performing transdisciplinary teams

Murphy and McVey (2010) define transdisciplinary team working as a more complex approach to team working where unique roles are integrated in order to achieve mutually independent goals. These authors describe how transdisciplinary team working is characterised by:

> 'clear channels of communication, robust decision making and good relations between team members and is underpinned by an integrated philosophy, shared values, and clear lines of accountability and responsibility outlined within an explicit operational policy.' (p158)

Murphy and McVey (2010) go on to describe four categories of tasks which will best ensure a high-performing transdisciplinary team. These are: (1) preparing for a team, (2) establishing clarity, (3) reducing unhelpful differences, and (4) ensuring participatory safety. It is likely that the governance principles outlined in this chapter will work to ensure that some of these objectives are met. For example, structures which enable a team to notice social defences and work to ensure containment of anxiety are likely to also enable one of Murphy and McVey's conditions (participatory safety). In addition, working to define how practice serves the primary task is also likely to contribute towards establishing clarity for the team.

Having a set of shared values is frequently cited as an important framework for teams aiming for a high level of integration. In our team, the importance of values is upheld as being 'the things that help you when nothing else does'. We understand the work to sometimes be confusing, frightening and overwhelming and, to help individual team members to make decisions under pressure that are likely to be consistent with each other and with the primary task, we stress the importance of values. Values – and what those look like when they are enacted in practice – help team members to make good decisions in the moment even when they are compromised emotionally. They help individual workers to stay wise even at times when they are unable to remember a policy, instruction or procedure or when the work takes an unexpected turn. Having an explicit set of values and helping the team to understand what those look like in practice (values into action) is a helpful way of ensuring a highly integrated team.

For those working in partnerships, we would suggest that there are added pressures on the integration of the team. One of those pressures stems from the fact that professional roles evolve through partnership work but remain subject to the governing rules of one organisation. This means that roles may become confusingly conflicted. Working to provide clarity for people working in partnership is difficult and often the overriding concern for the team shouldn't necessarily be to seek to provide absolute clarity, but to be able to notice and name the conflict for the individuals involved.

> Tom, a probation officer, had worked closely in partnership with a psychologist to understand more about an offender (Terry) who was coming out of prison. Terry had a history of serious domestic violence. Together the psychologist and Tom constructed a formulation which brought to the fore the impact of the domestic violence that Terry had witnessed between his parents as a child. Tom shared and developed the formulation with Terry, who conveyed the fact that the process had been immensely validating. Terry said that, in all his years within the criminal justice system, nobody had ever truly sought to understand him as a person before this. When Terry came out of prison he was restricted from contacting his previous partner. Tom visited him regularly at what he assumed was Terry's home and continued with some of the formulation-based work they had begun. This involved talking to Terry about how he was managing emotional responses that had been identified and associated with the abuse he had witnessed and suffered when young. Some months later the police informed Tom that they had been called out to a report of domestic dispute between Terry and his ex-partner. On investigation it was found that Terry had been living with her for some months.

In the example above, it could be argued that the probation officer became overly focussed on a formulation-led therapeutic process and neglected his public protection responsibilities. It is understandable how, in partnership, his role may have been influenced and how the mental health priorities for the psychologist affected the judgement of both about the focus for his intervention. Evidently, both organisations' priorities are important and likely to be mutually beneficial so a well-integrated, highly functioning partnership team requires clarity for workers about how their roles should function to bring relevant skills and expertise to the joint endeavour. How their roles might be influenced should be explicit and there should be forums for noticing when this is occurring. The focus for partnerships in creating a high level of integration between teams is on ensuring flexibility for learning and developing while also maintaining a high degree of role clarity.

Good communication and shared goals are essential for effective partnership working. However, communication and mutually established goal-directed work are likely to suffer through the emotional labour of the work. Nowhere are splits more likely than between organisations working in partnership. In our partnership team efforts are made, therefore, to ensure that there is a narrative in place about the complexity of partnership working. Efforts are made to ensure that we are orientated towards 'partnership tensions' and to ensure that some of the complex decision-making that has to occur can be done respectfully. Practical suggestions for doing this might include jointly led governance committees and active stakeholder engagement from within the partnership with others from each partnership organisation. Striving to co-produce and co-deliver interventions as well as teaching and training helps to ensure that partnership priorities continue to be thoughtfully attended to.

Summary

This chapter has sought to stress the importance of the work that is required of teams if they are to work effectively with the emotion that is inevitably involved when working to care for or manage other human beings. Where the work is especially complex and involves a high level of interpersonal stress, the emotional labour required is all the more important if teams are to manage the social defences which are likely to emerge and distort compassionate practice. Suggestions have been made within the chapter that are summarised under three main areas which should form the focus for governance committees. These are: working to notice and contain anxiety; working to ensure that practice serves the primary task; and working to ensure a high level of integration within teams. Practical suggestions include a process for clinical discussion informed by Balint group processes, a high level of stakeholder engagement and an explicit set of values which are augmented by values into action statements.

References

Balint M (1957) *The Doctor, His Patient and the Illness*. London: Pitman; Millennium edition, 2000, Churchill Livingstone, Edinburgh.

Bateman A & Fonagy P (2004) *Psychotherapy for Borderline Personality Disorder: Mentalization Based Treatment*. Oxford: Oxford University Press.

Bateman A & Fonagy P (2009) Randomized controlled trial of outpatient mentalization-based treatment versus structured clinical management for borderline personality disorder. *The American Journal of Psychiatry* **166** (12) 1355–1364. Doi: 10.1176/appi.ajp.2009.09040539

Bateman A, Gunderson J & Mulder R (2015) Treatment of personality disorder. *The Lancet* **385** (9969) 735–743.

Bateman A & Tyrer P (2004) Services for personality disorder: Organisation for inclusion. *Advances in Psychiatric Treatment* **10** 425–433. Doi: 10.1192/apt.10.6.425

Blumenthal S, Wood H & Williams A (2018) *Assessing Risk: A Relational Approach*. London/New York: Routledge.

Bohus M, Haaf B, Simms T, Limberger MF, Schmahl C, Unckel C, Lieb K & Linehan MM (2004) Effectiveness of inpatient dialectical behavioural therapy for borderline personality disorder: A controlled trial. *Behaviour Research and Therapy* **42** (5) 487–499.

Davies S, Clarke M, Hollin C & Duggan C (2007) Long term outcomes after discharge from medium secure care: A cause for concern. *British Journal of Psychiatry* **191** 70–74. Doi: 10.1192/bjp.bp.106.029215

Department of Health (2009) *Recognising Complexity: Commissioning Guidance for Personality Disorder Services*. London: Department of Health/Care Pathways Branch/Mental Health Division.

Department of Health (2014) *Meeting the Challenge, Making a Difference. Working Effectively to Support People with Personality Disorder in the Community*. London: Department of Health.

Evans S, Sethi F, Dale O, Stanton C, Sedgwick R, Doran M, Shoolbred L, Goldsack S & Haigh R (2017) Personality disorder service provision: A review of the recent literature. *Mental Health Review Journal* **22** (2) 65–82. DOI 10.1108/MHRJ-03-2016-0006

Evershed S (2011) The grey areas of boundary issues when working with forensic patients who have a personality disorder. In: P Willmot and N Gordon (2011) *Working Positively with Personality Disorder in Secure Settings: A Practitioner's Perspective*. Chichester: John Wiley & Sons Ltd.

Fonagy P & Bateman A (2006) Progress in the treatment of borderline personality disorder. *British Journal of Psychiatry* **188** 1–3.

Foster A (2001) The duty to care and the need to split. *Journal of Social Work Practice* **15** (1) 81–90.

Freestone MC, Wilson K, Jones R, Mikton C, Milsom S, Sonigra K, Taylor C & Campbell, C (2015) The impact on staff of working with personality disordered offenders: A systematic review. PLoS ONE; Aug 2015; vol. 10 (no. 8).

Hinshelwood RD (2002) Abusive help – helping abuse: The psychodynamic impact of severe personality disorder on caring institutions. *Criminal Behaviour and Mental Health* **12** S20–S30.

Hong V (2016) Borderline personality disorder in the emergency department: Good psychiatric management. *Harvard Review of Psychiatry* **24** (5) 357–366.

Johnstone L & Boyle M with Cromby J, Dillon J, Harper D, Kinderman P, Longden E, Pilgrim D & Read J (2018) *The Power Threat Meaning Framework: Overview*. Leicester: British Psychological Society.

Joseph N & Benefield N (2012) A joint offender personality disorder pathway strategy: An outline summary. *Criminal Behaviour and Mental Health* **22** (3) 210–217 Doi: 10.1002/cbm.1835

Kellett S, Bennett D, Ryle A & Thake A (2011) Cognitive analytic therapy for borderline personality disorder: Therapist competence and therapeutic effectiveness in routine practice. *Clinical Psychology and Psychotherapy* **20** (3) 216–225 Doi: 10.1002/cpp.796

Liberman RP, Hilty DM, Drake RE & Tsang HWH (2001) Requirements for multidisciplinary teamwork in psychiatric rehabilitation. *Psychiatric Services* **52** (10) 1331–1342.

Main T (1990) Knowledge, learning and freedom from thought. *Psychoanalytic Psychotherapy* **5** (1) 59–78.

Masley SA, Gillanders DT, Simpson SG & Taylor MA (2012) A systematic review of the evidence base for schema therapy. *Cognitive Behaviour Therapy* **41** (3) 185–202 Doi: 10.1080/16506073.2011.614274

McCarthy L, Huband N, Patel S, Banerjee P & Duggan C (2012) Personality disorder and psychopathy as predictors of psychosocial and criminological outcome in mentally disordered offenders. *International Journal of Forensic Mental Health* **11** 227–237 Doi: 10.1080/14999013.2012.739262

Menzies IEP (1960) A case study in the functioning of social systems as a defence against anxiety: A report on a study of the nursing service of a general hospital. *British Psycho-Analytical Society* **13** (2) 95–121 doi.org/10.1177%2F001872676001300201

Miller EJ (1993) The healthy organisation. Creating a holding environment: Conditions for psychological security. Retrieved from https://www.johnwhitwell.co.uk/child-care-general-archive/the-healthy-organisation-by-eric-miller/

MIND (2015) Restraint in mental health services: What the guidance says. London, UK: MIND.

Murphy N & McVey D (2010) *Treating Personality Disorder: Creating Robust Services for People with Complex Mental Health Needs*. London/New York: Routledge.

National Institute for Mental Health in England (2003a) *Personality Disorder: No Longer a Diagnosis of Exclusion*. London: Department of Health.

NHS England and NOMS (2015) Working with offenders with personality disorder: A practitioners guide (2nd edition). Retrieved from https://www.gov.uk/government/uploads/system/uploads/attachment_data/file/468891/NOMS-Working_with_offenders_with_personality_disorder.pdf

Obholzer A & Zagier Roberts V (eds) (1994) *The Unconscious at Work: Individual and Organizational Stress in the Human Services*. London/New York: Routledge.

Pegortwo (2017) It's all about the relationship, dammit! [Blog post] Retrieved from https://pegortwo.wordpress.com/2017/08/22/its-all-about-the-relationship-dammit/

Ramsden J (2018) "Are you calling me a liar"? Clinical interviewing more for trust than knowledge with high risk men with antisocial personality disorder. *International Journal of Forensic Mental Health* **17** (4) 351-361.

Ramsden J & Lowton M (2014) Probation practice with personality disordered offenders: The importance of avoiding errors of logic. *The Probation Journal* **61** (2) 148–160.

Royal College of Psychiatrists (2019) Enabling Environments quality improvement process. https://www.rcpsych.ac.uk/docs/default-source/improving-care/ccqi/quality-networks/enabling-environments-ee/the-enabling-environments-process-document-2019.pdf?sfvrsn=10b4616c_2

Stokes J (1994) The unconscious at work in groups and teams: Contributions from the work of Wilfred Bion. In: A Obholzer & V Zagier Roberts (eds) *The Unconscious at Work: Individual and Organizational Stress in the Human Services*. London/New York: Routledge.

Tyrer P (2004) Borderline personality disorder requires a team based approach. Retrieved from https://www.guidelinesinpractice.co.uk/mental-health/borderline-personality-disorder-requires-a-team-based-approach/309087.article#.XFQpfNIEqC8.twitter

Wilmot P & Evershed S (2018) Interviewing people given a diagnosis of personality disorder in forensic settings. *International Journal of Forensic Mental Health* **17** (4) 1–13 DOI: 10.1080/14999013.2018.1508 097(18)

Wlodarczyk J, Lawn S, Powell K, Crawford G, McMahon J, Burke J, Woodforde L, Kent M, Howell C & Litt J (2018) Exploring general practitioners' views and experiences of providing care to people with borderline personality disorder in primary care: A qualitative study in Australia. *International Journal of Environmental Research and Public Health* **15** (12) 2763.

Young JE, Klosko JS & Weishaar ME (2003) *Schema Therapy: A Practitioner's Guide*. New York/London: The Guilford Press.

Zagier Roberts V (1994) The organisation of work: Contributions from open systems theory. In: A Obholzer & V Zagier Roberts (eds) *The Unconscious at Work: Individual and Organizational Stress in the Human Services*. London/New York: Routledge.

Chapter 13:

Co-Produced 'Practice Near' Learning: Developing Critically Reflective Relational Systems

Neil Scott Gordon

Governance principles
- Organisations will learn when 'practice near' critical reflections are used to inform care.
- Organisations will learn when they work to maintain a mentalising capacity
- Learning processes will be enhanced through being co-produced

Introduction

'In the varied topography of professional practice there is a high, hard ground where practitioners can make effective use of research-based theory and technique, and there is a swampy lowland where situations are confusing "messes" incapable of technical solution. The difficulty is that the problems of the high ground, however great their technical interest, are often relatively unimportant to clients or to the larger society, while in the swamp are the problems of greatest human concern.

> *There are those who choose the swampy lowlands. They deliberately involve themselves in messy but crucially important problems and, when asked to describe their methods ... they speak of experience, trial and error, intuition, and muddling through.'*
>
> (Donald Schon, The Reflective Practitioner, 1983)

This quote introduced my doctoral thesis, 'The Swamp Workers' Stories' (Gordon, 2003), which focused on therapists working with the challenges of trauma and 'personality disorder' in high secure settings. It remains relevant here because frontline practice still predominantly occurs in those messy 'swampy lowlands', and any credible approach to learning and development must engage with this reality. Being one who chose the swampy lowlands, I have worked in these complex practice worlds for 40 years. As my career in mental health comes to an end, inevitably I find myself reflecting on my own professional journey and wondering what we have come to know about the process of learning itself, and how it can be nurtured in the organisations and systems that care for those with complex needs and trauma-related emotional distress. It seems clearer than ever that the creation of compassionate relationships and an ability to respond sensitively to the distress of others remains the essence of good practice, and therefore creating and sustaining this kind of relational culture is the real work of learning and development interventions.

The core theme of this book, new paradigms of practice, seems particularly relevant to the subject of learning, as many of the insights we have gained have evolved from a willingness to think about things differently and challenge taken-for-granted assumptions. This is apparent in the acknowledgement that authentic involvement and co-production focused on creating trauma-informed systems should represent the foundational elements of our organisational development efforts (Sweeney *et al*, 2018). This requires a fundamental shift in how we think about practice – to focus on people in their social context and examine the barriers or opportunities that enable them to reclaim a positive 'place in the world'. Such a perspective concerns issues of empowerment, collaboration and transformation, and has the potential to create a more service user-focused and responsive mental health system. Building on these foundational aspects, this chapter will elaborate how we can cherish the humanity of those we care for by promoting continuous learning within systems and organisations working with the challenges of 'personality disorder' and trauma. Keeping up with constantly evolving knowledge is essential in these fragile social contexts, where practitioners are often emotionally invested in ideas that may have outlived their usefulness and can then end up being applied in unthinking and unhelpful ways (Main, 1990). In this chapter I will highlight the importance of what I call practice near learning opportunities to enhance the relational capacities of the workforce by maintaining the system's capacity to reflect critically on the interpersonal and emotional demands of the work.

I begin by reflecting on my personal experiences as a facilitator of learning with reference to the practice-based insights that inform this work. While it is important to draw attention to what has been effective in how we help professionals learn, I will also argue that our evolving understanding of the impact of wider socio-political issues has illuminated new challenges that require attention. The related issue of the legitimacy of professional expertise will be discussed, arguing that we need to be more humble and collaborative in the ways in which we produce and use knowledge. The importance of creating containment through system-wide reflective practices that enable workers to process their experience of the work will be highlighted, before advocating for extended learning opportunities through the creation of communities of practice. In conclusion, I will argue that connecting to other systems ensures that organisations remain healthy and continue to evolve, based on developing shared values and co-produced knowledge.

Setting the scene: reflecting on lessons learned

I have spent most of my professional life facilitating the learning of others around these complex topics, but I begin writing with a sense of regret that, although well intentioned, we may as a community of practitioner/educators have been overly narrow in our approach. In our efforts to date perhaps we have not sufficiently engaged with how the intra-psychic and relational wounds (Frost & Hoggett, 2008) inflicted through coercive social policies, such as austerity, have impacted on the lived experience of those who use our services (Cooper & Whyte, 2017). This results in a narrow focus on faulty cognitions and behavioural self-control and risks situating the problem within the person and fails to address how the environment and social context they live within impacts on their capacity to cope with, and recover from, traumatic experiences. In acknowledging this, I accept that much of our educational work in recent years involved designing and delivering learning packages at local and national levels with an overt focus on dealing with (and managing) the challenging and disruptive service user. Despite these shortcomings, I remain proud of what these inputs have achieved in improving the experience of service users labelled with the contested diagnosis of personality disorder. Our students have been inspiring, and many, including those with lived experience, are making significant impacts in mental health and criminal justice services across the country. We made a genuine attempt to change the negative experiences of service users, but acknowledge that for more radical critics, the narrow focus and connotations of 'othering' carried by the use of diagnostic labels may have bolstered the inadequate diagnostic framework of 'personality disorder' and its undesirable trappings. So, while being involved in what I argue were positive educational interventions informs the narrative that follows, I am left with a nagging concern that using the term 'personality disorder' allowed some practitioners to over-identify complex traumatic experience with this, mainly, unhelpful diagnostic label that encourages workers to situate the problem within the service user.

Over the past ten years the contested nature of the diagnosis and the limitations of the current system have come much more sharply into focus, particularly following the recent publication of the British Psychological Society's Power, Threat, Meaning Framework (Johnstone & Boyle, 2017), which has challenged the uncritical use of medical diagnostic categories and furthermore questioned their validity and usefulness. Further issues concerning diagnostic terminology include the ways in which it individualises and medicalises the problem, encouraging a narrow focus on intra-psychic and interpersonal issues, with limited attention to the wider socio-political and economic realities of people's lives (Frost & Hoggett, 2008). It is evident that this neglect has been particularly apparent in these times of austerity, where systematic structural violence has damaged the most vulnerable (O'Hara, 2017). The lack of attention to the violence of austerity (Cooper & Whyte, 2017) within our educational endeavours is perhaps understandable, as commissioned programmes emerged through an existing system recognising the poor quality of care it was providing and wanting to improve things. However, as staff development is usually funded and supported by the system itself, learning initiatives are not always well placed to look critically at how that system operates to maintain the social order through efficient management of the vulnerable and risky.

In view of this, much of our development work considered issues rooted in the attitudes, knowledge and skills of the workforce, while the theories, policies and power relationships shaping these systems have to date received minimal attention. More recently I have come to the view that the negative social experiences of those cared for and/or contained in mental health and criminal justice systems needs to become more central to the agenda of workforce learning. It seems clear that we cannot improve services without also acknowledging the psychosocial and economic factors that shape individual experiences of personal distress and mental ill health (Smail, 2005). With this in mind, it is important that the critique offered by those who define themselves as mental health survivors is acknowledged to ensure future learning initiatives are always co-produced, are trauma-informed and engage with the socio-political dimensions of service users' lives.

In terms of things we need to get right, the centrality of co-production in our learning interventions and the 'practice near' philosophical position that informs them is vital. Attention to these issues will ensure that direct relational contacts with service users and colleagues remain the focus of education and training inputs, rather than an emphasis on diagnostic labels and symptoms. I believe what we have provided to date has been a good starting point in improving service user experience, particularly in the way we have advocated for more therapeutic and compassionate relationships. However, part of our future responsibility is to problematise professional discourse as part of any learning initiative; this can be achieved by encouraging a more critically informed workforce able to question the validity and politics of psychiatric diagnosis and professional authority (Reeve, 2015).

There is a desperate need for more informed socio-economic and political thinking to address MH issues, but this wider agenda is beyond the scope of this chapter. There are no quick fixes to address the failings of our care and criminal justice systems in dealing humanely and effectively with vulnerability and trauma. However, I believe that critically informed, system-focused team learning can make a real difference to those who find themselves embedded in, and affected by, the impersonal organisations and services created to deal with suffering and emotional distress. In terms of organising and delivering this system-focused approach, I aim to explore the key principles that should inform this work. This includes some of the challenges of bringing this to life in over-stretched organisational contexts.

Creating relational learning environments: guiding principles

I have written previously (Gordon, 2010) about Mahrer's (2004) conceptual distinction between theories of truth and models of usefulness, where he explores how professionals become committed to a particular theoretical perspective, pursuing a narrow epistemological path to prove it represents the truth. The consequence of this is an obsession with a particular model of delivery and the creation of rigid treatment and practice protocols that often miss the essence of messy practice that is difficult to objectify and capture in this positivistic frame. Alternatively, Mahrer advocates for models of usefulness defined as ways of thinking about what we are doing to help us to achieve our goals and increase understanding of our own and others' experiences.

In the spirit of the idea of models of usefulness, I offer some personal thoughts about the creation of consistent and healthy development processes by suggesting some core principles that have the potential to shape our learning interventions (see **Figure 13.1**). These are not offered as theoretical 'truths' to be applied in a decontextualised way, but rather to provide a useful framing of the issues that reflect my experience of working with systems that do this well. The common theme that connects them is the concept of relational learning, which I define as the capacity to use our reflections on our direct experience of relationships with others to inform our practice. I will outline each principle and discuss their importance in working with individuals who often have an extensive trauma history and have struggled to engage with, and experience safety and security in, the systems that have been created to care for them.

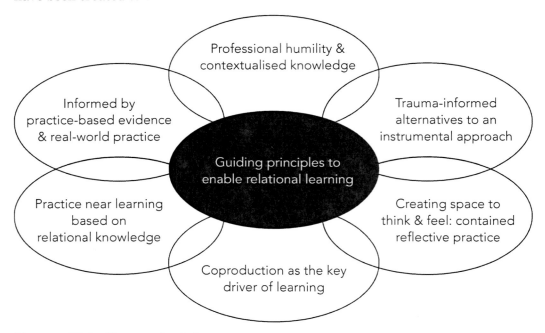

Figure 13.1: Core principles

Professional humility and contextualised knowledge

It is important to begin by reflecting on the contested nature of professional expertise itself, particularly how abstract professional knowledge applied in a narrow and decontextualised way can become the anathema of good practice. Mahrer (2004) encourages a move to more tentative and speculative conceptualisations of professional knowledge centred on the unique person with whom we are working. Such a shift challenges the way we utilise research-based academic theory by recognising the importance of developing understanding through relational contact. This capacity to learn from our practice encounters is supported by the work of Polkinghorne (1992, 2004), who describes what he refers to as 'practitioner epistemology' as the way practice-based helping professionals develop and learn from their direct experiences with service users. He argues for challenge of the dominant technical-rationalist approach where practice involves the application of theoretical knowledge, and to instead embrace a judgement-based approach, where practice consists of actions informed by situated context-sensitive judgments and the uniqueness of the individual service user. In such a judgement-based approach, it is the person rather than the technique that is viewed as the factor producing change. Discussing therapeutic interviewing, Ramsden (2018) observes the driver for therapeutic change in our work is not abstract expert knowledge but the one-to-one relationship process itself. She suggests that this does not mean that the clinician's expertise and training are unimportant, but they should be used and applied to 'being with' rather than 'knowing about'. This is a good example of using our knowledge in more humble ways, where professional theories are used as models of usefulness to help the practitioner remain hopeful and compassionate, while making an authentic connection with the lived experience of the service user.

This humility is increasingly relevant, as professional discourse within mental health tends to privilege the worker's definition of the problem and solutions over service users' personal understanding of their difficulties and desired outcomes (Perkins & Repper, 2016). The language of these dominant discourses can have an oppressive effect on vulnerable and traumatised people, leading them to feel excluded and marginalised, unable to contribute to the conversation. Equally, professional socialisation can condition practitioners to neglect the meaning of the service users' stories because they are viewed as irrelevant (Grant, 2015). Operating within a deficiency model of pathology, focused primarily on deficits and problems, discourages the exploration of service user narratives, thus ignoring individual strengths and possibilities for a re-authoring of damaged social identities (Carr, 2018). I recognise that the theoretical conceptualisations offered by, for example, attachment theory, early maladaptive schemas and mentalisation might offer useful ways of thinking about the presenting distress and experience of those we work with, and I believe that staff development should address these ideas. However, while these abstract concepts or theories of truth are relevant as a guide, I am arguing that where the realities of the work itself need to be understood in the context of unique relationships, we need to pay particular attention to service user narratives and personal meaning (Grant, 2015). For too long, professionals have developed theoretical accounts of distress independently of service users and then assumed these could be applied regardless of context and the experiences of the individual they happen to be working with. This has implications for learning interventions, where front-line practitioners are often unrealistically searching for theoretical explanations to apply directly to the challenging service user they are struggling to connect with relationally. The idea of humbler knowledge challenges this technical-rational and instrumental approach (Schon, 1983) by bringing the struggle with relational connection to the centre of the learning process, promoting a deeper understanding of individuals' experience and the historical and current factors that may be shaping it.

Informed by practice-based evidence and real-world practice

In articulating the essential principles informing a pragmatic and reality-based relational approach to learning, I want to emphasise that the roots of these ideas have evolved from my personal practice-based experience (Fox, 2011) gathered from intimate involvement with frontline practitioners, service users and facilitators in a range of contexts. This has provided an opportunity to engage with individual and team narratives regarding how their educational experiences have impacted on their personal and professional worlds, and, most importantly, shaped the relationships they create with service users. Informing my thinking is a realisation that my experience of delivering national training in different contexts across the UK has provided me with a unique educational ethnography (Carspecken, 1996) of personality disorder service provision. Interestingly, the 'data' generated through these experiences has revolved around recurring individual and organisational themes that highlight the challenges, rewards and core features of working with this marginalised group. A further influence on my understanding of the learning challenges that we face relates to being involved in the supervision of more than 50 practice-focused Masters' dissertations (produced by service users, probation officers, prison officers, psychologists, occupational therapists and mental health nurses), all of which explored the micro-processes of complex practice worlds dealing day to day with human distress, trauma interventions and risk-related issues. When synthesising the insights emerging from this body of work, the core learning themes and ideas can be framed around interpersonal, team and organisational layers. Using these practice-based evidence layers (Collins & Crowe, 2017) to frame the remainder of the chapter, I will explore how they can inter-relate to create systemic learning interventions that attend to the interpersonal complexity of the work and create the essential reflective spaces and processes required to nurture and sustain it.

An important insight which I have gleaned from many years of facilitating learning within systems working with complex trauma, in all its manifestations, is the need to ensure that the people within the system understand and bring to life the values of being person-centred and trauma-informed. What follows explores ways of effectively achieving this kind of culture change. A focus on relational processes does not involve creating a curriculum of topics to be covered, rather it involves meaningful, educational interventions that have a capacity to influence day-to-day encounters through shaping how these are managed and experienced by those involved. As highlighted above, the swampy lowlands of practice are always messy and complex. Effective work in these conditions is dependent on the quality of relationships that can be developed; and more importantly how these can be sustained and contained in the face of the emotional labour implicit in the work (Bondarenko *et al*, 2016). Central to this critical agenda is the need for a co-production model to shape the learning philosophy and challenge instrumental professional cultures and invalidating systems of care. Such an approach enables professionals to reconnect with the personhood and background of those who are trying to overcome a history of interpersonal trauma, frequently amplified by further negative experiences within the systems created to help them (Sweeney & Taggart, 2018). This makes our primary task (Barrett, 2014) a relational one that recognises the importance of every interaction and the constant battle to engage with the vagaries of 'bilateral miscommunication' (Zanarini *et al*, 2010) and the interpersonal misunderstandings so common in this work.

Co-production as the key driver of learning

A feature of my recent training delivery experiences has involved following the principle of co-facilitating with a person with lived experience. This often has a significant impact on the audience who are confronted with a competent and able service user who challenges their existing stereotypes and negative attitudes regarding people labelled in this way (Blazdell & Morgan, 2015). Any credible approach aimed at creating a relational learning environment depends on meaningful co-production. While it can be argued that co-production remains a contested concept (Farr, 2018), it is commonly presented as a normative and desirable approach by both practitioners and policy-makers. It is not surprising that this emphasis on partnership and equal relations between staff and service users is viewed in this positive way. In contrast, a more critical perspective views co-production as an extension of neoliberal free market policies, helping governments manage austerity (McGimpsey, 2016). This plays out, for example, where peer workers are substituted for paid personnel within MH services. Beresford and other more radical advocates believe that authentic co-production only occurs where collaborative alliances are forged between practitioners, service users and carers. He goes on to argue that such alliances help us to challenge 'damaging policies' and promote 'genuinely user-led services' (Beresford, 2016).

Co-production is essential because the intrinsic knowledge associated with lived experience has traditionally been excluded from service development agendas. Collaborative working and power sharing can 'bring air into a closed system' (Bell & Pahl, 2018) by empowering 'communities' to collectively construct new understandings, challenge potentially alienating practices, while unleashing alternative social forces to shape and improve service provision. However, as Bell and Pahl (2018) suggest, the implementation of co-production often seems to be dependent on the professionals' willingness to co-produce, and there is some evidence within the co-production literature that professionals resist because it involves the ceding of power (Bovaird & Löffler, 2012). Carr (2016) points to the difficulties of implementing a radical type of 'transformative' co-production in mainstream UK mental health services because of the medicalised system, which she suggests is riven with vast and varied inequalities, ingrained stigma and a history of rigid power and role relations. This highlights the importance of involving service users in designing and delivering learning and development inputs that encourage critical exploration of potential power struggles, addressing the attitudes and vested interests that impede meaningful change.

To move beyond tokenism to ensure authentic involvement, the work of Needham and Carr (2009) is helpful. Their typography comprises three levels. The first is basic co-production, which recognises the nature of passive participation of being treated or cared for in a system – for example, service users complying with medication regimes or turning up for appointments. However, 'compliant' service users are unlikely to have any influence or involvement in shaping how these services are designed or delivered. The next level, intermediate co-production, recognises that people using services have skills to offer and their contributions and ideas for improvement are sought. However, they suggest that such inputs are invited only if they are seen as assisting professionals to deliver services more efficiently. The third, and in the context of this chapter the most important, level is transformational co-production, where issues of power and control are worked with explicitly to create change. In this scenario service users are involved in all aspects of designing, commissioning and delivering those services in terms of introducing a new culture of learning into an organisation. I believe that this latter approach is the only one that can lead to meaningful change, but is challenged in our current systems and organisations where control of resources and anxiety about managing risk and maintaining professional omnipotence and authority resists radical involvement initiatives (Repper & Perkins, 2003).

From my experience of working with systems that have overcome these challenges, the key feature seems to be how integrated the service user voice is throughout the system, both formally, in terms of specific job roles, and informally, in terms of representation in all decision making within the organisation. Strategic approaches to staff development must make central the importance of meaningful involvement. This can include workshops on effective strategies for empowering others and how to involve service users in collaborative relationships. It is also important to address ways of increasing confidence regarding sharing power and understanding and incorporating service user expertise and knowledge. Regular review meetings offer an opportunity to critically reflect on the benefits of co-production, where staff can be supported in positive risk-taking and encouraged to identify new opportunities for collaboration. A wide range of people should be recruited to access co-productive initiatives to ensure diversity among the people who use services. Within the organisation itself new structures need to be created, including commissioning practices and financial resources to ensure that co-production philosophy and practice are integrated as long-term initiatives. The principles of effective organisational learning in this area centre on the core themes of partnership and co-design, acknowledging that service users have the capabilities to offer a positive and unique contribution to programme design and delivery. The importance of mutuality and the creation of peer and personal support networks should be encouraged and the boundaries between those who design and deliver services and those who use them need to be more fluid, encouraging people working at all levels of the system to pool expertise in collaborating to achieve positive change. At its most radical, co-production advocates a form of peer support between the people who use services, which can act as a challenge to the dominant role of the professional. As Sweeney *et al* (2016) have suggested this would also lead to professionals moving from being interventionists who focus on problems, to becoming catalysts and facilitators who focus on the abilities of service users to support and help each other.

Practice near learning based on relational knowledge

I have chosen to describe this model of learning as 'practice near' as it is directly concerned with people, relationships and organisational environments comprising social systems involving teams and networks. These practice settings are not only places of knowledge application, but also where relational encounters generate important information for building new knowledge and experience (Kinsella, 2007). This has particular resonance in systems where those being cared for have often experienced developmental trauma in the context of toxic attachment relationships with caregivers (Adshead, 2015). The echoes of these experiences are always active within these environments and require a response of compassion and understanding. Following Rolfe (2006), I believe that practitioners develop knowledge from three broad sources when engaging in such relational work. First, there is personal knowledge, knowledge about specific service users they are working with, gained mostly from the therapeutic relationships built with these individuals. Personal knowledge also includes relational knowledge, in terms of self–other awareness. Second, there is experiential knowledge, knowledge that the practitioner brings to the encounter from other, similar situations from their past experiences or repertoire of practice memories and their own attachment history. Third, there is propositional knowledge, more formal knowledge from research findings and professional training that affirm information about general situations in which practitioners find themselves. Unfortunately, this formal knowledge has often been idealised and viewed as superior in professional discourse despite its limitations to those occupying the context-dependent 'swampy lowlands' of practice.

An epistemology of practice, however, re-weighs this balance between different sources of evidence and knowledge, placing emphasis on practice, recognising that it is not merely the site for applying theory and research knowledge but also for developing knowledge, particularly experiential and relational knowledge (Polkinghorne, 2004). The missing dimension of this interpersonal model of learning is the shaping influence of the wider organisational and socio-political system where practice is situated. I would suggest that all these dimensions need to be addressed in some way to create a multi-layered learning process.

A deeper understanding of what it might mean to get 'near' to practice needs a focus on what happens when we get close, emotionally or physically, to people who have experienced trauma and have difficulties in relationships, who often become labelled or diagnosed within our systems as personality disordered. The themes outlined below are central to creating learning environments where practitioners are encouraged to grow and learn in ways that have the potential to re-shape and positively impact on their relational capacities: the very essence of trauma-informed care. In this context, the focus is on dialogue where both those giving and those receiving care can share their experiences in a range of formal and informal forums to better understand what is going on between them. One of my concerns about the current polarisation of perspectives is the lack of attention to issues emerging in a relational context. Ironically, where in the past service users rightly rebelled against the idea of situating the problem within them, activist groups have now situated the entire problem within the system and professionals. Neither position is helpful, and the situation cries out for deeper analysis of bilateral mis-communication (Zanarini, 2009). The key to effective learning is ensuring that all parts of this interpersonal system continue to mentalise (Bateman & Fonagy, 2004) and think about the experiences of 'the other'. This is the primary goal of development work in this area. Secure attachments provide the ideal conditions for fostering mentalising. Such relationships are characterised by staff showing interest in the service user's mind, creating the interpersonal safety for the individual to engage with and learn from meaningful connection with other minds (Bateman & Fonagy, 2004). Providing such containing relationships is essential as this connected experience was rarely available to those who experienced developmental trauma and neglect.

Essentially this kind of learning needs to be up close and personal – practice-near education will therefore always be co-produced and co-facilitated, bringing us close to people in a live emotional way. This could be exciting or challenging or both, but whichever, it is likely to be hard to stay detached or dispassionate in shared learning endeavours of this kind. Practice-near education requires a relationally informed dynamic model at its heart, where people are encouraged and contained in a safe trusting environment in which they are able to explore their own and others' experiences in reflective and honest dialogue. This is in direct contrast to the more traditional 'what is personality disorder' type workshop, where often a didactic, information-giving style is adopted and learners are seen as passive recipients of knowledge: a 'banking' concept of education (Freire, 2000). Practice-near learning involves a meeting of minds, whereby the closer we come to other people the greater the likelihood that we will become emotionally connected to them. The processes involved can be captured by returning to the concept of mentalisation (Bateman & Fonagy, 2004), which has become a core idea in the understanding of how we learn from and with others, including exposing the difficulties we might have in trusting others during this process. Fonagy refers to this as epistemic mistrust (Fonagy & Allison, 2014), a sense that it is not safe to learn from others in the social world, often for good reason. This processing of emotional dynamics represents the heart of relational practice, making sense of how the work impacts on us emotionally while trying to understand what is going on, and using this understanding to keep difficult conversations going and find new ways of connecting helpfully with others.

Accepting the inevitability of personal change is intrinsic to this approach as the psychological intensity of these reflective learning encounters has the capacity to transform our experience. This is an important aspect of practice-near learning; the process itself leads to altered behaviour and attitudes towards our practice and those we care for and work with, highlighting the importance of safe and containing teams where shared values and understandings can grow. It is not possible to work effectively in these types of systems without creating meaningful attachments with service users and colleagues. These bonds, by their very nature, impact on sense of self and ability to cope with, and continue to learn from, the emotional realities (Hochschild, 2001) of interpersonal work. This is facilitated by creating a range of reflective spaces where experiences can be processed and critically reviewed on a regular basis.

Finally, this type of live relational learning develops an increased sensitivity to context and personal meaning. Being close enough to service users and colleagues for the above to be happening, rather than relying on detached theoretical accounts, allows more personal and contextualised understandings to emerge. The closer one comes to the lived experience of another, the more its uniqueness and particularity demands to be understood; but equally its value for the illumination of other situations where there are familiar patterns becomes clearer (Cooper, 2009). This fits well with the idea of a humbler approach to professional knowledge. Constantly working in a context-sensitive and person-centred way negates reliance on abstract theoretical explanations to distance us from the lived experiences we are confronted with. This experiential model of learning (Beard & Wilson, 2018) poses a fundamental challenge to the continuing dominance of the positivist and behaviourist paradigm that has tended to dominate learning in mental health (Pilgrim, 2015). The centrality of life narratives and personal meaning making take centre stage. Direct experience of peers becomes available for critical review through dialogue and reflection on practice, including attending to the learning process itself. Brookfield (2005) describes 'knowing how we know what we know' as an essential feature of such an adult learning approach. He links this to the idea of reflective practice and the capacity to continue learning from our relational encounters by creating safe spaces to explore personal meanings and interpretations and the factors shaping them.

When developing a learning strategy to assist people working in trauma-focused services, we might ask what they need to know about, and how might this be helpful to them in their attempts to help others. The traditional instrumental approach often involves education about the presenting issues, focusing on diagnoses, signs and symptoms, pervasive common problems and behaviours. In this context, this received wisdom should be challenged to ensure a re-focus on the relational dynamics at the heart of this work. The nature of relational work requires a reflexive and engaging learning methodology that brings interpersonal dynamics centre stage, where they can be explored and assimilated both experientially and practically. The practice-near approach is founded on co-production and transformative adult learning. Its aims are to create psychologically minded workers who can reflect critically on their own practice while working collaboratively with service users and other professionals.

Trauma-informed alternatives to an instrumental approach

Relational learning also needs to be trauma-informed. Recent research confirms that trauma is widespread across society, is related to the development of mental health difficulties and has high economic costs (Sweeney, 2018). Recognising this, the Power Threat Meaning Framework (Johnstone & Boyle, 2018) advocates a fundamental shift to providing a trauma-informed approach through moving from the question 'what is wrong with you?' to 'what happened to you?'. Sweeney and Taggart (2018) caution that this should be seen as an orientating ambition as opposed to a literal instruction. Others are also hesitant regarding the usefulness of the trauma-informed mantra. For example, Pilgrim (2018) argues that acknowledging the corrosive or traumatic impact that different forms of power have on our lives would represent a radical shift of ethos in mental health services. For him, the question of the relationship between experiencing trauma and receiving a psychiatric diagnosis needs more research, and he cautions that the call for trauma-informed services, although positive, needs to be wary of 'simplistically replacing bio-reductionism with trauma-reductionism, as a blanket explanation for all mental health problems' (Pilgrim, 2018, p3). Sweeney and Taggart (2018) express a related concern that mainstream MH systems have a history of corrupting and assimilating new ideas, and they warn against the risk of co-option, where trauma-informed approaches become little more than treatment as usual packages re-labelled as trauma-informed.

Interestingly, from my own clinical experience the concept of 'what happened to you?' has always been central to our understanding of the phenomena that become labelled as personality disorder. Those doing this work well have, in my view, tended to be trauma-informed in their approach. In saying this, I accept that it can be problematic to assume that this is what practitioners and services do already. While many practitioners, particularly in specialist services, do work in trauma-informed ways, and a number of organisations are implementing trauma-informed approaches, we know that many people are still faced with stigmatising rejection and pejorative staff attitudes across the health, social care and criminal justice systems.

While it is evident that past trauma may be a contributing cause of mental distress for many service users receiving a personality disorder diagnosis, it is also clear that for some, their experiences in care systems and interactions with professionals can lead to retraumatisation. Sweeney and Taggart (2018) discuss the liability of 'trauma-uninformed' staff and the negative impact their poor understanding of the triggering nature of restrictive and invasive care practices can have. From Sweeney and Taggart's (2018) perspective, the primary goals of a trauma-informed approach are to improve service users' experiences and improve working environments for staff. This leads to increased job satisfaction, reduces stress and, through greater understanding, respect and trust, improves relationships between staff and service users.

So, while the idea of trauma-informed practice is certainly important, to avoid it becoming empty rhetoric we need to be clear about what it actually means in terms of individual behaviour and the team and organisational structures required. Trauma-informed services are those in which service delivery is influenced by an understanding of the impact of interpersonal and structural violence and victimisation on an individual's life and development. To provide trauma-informed services, all staff in the organisation, from the receptionist to the direct care workers to the senior managers, must understand how developmental trauma impacts on the lives of the people being served, so that every interaction is consistent with the recovery process, thus reducing the possibility of retraumatisation. To do this effectively, we need organisations and management systems that ensure the resources are available to create co-designed development inputs that shape the culture of practice.

When organisations are informed enough to do this well, it will infuse the plans they make, shape the development opportunities they provide and inform direct work with service users. The analytical idea of parallel process thinking (Hughes & Pengelly, 2003) suggests that the dynamics of one system will be picked up and re-enacted by associated systems. It seems obvious that if we want our service users to feel contained and empowered, it is critical that those working with them feel supported and held. This means the leadership style, organisational culture and policies, including how change and conflict are handled, must also reflect a trauma-informed approach. We cannot expect professionals working in toxic team environments where blame, fear and shame predominate to be able to engage meaningfully with service users struggling with emotional distress. Developing a responsive culture takes time and needs significant ongoing resources. The all too familiar scenario where professional supervision and reflective space is gradually eroded due to lack of time or expertise available to facilitate these processes was a recurring topic in the practice-focused Masters research I have recently been involved with. Despite many of these students working in innovative, leading-edge services, the constant tension between maintaining a trauma-informed approach to practice versus resource-driven organisational sabotage of these efforts was a recurring theme.

Our organisations need to be trauma-informed from top down and ground up, with a commitment to extended support networks and team reflection processes (Treisman, 2017). Such structures create sufficient emotional containment to enable staff to get 'up close and personal' with service users. This closeness offers the securely attached relationships that service users need, assisting them with managing their own distress in ways that facilitate personal growth and positive change (Adshead, 2015). A focus on learning when faced with working with trauma is crucial, given that personal development through self–other awareness is the central feature of good relational practice. This results in connected relationships within our systems that have the capacity to create containment and a sense of hope for service users.

Creating space to think and feel: contained reflective practice

Creating meaningful relational connections with service users is associated with significant emotional labour (Freestone *et al*, 2015). The experiences associated with this require to be processed through critical reflective dialogue with peers. Professionals working with trauma need to confront the powerful and primitive emotional states that underpin helping relationships, particularly with the most vulnerable (Barrett, 2012). Reflective space offers an opportunity to confront the pain and despair associated with the work, which can be amplified by the increasingly turbulent social and political processes that place relentless demands on workers and their organisations (Cooper and Lousada, 2005). Reflective engagement with direct interpersonal experience offers opportunities to explore the complexity of trauma-related work. Lack of attention to the complex interplay between persons and context increases the emotional and relational distance between staff and service users, as without this crucial sense-making space it is easy to get caught up in the powerful emotional dynamics associated with getting close to others' distress.

It is concerning that professional discourse about the nature of working with vulnerable people tends to 'other' service users, often viewing them as maliciously inflicting distress on caring and dedicated staff. The narrative then moves to the importance of building resilience and focuses on how staff can be assisted to withstand these psychological attacks. Unsurprisingly, critiques of the legitimacy of this narrative have come from service user groups who are antagonistic to diagnostic labels and see this othering as punitive and oppressive (PDintheBIN, 2016). This is further illuminated by Green (2018), who explored the concept of 'splitting' and how it is currently used within services working with 'personality disorder'. Green articulates how the term, originally a relational concept, has become a blaming accusation about a service user's malign intent. He concludes that an integrated psychological theory of team-splitting needs to move beyond focusing on individual service user psychology and pathology, to incorporate the predispositions, motivations and sensitivities of everyone involved. This example highlights the importance of ongoing learning and reflection within care systems and how this can be achieved through exploring the differing perceptions of those involved. Ideally, being critically reflective should become integrated within the general organisational culture, rather than being something that particular individuals or groups do. Creating this culture can happen in a variety of ways, but these processes need to be co-produced and co-facilitated to ensure a creative collaboration. It is also important that these initiatives are closely aligned with practice-near learning opportunities such as reflective work discussion groups, supervision, formulation forums and interagency and multidisciplinary team reviews (Daykin & Gordon, 2011).

These work-based learning processes need to be transformative (Mezirow, 2009) if the relational capacities of individuals and teams are to increase. Transformative learning involves adapting our taken-for-granted frames of reference (meaning perspectives, habits of mind, mindsets) to make them more inclusive, discriminating, open, emotionally capable of change and reflective so that they generate beliefs and opinions that more accurately guide our actions (Taylor, 2012). Transformative learning involves participation in reflective conversations, using the experience of others to understand and analyse our assumptions while reviewing our behaviour and actions.

To keep the learning process dynamic while ensuring the social ecosystem stays healthy and nurtured, it is imperative to create connections through engagement with external networks and like-minded professionals and service users. For example, Lave and Wenger (1991) depart radically from traditional ways of conceiving learning and the development of knowledge. For them, learning arises from participation in a community of practice (CoP), which is a community engaged in a common activity with its associated ways of working, narratives and traditions. Practice is negotiated between individuals and the community and learning 'is distributed among co-participants and not a one-person act' (Lave & Wenger, 1991, p15). The knowledge that develops is co-produced within the group through a process of participation leading to the adoption of shared values and practices.

Conclusion

This chapter has explored key relational principles to inform learning and development interventions in systems working with complex needs and trauma. I have used my experience as a facilitator and designer of learning to make the case for the importance of creating practice-near learning processes that are co-produced and trauma-informed, highlighting the need to interpret these terms in a pragmatic and context-sensitive way. The central role of connected and compassionate relationships, which I argue are the heart of this work, has been emphasised and the dynamics and potential learning within co-produced, safe reflective spaces has been articulated. Nurturing and sustaining a responsive care environment relies on maintaining thinking and mentalising capacity when responding to traumatic experience and distress. Throughout I have stressed the importance of attending to wider social and psycho-political realities of service users' lives. I advocate for a more critically thoughtful and humble approach to counter the dominance of professional frames of reference, encouraging more meaningful work with the lived experience narratives of service users. The imperfect systems created to deal with our most vulnerable citizens need to be reflexively aware of the tension between the potential to make a difference and the ever present danger of causing iatrogenic harm. Creating collaborative co-productive relationships and commitment to reflective lifelong learning remain the most effective strategies to ensure this tension can be managed within trauma-informed mental health systems.

References

Adshead G (2015) Security and the social mind: attachment and therapeutic communities. *Therapeutic Communities* **36** (1) 12–20.

Barrett J (2012) Sustainable organizations in health and social care: developing a 'team mind'. In: A Rubitel and D Reiss, *Containment in the Community: Supportive Frameworks for Thinking about Antisocial Behaviour and Mental Health*. London: Karnac.

Bateman A, Fonagy P (2004) *Psychotherapy for Borderline Personality Disorder: Mentalisation Based Treatment*. Oxford: Oxford University Press.

Beard C & Wilson JC (2018) *Experiential Learning: A Practical Guide for Training, Coaching and Education* (4th edition). London: Kogan Page.

Beresford P (2016) Social workers must fight for service user rights and the profession's soul. *Community Care*, 29 February. Retrieved from www.communitycare. co.uk/2016/02/29/social-workers-must-fight-service-user-rights-professions- soul/

Bell D & Pahl K (2018) Co-production: Towards a utopian approach. *International Journal of Social Research Methodology* **21** (1) 105–117.

Blazdell J & Morgan L (2015) Developing personality disorder training – a collaborative process – Co-production as a Process for Developing and Provoking Learning, *Prison Service Journal*, Special edition, Working with people with personality disorder **March** (218) 54–60.

Bondarenko P, du Preez E, Shepherd D (2017) Emotional labour in mental health field workers. *New Zealand Journal of Psychology* **46** (1) 4-13.

Bovaird T & Loeffler E (2012) From engagement to co-production: The contribution of users and communities to outcomes and public value. *International Journal of Voluntary and Nonprofit Organizations* **23** (4) 1119–1138.

Brookfield S (2005) *The Power of Critical Theory for Adult Learning and Teaching*. Maidenhead: Open University Press.

Carr S (2016) Position Paper: Are mainstream mental health services ready to progress transformative co-production? Bath: NDTi.

Carr S (2018) Who owns co-production? In: P. Beresford and S. Carr (eds) *Social Policy First Hand – An International Introduction to Participatory Social Welfare*. Bristol: Policy Press.

Carspecken P (1996) *Critical Ethnography in Educational Research: A Theoretical and Practical Guide*. New York: Routledge.

Collins P & Crowe S (2017) Recovery and practice-based evidence: Reconnecting the diverging discourses in mental health. *Mental Health and Social Inclusion* **21** (1) 34–42.

Cooper A (2009) Hearing the grass grow: Emotional and epistemological challenges of practice-near research. *Journal of Social Work Practice* **23** (4) 429–442.

Cooper A & Lousada J (2012) *Borderline Welfare: Feeling and Fear of Feeling in Modern Welfare*. London: Karnac.

Cooper V & Whyte D (2017) *The Violence of Austerity*. Northampton: Pluto Press.

Daykin A & Gordon N (2011) Establishing a supervision culture for clinicians working with personality disordered offenders in a high secure hospital. In: P Wilmott and N Gordon (eds) *Working Positively with Personality Disorder in Secure Settings: A Practitioner Perspective*. London: Wiley.

Farr M (2018) Power dynamics and collaborative mechanisms in co-production and co-design processes. *Critical Social Policy* **38** (4) 623–644.

Fonagy P & Allison E (2014) The role of mentalizing and epistemic trust in the therapeutic relationship. *Psychotherapy* **51** 372–380.

Fox M (2011) Practice-based evidence – overcoming insecure attachments. *Educational Psychology in Practice* **27** (4) 325–335.

Freestone MC, Wilson K, Jones R, Mikton C, Milsom S, Sonigra K, Taylor C & Campbell C. (2015) The impact on staff of working with personality disordered offenders: a systematic review. PloS One 10 (8) 0136378.

Freire P (2000) *Pedagogy of the Oppressed*. New York: Continuum.

Frost E & Hoggett, P (2008) Human agency and social suffering. *Critical Social Policy* **28** (4) 438–460.

Gordon NS (2003) The swamp workers' stories: An exploration of practitioners' perspectives as a foundation for the development of a context sensitive development programme in a forensic setting. Unpublished PhD dissertation. Metanoia Institute/Middlesex University.

Gordon NS (2010) The 'unthought known': Working with men with personality disorder in a high secure setting. In: A Aiyegbusi and J Clarke-Moore (eds) *Therapeutic Relationships with Offenders: An Introduction to the Psychodynamics of Forensic Mental Health Nursing*. London: Jessica Kingsley.

Grant A (2015) Demedicalising misery: Welcoming the human paradigm in mental health nurse education. *Nurse Education Today* **35** e50–e53.

Green H (2018) Team splitting and the 'borderline personality': A relational reframe. *Psychoanalytic Psychotherapy* **July** 1–18.

Hochschild AR (2001) Emotion work, feeling rules, and social structure. In: A Branaman (ed) *Self and Society*. Malden: Blackwell.

Hughes L & Pengelly P (1997) *Staff Supervision in a Turbulent Environment: Managing Process and Task in Front-Line Services*. London: Jessica Kingsley.

Johnstone L & Boyle M (2018) The Power Threat Meaning Framework: An alternative nondiagnostic conceptual system. *Journal of Humanistic Psychology*. Online first.

Kim S (2015) The mind in the making: Developmental and neurobiological origins of mentalizing, *Personality Disorders: Theory, Research, and Treatment* **6** (4) 356–365.

Kinsella EA (2007) Embodied reflection and the epistemology of reflective practice. *The Journal of Philosophy of Education* **41** (3) 395–409.

Lave J & Wenger E (1991) *Situated Learning: Legitimate Peripheral Participation*. Cambridge: Cambridge University Press.

Mahrer AR (2004) *Theories of Truth and Models of Usefulness*. London: Wiley.

Main T (1990) Knowledge, learning, and freedom from thought. *Psychoanalytic Psychotherapy* **5** (1) 59–78.

McGimpsey I (2016) Late neoliberalism: Delineating a policy regime. *Critical Social Policy* **36** (4) 1–21.

Mezirow J (2009) Transformative learning theory. In: J Mezirow & EW Taylor (eds) *Transformative Learning in Practice: Insights from Community, Workplace, and Higher Education*. San Francisco, CA: Jossey-Bass.

Needham C & Carr S (2009) SCIE Research briefing 31: co-production: an emerging evidence base for adult social care transformation. Retrieved from www.scie.org.uk

O'Hara M (2017) Mental health and suicide. In: V Cooper and D Whyte (eds) *The Violence of Austerity*. London: Pluto Press.

PD in the bin (2016) A simple guide to avoiding a diagnosis of personality disorder. Retrieved from https://personalitydisorderinthebin.wordpress.com

Perkins R, Repper J (2016) Recovery versus risk? From managing risk to the co-production of safety and opportunity. *Mental Health and Social Inclusion* **20** (2) 101–109.

Pilgrim D (2015) *Understanding Mental Health: A Critical Realist Exploration*. London: Routledge.

Pilgrim D (2018) Are kindly and efficacious mental health services possible? *Journal of Mental Health*, Early online.

Polkinghorne DE (1992) Postmodern epistemology of practice. In: S. Kvale (ed) *Inquiries in Social Construction: Psychology and Postmodernism*. Thousand Oaks: Sage Publications, Inc.

Polkinghorne DE (2004) *Practice and the Human Sciences: The Case for a Judgment-Based Practice of Care*. Albany: State University of New York Press.

Ramsden J (2018) 'Are you calling me a liar?' Clinical interviewing more for trust than knowledge with high-risk men with antisocial personality disorder. *International Journal of Forensic Mental Health* **17** (4) 351–361.

Reeve D (2015) Psycho-emotional disablism in the lives of people experiencing mental distress. In: H Spandler, J Anderson and B Sapey (eds) *Madness, Distress and the Politics of Disablement*. Bristol: Policy Press.

Repper J & Perkins R. (2003), *Social Inclusion and Recovery*. Edinburgh: Bailliere Tindall.

Rolfe G (2006) Nursing praxis and the science of the unique. *Nursing Science Quarterly* **19** (1) 39–43.

Schön DA (1983) *The Reflective Practitioner: How Professionals Think in Action*. New York: Basic Books.

Smail DJ (2005) *Power, Interest and Psychology: Elements of a Social Materialist Understanding of Distress*. Ross on Wye: PCCS Books Ltd.

Sweeney A, Clement S, Filson B, *et al* (2016) Trauma-informed mental healthcare in the UK: What is it and how can we further its development? *Mental Health Review Journal* **21** 174–192.

Sweeney A, Filson B, Kennedy A, Collinson L & Gillard S (2018) A paradigm shift: Relationships in trauma-informed mental health services, *BJPsych Advances* **24** 319–333.

Sweeney A & Taggart D (2018) (Mis)understanding trauma-informed approaches in mental health. *Journal of Mental Health*, **27** (5) 383-387.

Taylor EW (2012) *The Handbook of Transformative Learning: Theory, Research, and Practice*. New York: Wiley.

Treisman K (2017) *Working with Relational and Developmental Trauma in Children and Adolescents*. Oxford: Routledge.

Zanarini MC (2009) Psychotherapy of borderline personality disorder. *Acta Psychiatrica Scandinavica* **120** 373–377.

Zanarini MC, Frankenburg FR, Reich DB & Fitzmaurice G (2010) Time to attainment of recovery from borderline personality disorder and stability of recovery: A 10-year prospective follow-up study. *Am J Psychiatry* **167** 663–667.